"Our generation has inherited an incredibly beautiful world from our parents and they from their parents. It is in our hands whether our children and their children inherit the same world."

—*Richard Branson*

Kick the Fossil Fuel Habit

10 Clean Technologies to Save Our World

Tom Rand

WHERE IT ALL BEGINS

Solar

An Introduction

The ancient Romans called it Sol; the Greeks, Helios. Its gods were plentiful—in Greece, they worshipped Apollo, the Norse had Freyr, and the Incas paid homage to Inti. Icarus was said to have tried to fly there, but his wings melted long before he arrived.

The sun is the star of our solar system and the source of almost all forms of energy on Earth. Plants use sunlight to grow. Wind is generated by temperature differences in the air. Waves form from wind over long stretches of ocean. And the sun's rays evaporate water from the oceans, which returns as rain and give us hydropower.

Fossil fuel itself is really just stored solar energy, since natural gas, oil and coal are derived from the remains of things that lived long ago. Even the uranium atoms that power our nuclear reactors were created when a sun much larger than ours exploded in a supernova.

The sun is a nuclear furnace, the size and strength of which beggars the imagination—almost a million miles (1.6 million kilometres) across, with an internal temperature that exceeds 27 million F (15 million C). Even on the surface, it's still a scorching 9,000 F to 11,000 F (5,000 C to 6,000 C).

Apollo was recognized in both Greek and Roman mythology. In Hellenistic times, especially during the third century BC, as Apollo Helios he became identified among Greeks with Helios, god of the sun.

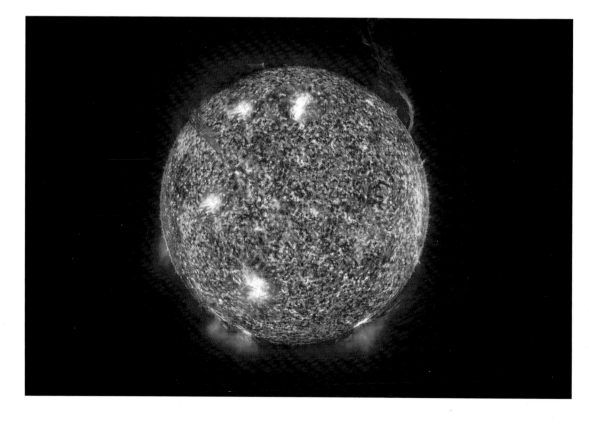

The surface of the Sun is made up of hydrogen (about 74% of its mass), helium (about 24%) and trace quantities of other elements. The energy of the sun supports almost all life on Earth via photosynthesis, and drives the Earth's climate and weather.

Stars are one of the only natural phenomena powerful enough to forge matter itself. Most larger atoms—including those that make up human flesh—are formed by the nuclear might of a sun.

Fossil fuel itself is really just stored solar energy.

Giant explosions regularly burst outward from the sun's surface, shooting out fiery tentacles that stretch for millions of miles. Only a tiny fraction of the sun's energy reaches our planet, in the form of photons. These tiny particles fly through space at the speed of light for a full eight minutes, covering a distance of 93 million miles (150 million kilometres). And they deliver an astounding amount of energy when compared to what we need to power our entire civilization.

High in the Peruvian Andes, at the remains of the city of Machu Picchu, there's a shadow clock that describes the course of the sun personified by Inti, thought to be the ancestor of the Incas.

By the end of 2008, over one million solar thermal systems had been installed on German roofs. Their combined power output amounted to some 7,300 megawatts, and the manufacturing and installation of them created 20,000 jobs.

According to David Faiman, a professor at Israel's Ben Gurion University Solar Energy Center, "A square yard of desert absorbs as much energy over a year as you can get out of a barrel of oil." That's nothing to sneeze at. And it means that an area of desert the size of tiny Connecticut absorbs enough energy to replace the entire oil output of the OPEC countries[8] (that annoying oil cabal). We fight wars over oil, yet the Arizona desert sits peacefully under an American sky. Solar energy that can deliver huge amounts of power is not science fiction. This technology is available today—a fact that's already been proven by projects the world over.

A square yard of desert absorbs as much energy over a year as you can get out of a barrel of oil.

I remember quite vividly as a child my father gesturing to the expanse of gravel that was our driveway. "Enough sun lands here to power our house, if we could only grab it," he'd exclaim. We settled for winding black pipe on the roof and attaching it to the pump that heated our pool. It may sound primitive, but the water that jetted out of there was often too hot to touch. We've come a long way since then—there are now lots of ways to grab the sun's energy. Long gone are the days of simple black tubes, or toy-like solar panels that captured just enough energy to power a radio or flashlight.

In the Mojave Desert, fields of reflective troughs and parabolic dishes cover the ground, tracking the desert sun. In Spain, giant mirrors cover the ground for acres, focusing the sun's rays on a giant tower, generating heat so intense, it melts salt.

Solar vs. Coal

Energy Type	Use	Scale of Power Generation	Capital Costs[1]	Fuel Costs[2]
		Small – a house Medium – a neighborhood Large – a large city	$/watt of capacity	$/kilowatt hour of production
Coal	Electricity	Large	$1.5 - $4[3]	$0.0175[4]
Solar - Photovoltaic	Electricity	Small to Medium	$6 - $12[5]	free
Solar - Thermal	Hot Water	Small to Medium	$1 - $3[6]	free
Solar - Concentrated	Electricity	Medium to Large	$4[7]	free

This chart compares solar to coal, with no cost attributed to carbon emissions and using only current economies of scale for solar. In other words, this is the picture that exists today—and the picture can only get better for solar. For every pound of coal consumed, a coal plant will emit around three pounds of CO_2. So if CO_2 emissions were to cost $35 per ton, the fuel costs for coal would effectively quadruple, to seven cents per kilowatt hour. Solar fuel remains free.

In Australia, they plan to construct the world's largest tower, a "solar chimney." These solar projects store energy and keep producing electricity well into the night. Germany is well on its way to covering its rooftops with highly efficient solar panels. Europe plans projects in the northern African desert, big enough to power all of the UK. It doesn't stop there...

These solar projects store energy and keep producing electricity well into the night.

Developing large-scale solar energy is even cost-competitive with developing the tar sands of Alberta, Canada, the world's largest—and dirtiest—oil reserve.

Solar power is big, and tomorrow, it will get even bigger. Literally. We must think big about solar power the way we used to think about securing Gulf oil, saving the world banking system or going to the moon. And thinking big is not just about big projects, but lots of them.

A Dish Stirling Solar power system is being tested at the Solar Test and Research Center in Tempe, Arizona. Its mirrors focus sunlight onto a thermal receiver, where a Stirling heat engine drives a generator producing 25 kilowatts of electricity.

Concentrated Solar Power

Using heat accumulators, the current production of solar thermal power stations can be independent of the vagaries of the sun. They can supply energy even at night and in overcast conditions.

The Giant Magnifying Glass

Give a kid a magnifying glass on a sunny day and you're asking for trouble. From time immemorial, magnifying or concentrating the rays of the sun has served as both boon and bane.

The Chinese first used mirrors to light fires back around 700 BC. In ancient Greece, Archimedes was said to have used soldiers' shields as a giant mirror, reflecting sunlight onto Roman ships and setting them on fire. While this tale may seem more tall than true, the Greek Navy did confirm some years back that 60 mirrors could indeed ignite a wooden ship from a distance of 165 feet (50 metres).

Italy was once a solar pioneer (though it's now fallen behind in the solar race). During construction of the Santa Maria del Fiore cathedral in Florence, mirrors were used to melt copper. And no less a figure than Leonardo da Vinci foresaw the power of concentrated solar, evidenced by drawings in his famous notebooks.

Today, concentrated solar is serious business, commonly generating temperatures hot enough to melt bricks and even salt. The heat captured is used to generate electricity, and with means to store that heat now being developed, the electricity will flow long after the sun goes down.

Are the experts excited about concentrated solar thermal? You bet. "This is just so obvious it's going to be huge," says Terry Collins, the Thomas Lord Professor of Chemistry at Carnegie Mellon and director of the university's Institute for Green Science. "It's going to completely change the country."

There are three common ways of concentrating the heat of the sun. This is a story of the trough, the tower and the dish—with a dash of molten salt.

The Trough

During the OPEC oil crisis of the 1970s, when Jimmy Carter wore sweaters in the White House to conserve energy and put solar panels on its roof, I had a science teacher who came to class one day with what he called the "solar hot dog cooker." A hot dog lay skewered inside an open tube, or parabolic trough—a special shape that reflected light from the open top along the same line as the hot dog. It took hours to cook and was more novelty than stove, but my old teacher had the right idea.

Today, an Israeli company called Solel Inc. is building some pretty serious troughs—ones that could *vaporize* a hot dog. The Mojave Solar Park, expected to be operational by 2011, will be the largest solar thermal electricity plant in the world. Eventually, it will cover nine square miles, and employ 1.2 million mirrors and 317 miles of vacuum tubing. At Solel, they think big. With an estimated cost of $2 billion, the Mojave Solar Park (contracted by Pacific Gas and Electric) can generate 553 megawatts of electricity, or half a medium-sized coal plant—more than enough to power half a million homes.

Devoid of energy sources, the remote regions of the world lend themselves to solar cooking. This simple parabolic unit in Kashmir, in northern India, is one of over 70,000 solar cookers that were distributed throughout the country between 2002 and 2007.

The largest solar thermal electricity plant in the world is currently under construction in California's Mojave Desert—it's due to come online in 2011. Pacific Gas and Electric, in partnership with Israel's Solel Inc., plans to generate enough electricity to power 400,000 homes.

Existing parabolic fields in the Mojave Desert —at Harper Lake, Kramer Junction and Daggett—have been in operation for years, generating enough power for more than 350,000 homes and reducing California's annual oil consumption by two million barrels.

We can build as many as we want, and fast. We could cover the desert in these things long before we could get another nuclear plant built, or find a new patch of offshore oil.

The Mojave Solar Park is simply the latest, largest and most modern project out there. Add it to the mix, and these parabolic solar farms alone replace over 3.5 million barrels of oil annually.

How does it work? High-tech reflective silver coatings cover the surface of long lines of massive parabolic troughs that are many times taller than the people who built them. Each trough tracks the sun, so that the sunlight reflects onto a tube containing an oil-like fluid, which heats to around 750 F (400 C). The fluid passes through a heat-exchanger that draws heat from the oil and uses that heat to turn water into steam, which in turn powers a turbine.

Andasol One, Europe's first parabolic trough plant, went online in November 2008 near Granada, Spain. The Spanish have also figured out a way to store the heat produced during the day, in a kind of molten salt mixture. That heat is released at night or when it's cloudy, almost doubling the amount of time the plant produces power.

Simple—make some heat with a hot dog

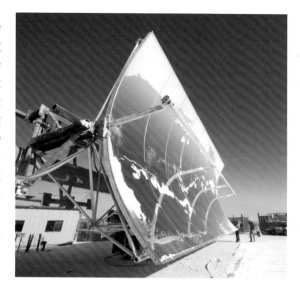

The highly reflective, silver-metalized film of this solar tracker is lighter and less expensive than the breakable glass mirrors traditionally used in parabolic troughs. It's being tested atop South Table Mountain in Golden, Colorado, for the National Renewable Energy Laboratory.

Nine trough power plants in California's Mojave Desert—at Harper Lake, Kramer Junction and Daggett—have been in operation for years, generating 354 megawatts and reducing California's annual oil consumption by two million barrels.

cooker. Boil some water. Spin a wheel. Or, if you're really ambitious, add another step: Make some heat. Put some of it into a thermos. When you need it, open the thermos.

The key to efficiency is the reflectivity of the surface coatings, the absorption of the heat-carrying tube, and the tracking of the sun. In other words, bounce lots of photons from the trough onto the tube, where they stick. As coating technologies improve, they will be applied to existing parabolic fields—over

the past 10 years, output of the older Mojave Desert plants have increased by 35%.

A big advantage of this type of plant is that there are no hard-to-find materials and no bottlenecks in the supply chain. According to Avi Brenmiller, the CEO of Solel, "The raw materials we are using—glass, metal, cement—are commodities. There are almost no limits to the amount we can use." What this really means is: We can build as many as we want, and fast. We could cover the desert in these

Andasol-1 and Andasol-2 are thermal solar power plants that came online in Granada, Spain, in 2008. Their collector troughs cover more than a million square metres—about 140 soccer fields—and will have a capacity of 49.9 megawatts, with 7.5 hours thermal storage.

things long before we could get another nuclear plant built or find a new patch of offshore oil.

Ease of large-scale supply applies equally well to the following two processes—the tower and the dish.

Abengoa Solar's PS10 solar tower near Seville, Spain, focuses the radiation of 624 heliostats onto a receiver at the top of a 40-story concrete tower. Concentrated steam drives a turbine generator delivering 11 megawatts. It's the first solar tower in the world to generate electricity commercially.

The Tower

Archimedes may or may not have managed to set Roman ships on fire with his soldiers' shields, but deep in the New Mexico desert sits a facility that takes the science behind his legendary attempt seriously. And they'd have no problem lighting a fire or two.

Sitting next to an abandoned bombing target is the National Solar Thermal Test Facility, run by the US Department of Energy. Eight acres of mirrors (called heliostats) track the sun and aim their beams at a looming concrete tower 200 feet tall. An object placed in the path of that beam of concentrated sunlight would reach temperatures of more than 4,000 F (2,200 C).

How does it work? Tubes inside the tower are filled with molten salt that carries the heat away—much like the oil in the parabolic troughs, but far hotter. And like the troughs, the molten salt heats water, creates steam and turns a turbine.

A plant like this would cost around $100 million, and with economies of scale would be cost-competitive with coal.

What a sight—sometimes, when there's dust in the air, the concentrated light is so intense, the air itself seems to glow brightly, and a halo of sorts surrounds the tower. Virtuous power, indeed.

That facility has spawned a number of spin-offs, including two installations in the Mojave Desert that date back to the 1980s and '90s. Two other spin-offs sit side by side in Spain and produce power for more than 30,000 homes.[9] A third project, called Solar Tres, will have 15 hours of storage and drive a turbine that can power 17,000 homes. The storage thermos for Solar Tres will hold over 6,000 tons of molten salt. And there's more coming.

Where is all this going? A solar tower with 12 hours of storage, capable of powering 100,000 homes, would take up 1,000 acres of land. In the US southwest alone, there are millions of acres just sitting empty. A plant like this would cost around $100 million, and with economies of scale would be cost-competitive with coal—that's only $1,000 per powered home.

Plataforma Solar de Almería in southern Spain is Europe's largest research center for concentrated solar technologies. The 17-megawatt Solar Tres is currently under development there. When completed, it will be the world's first commercial molten-salt central receiver plant, and will feature a field of 2,600 heliostats and a 15-hour molten-salt storage system.

Stirling Energy Systems has developed the SunCatcher solar dish for utility-scale power plants. Its mirrored concentrator dish focuses sunlight at a high-efficiency Stirling engine that powers a generator to produce electricity.

The Dish

The Stirling SunCatcher looks like something designed to scan the skies for signals from extraterrestrials or eavesdrop on the conversations of dodgy military regimes. It's neither. Instead, this bunch of large parabolic mirrors is the heart of a sunlight engine.

How does it work? The dish works like other concentrating technologies: Large areas of sunlight are focused on a single point, and the heat is used to generate electricity.

Instead of heat-transferring liquid, though, the target is the Stirling engine, an external combustion engine that burns sunlight instead of petroleum.

Unlike the internal combustion engine under the hood of your car, which harnesses the power of a controlled explosion inside the engine's cylinders, the Stirling engine uses heat generated *outside* the cylinder to heat the expanding gas. The heat here is sunlight.

Hence, it is, quite literally, a sunlight engine. The engine drives a turbine, and you know the rest of the story.

The Stirling engine burns sunlight instead of petroleum.

What's great about this technology is its efficiency. Parabolic dish solar power was, until recently, the record-holder for most efficient conversion of sunlight to electricity, at 31%.[10] Though it was recently beaten by modern photovoltaic (PV) cells (see the next section), it still holds the record for concentrated solar thermal electrical generation.

These first stabs at big solar are already roughly equivalent to a medium-sized coal plant.

Another advantage is that the dishes are modular—you can run just one to power a neighborhood or small building,[11] or build a massive field of them, or anything in between.

Stirling Energy Systems (SES) plans some big, utility-sized fields. SES Solar One in the Mojave Desert will be run by Southern California Edison Co., producing power for 500,000 homes to start, and scaling up to just under a million.[12] SES Solar Two, in California's Imperial Valley, will be run by San Diego Gas & Electric and will start by producing enough power for 300,000 homes, again scaling up to close to a million.

These are big fields, capable of powering a small city. Between 12,000 and 36,000 of these SunCatchers, each over 35 feet (11 metres) in diameter, will cover several thousand acres[13] of the desert floor. An equal number of Stirling engines will drink that sunlight, converting it to electricity and feeding the grid.

To put this into perspective, these first stabs at big solar are already roughly equivalent to a medium-sized coal plant.

The Infinia Solar System, a small-scale, three-kilowatt Stirling solar dish designed for commercial and private use, is under development in Kennewick, Washington. The self-contained system, which tracks the sun throughout the day, is easy to install, operates unattended and requires no water for cooling.

This artist's rendering shows how the SES Solar One installation in the Mojave Desert and SES Solar Two in California's Imperial Valley will look when thousands of mirrored SunCatcher concentrator dishes go to work to generate several hundred megawatts of power for two major utilities.

Solar Photovoltaic

Hitting the Electron Out of Orbit

GreenVolts is striving to achieve the highest solar-to-electricity ratio by integrating innovative optics with two-axis solar tracking. An array of small parabolic mirrors mounted on a rack at ground level focuses sunlight onto a row of PV chips.

Jimmy Carter put them up, and Ronald Reagan tore them down. Now it looks like the Pope wants in on the action. The roof of Nervi Hall in Vatican City is now covered

The next generation of PVs will be thinner, bendable, and incorporated into building structures.

with 2,400 solar photovoltaic (PV) cells, the Vatican's vote for solar. The American military, for its part, has weighed in with a field of them at Nellis Air Force Base in Nevada. Solar PV is what most people think of when they think of solar energy—the kind of panels that power our calculators.

How does it work? Electricity is a stream of moving electrons—tiny charged particles that orbit the nucleus of an atom like planets around the sun. Solar PVs are normally made from silicon, with more advanced materials on the way. They're built so that the incoming photons knock electrons out of their orbit. Those electrons are sucked away by an electromagnetic field, generating an electric current. The record for efficiency—how much of the sun's energy is converted to electricity—was set by researchers at the University of New South Wales, Australia, at 25%.

Later generations of PVs will be able to capture more of that sunlight. Spark Solar of Australia is using multidimensional surface structures designed to capture more wavelengths of light (or energy of photons). New cell designs can convert over 40% of the sunlight to electricity. The next generation of PVs will also be thinner, bendable and incorporated into building structures. One day, the shingles on our rooftops will help to power our homes.

There's a real treat on the horizon here. Take those high-tech, next-generation solar cells and combine them with a bunch of mirrors or magnifying glasses. Voilà—concentrated solar PV! A tiny California-based company called GreenVolts is doing just that. Its device, called the CarouSol, is made up of 172 mirrors that track the sun, magnify its light 625 times, and focus it on a superefficient, next-generation PV cell. Morgan Solar uses an injection-molded Plexiglas optic, instead of a lens, to guide sunlight onto the cell. Morgan's power could be far cheaper than coal.

Photovoltaic modules peek above the roof of the Solar Energy Research Facility in Golden, Colorado. The building faces 15 degrees east of due south to maximize its exposure to the sun, and its numerous energy-saving features reduce annual energy costs by 30% to 40%.

Solar PV is promising because enormous amounts of energy can be produced by millions of individual panels, on millions of individual roofs. Power to the people!

"It turns farms, homes and business into entrepreneurs."

Those little projects add up, but you have to give people a reason to do it. Germany is awash in solar PV. In 2007 alone, enough solar PVs were installed on farms and houses throughout the country to power more than 1.2 million homes. Why? Germany provides generous incentives—called feed-in tariffs—to

homeowners who install them. Feed-in tariffs pay you for the electricity you produce, and Germany has shown just how effective they can be.

Why are these incentives so effective? In the words of Terry Tamminen, former chief policy advisor to California Governor Arnold Schwarzenegger, the model "turns farms, homes and business into entrepreneurs." Solar PV lets all of us compete with the utilities.

An 82-acre tract in the San Luis Valley of south central Colorado—home to the state's best conditions for solar—is the site of the Alamosa Photovoltaic Plant. It went online in December 2007, and the array of single-axis tracking PV panels generates eight megawatts.

Solar Hot Water

A Warm Solar Shower

Stopping at a solar energy store on a camping trip one year, I bought what was touted as a "solar energy shower"—a black plastic bag you filled with lake water and hung in a tree for a few hours. Pricey for a bag and a bit of hosepipe, but it worked.

That's the basic idea behind the solar collectors that sit on rooftops to provide domestic hot water. Such systems are normally supplemented by another form of heat—particularly in northern countries during the winter months—but collectively, they can add up to an awful lot of energy.

How does it work? The most common method is to pump liquid through a black, insulated panel that faces the sun. When the liquid gets warm enough, it's returned to a heat-exchanger in the hot water tank.

Doesn't sound like much, but remember that the hot water you use starts at around 54 F (12 C), and every degree counts. Even in a notoriously cloudy—and often chilly—country like the UK, these systems can provide about half the power required for domestic hot water.

Because these are small systems that anyone

Even in a notoriously cloudy— and often chilly—country like the UK, these systems can provide about half the power required for domestic hot water.

can install, the real strength of this energy source is when you add them all together. Back in 2001, there were already almost 72 million square yards (60 million square metres) of these panels installed worldwide.

The solar hot water system at the Jefferson County Jail in Golden, Colorado, produces about 50% of the hot water used annually at the facility. Parabolic collectors heat a glycol ethylene mixture that's circulated in a coil system through a 4,000-gallon water tank.

How much energy pours out of these? It's hard to say with any precision, but even a conservative estimate would come in at an energy equivalent of more than 28 million barrels of oil a year.[14]

Commercial-scale systems on hospital and hotel roofs are common, and can provide energy more cheaply than natural gas.

Companies like Mondial Energy in Canada are installing arrays of these solar panels at no cost to the building owner, and charging them like a utility.

You can even use the warmed water to heat the building itself. These things are a no-brainer.

This array of 108 solar hot water collectors installed on a community services facility in Toronto, Canada, produces one-third of the building's annual hot water requirements. That's a reduction of 61 metric tons of CO_2 per year.

In 2001, as part of a United Nations Foundation initiative to help reduce the consumption of fossil fuels, solar water heater systems were installed on rooftops in Kunming, in China's Yunnan province. Now, more than 1,000 factories and dealers produce and sell solar water heaters in China.

Enviromission, an Australian company, plans to build the world's tallest structure, a giant, hollow chimney that will use the thermal wind created by rising hot air from a massive greenhouse to power a series of turbines. The project will deliver up to 200 megawatts of power.

Solar Chimneys

Heat Always Rises

We all know that heat rises. That's why our attics are hot and our basements cool. Seems pretty benign as an energy source, but a company in Australia doesn't think so. The people behind Enviromission think big—big enough to make that rising air a significant source of energy.

Enviromission plans to build the world's tallest structure—a giant, hollow chimney that will soar 2,600 feet (800 metres) into the sky. Rated at enough power for more than 200,000 homes and costing an estimated $700 million, the chimney would tower over the desert and be surrounded by a 1.5-mile-wide (2.5 kilometres) greenhouse canopy, open at the outer perimeter.

How does it work? The sun heats the air in the greenhouse, which fights to get up the chimney. That creates a thermal wind, driving turbines located around the chimney's base. Thanks to the sheer scale of the structure, the air could reach speeds of close to 30 miles per hour (50 kilometres per hour). It's possible to operate this sort of structure at night, and this time, the "battery" is warm ground, made black to absorb heat all day and release it at night.

Sound far-fetched? The sheer size of the project is indeed audacious, but the concept has been proven with a successful small-scale pilot plant in Manzanares, Spain. It was a collaboration between the Spanish government and a German civil engineering company, Schlaich Bergermann and Partner. The plant operated for seven years, between 1982 and 1989, and consistently generated around 50 kilowatts of clean energy.

There are advantages to this sort of solar. Aside from the turbines, it's entirely passive—it just sits there doing its thing. It may only convert 1.3%[15] of the sunlight to electricity, but it has a relatively high capacity factor of 40% to 50%.[16]

The key to this technology lies in the cost of building and operating the chimney. If it can be built cheaply enough to compete with other solar technologies (and it looks like it can), it may well spring from the drawing board to a desert near you.

Thinking Big

Cover the Deserts and Power the Cities

All you have to do is think big. The American southwest can produce solar at much the same level as the northwestern US and Quebec produce hydroelectricity. Australia could stop burning coal in quick order. Even Europe can incorporate huge amounts of solar.

Here's what thinking big can get you: A group called Trans-Mediterranean Renewable Energy Cooperation (TREC) has developed a plan they call the DESERTEC concept.

Near Seville, Spain, Abengoa Solar's PS10 and PS20 solar power plants will ultimately produce enough power for about 180,000 homes. PS10 went into production in 2007, delivering 11 megawatts. Second-generation technology will enable PS20 to double that figure when it's completed in 2013.

The key is to build a transmission "super-grid" based on high-efficiency direct current (DC) lines (see Chapter 10) that connect the North African and Middle Eastern deserts with Europe. Then cover those deserts with solar farms.

Solar thermal plants built on just 1% of the surface of the Sahara could provide the entire world's electricity demands.

The European Commission's Institute for Energy has confirmed what I alluded to earlier: Just 0.3% of sunlight from these deserts could power all of Europe. That's an area the size of Massachusetts! Pay the countries sitting on the deserts to put up massive solar farms, each enough to power between 50,000 and 200,000 homes, and feed those megawatts back to Europe.

This is not an idea resting on the loony fringes. British Prime Minister Gordon Brown and French President Nicolas Sarkozy have both expressed support, and the international research team has cooperated with the likes of the German Aerospace Center to make it happen. Plans are already afoot for undersea cables to Sicily and Spain. Costs for the initial lines are in the order of $60 billion.

Large-scale solar energy is highly competitive with the tar sands of Alberta.

How big can this get? Scientists working on the project estimate that by 2050, solar farms in North Africa could produce enough power for 100 million homes,[17] at a total cost of half a trillion dollars. Put a similar amount of money into the American southwest, build an American supergrid, and you'd get similar amounts of power. You might even get more, since the grid doesn't have to cross a sea. You

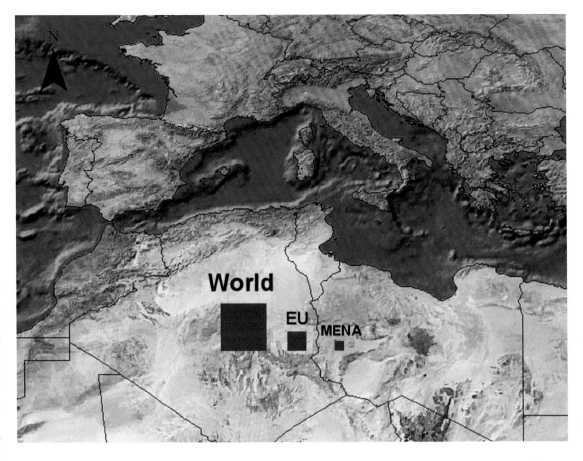

The red squares on this map, from the Trans-Mediterranean Renewable Energy Cooperation (TREC), show the area required for solar collectors to produce the present power needs for the world, Europe, and the Middle East and North Africa (MENA).

could even use the power to make hydrogen to run cars and trucks.

Want to think even *bigger*? According to Solel, solar thermal plants built on just 1% of the surface of the Sahara could provide the *entire world's* electricity demands.

It is often claimed that the only energy solution big enough to satisfy North America's growing energy appetite is the tar sands in Alberta, Canada. The tar sands are massive deposits of a tar-like substance that is mined, melted and refined. The process is notoriously dirty, not to mention ridiculously expensive. It turns out that large-scale solar energy is highly competitive with the tar sands, and dollar for dollar, we could get the same amount of *clean* energy from solar as we could from melting all that tar.[18]

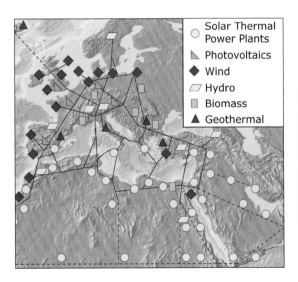

This sketch illustrates the DESERTEC plan for a transmission "supergrid" and the associated infrastructure for a sustainable supply of power to Europe, the Middle East and North Africa.

Potential and Pitfalls

Bottom line? There's no reason the sun couldn't fill up to half of our primary energy needs—heat, electricity, even hydrogen for our cars—if we just think big enough. Filling a quarter of all our energy needs is a conservative estimate.

But all solar requires sun, and there's the rub: It isn't always shining, and isn't always near the places that need the power. It also costs a fair bit, but that can be solved with mass production.

Concentrated solar requires lots of hot, direct sunlight, even with a giant thermos to store the energy. So the technology is limited to sunny, desert areas. The American southwest, Spain, the Australian outback, the Sahara, the Middle East—these are all great spots. New York City, London, Paris—not exactly prime solar real estate. The solution is to get the power to the cities that need it. Grid connections are expensive, but they aren't exactly rocket science.

Solar PV operates on cloudy days, but at reduced output. The energy can generally be stored in batteries, which are always improving, and could include hydrogen production (see Chapter 10). But solar PV is limited in two other ways. Manufacturing bottlenecks have already appeared, because there are only so many factories capable of producing the wafers. It's also the most expensive form of solar—costs need to come down significantly. With advanced manu-facturing techniques and mass-production incentives, these problems can be overcome.

As for solar hot water, that, as I said earlier, is a no-brainer. From Mexico City to Toronto to Paris, it can contribute significant energy by offsetting natural gas or electric heat.

Solar is already fast becoming cost-competitive with coal-based production. With economies of scale, lower capital costs and a price attached to emitting carbon, solar is clearly positioned to compete with our dirtiest source of electricity.

The Trillion-Dollar Question:

So, what do you get for $1 trillion?
As we've seen, solar energy comes in three types: concentrated solar for electricity, solar PV for electricity and solar thermal for heat. Funnily enough, they all come out roughly the same[19]—somewhere around a trillion kilowatt hours per year[20]—for a $1-trillion investment.

What does that get you? A trillion dollars invested in solar energy could replace half[21] of the coal-based electrical production in the United States.

These 20-kilowatt solar dishes dwarf visitors in Alice Springs, Australia. The array of concentrator mirrors focuses sunlight onto high-efficiency photovoltaic cells. New technology enables virtually the full spectrum of sunlight to be converted into electrical current.

A New Economics

A Price on Carbon

There's an old philosophical chestnut known as the "tragedy of the Commons." The story goes like this: There are a bunch of farmers, each with a herd of cows. But there's only one meadow, or Commons. Each farmer, acting in his own self-interest, puts as many of his cows as possible out to graze on the Commons, getting all the benefit, but bearing none of the cost. Since they all do the same thing, the Commons are soon destroyed by overgrazing. Everyone loses.

The lesson comes from a paradox (or conundrum) —actions that seem to be in our best interest are often the worst thing for us. Now think of the Commons as the environment, and all those grass-guzzling cows as CO_2 emissions. The free market, with every person acting in their own rational self-interest, can't by itself solve the global climate change problem. We need a new economics.

Coal plants emit carbon dioxide. Since the cost of those emissions doesn't directly impact the coal plant, why would the owner be motivated to turn it

The new economics says that emitting carbon can no longer be free.

off? The cost is shared by everyone, and the owner gets all the benefit. Whether we're talking about a plant owner, an entire country or any group in between, without some kind of intervention, everyone will sit around waiting for someone else to make the first move.

The new economics says that emitting carbon can no longer be free—paying to emit the stuff is like paying to graze. There are a few proposals out there that suggest how to do this: a carbon tax, a concept called "cap-and-trade" and straight regulation. The final formula will probably involve a bit of each.

A carbon tax is just what it sounds like—a tax on carbon that's cranked up over time. The idea is to motivate consumers and industry alike to emit less. To ensure that the poorest among us can still afford

Without some kind of intervention, everyone will sit around waiting for everyone else to make the first move.

to heat their homes—and to satisfy those who are ideologically opposed to big government and higher taxes—proponents of this model suggest redistributing the carbon tax dollars, making it revenue-neutral.

The benefits? The tax is clear to everyone, and they apply to all emissions. The downside? It's hard to link the tax rate to a specified cut in emissions.

Cap-and-trade applies to big industry. The idea here is to put a ceiling on how much carbon a specific sector can emit, and gradually reduce that cap over time. Factories would each get "carbon credits"—the right to pollute a certain amount. Any factories that exceed their cap must buy extra credits from factories that come in beneath their cap. Everyone is motivated to reduce emissions, since they not only save money, but can actually *make* money in the process.

The benefits? There's none of the guesswork that's involved in a carbon tax system, since the price determinant for carbon can be directly linked to

an emissions reduction target. And it unleashes the creative forces of the market as factories compete to find new ways to reduce emissions. The downside? Lots of bureaucracy.

Straight regulation is pretty simple: Just pass laws that require reductions in emissions, and enforce those laws with strong penalties and enforcement mechanisms.

The benefits? Again, they're pretty obvious. The downside? It would be very hard to enforce regulations in every economic sector, and there's little incentive for the creative entrepreneurial forces to come into play. If overused, straight regulation would probably result in a noticeable downsizing of the economy (if it worked at all). However, regulation will certainly play some role in specific targeted industries, activities and regions.

The hard part is not designing the new economy. The hard part will be to get every country to sign up. The key to carbon pricing is that it must be international and universal in scope. New international institutions will have to be built to set and enforce the price.

The creative forces of the market are unleashed as factories compete with each other to find new ways to reduce emissions.

That brings us right back to the tragedy of the Commons. Why would, say, China slap a new tax on industry, when it can just wait for everyone else to start? Why would the US? It's clear that leadership, diplomatic arm-twisting and outright coercion will be required. If, for example, one country doesn't sign up to a carbon pricing scheme, we'd see most of the high-carbon industry move there. And why not? It would be in any company's best interest to do so.

Finally, international tariffs linked to the carbon emissions embedded in products could be put in

The hard part is not designing the new economy. The hard part will be getting every country to sign up.

place. That's a kind of carbon tax. So we'll have to redesign the World Trade Organization (WTO), the General Agreement on Tariffs and Trade (GATT) and other international institutions that govern trade.

It's going to be hard, but it can be done. The tools are there to build a new, carbon-light economy.

Wind

GOING WITH THE FLOW

Wind

An Introduction

Any doubts I once had that wind was a constant thing—like the rising of the sun or the phases of the moon—were dashed one summer on a bicycle. After graduating from university (for the first time), I packed my bike with camping gear and headed west from Toronto. My destination was the West Coast, more than 3,000 miles (5,000 kilometres) away. To get there, I had to cross the great Canadian Prairies. Under that vast Prairie sky, I pedaled furiously, *against the wind*, hour after hour, day after day. It never let up. It would start each morning around 8:30, and be my constant and unwanted companion until early evening. The odd cyclist coming the other way would just *fly* past, invariably yelling gleefully, "You're going the wrong way!"

What is the wind, and what makes it so relentless?

We've all looked up at the sky and been transfixed by how immense it is—particularly in the Prairies, where clouds dot the sky from one horizon to another, and the majesty of the blue expanse above takes your breath away.

Climb a decent-sized mountain, though, and things change—after a few days of climbing, the sky looks darker, as the layer of air that scatters the blue part of the sun's light starts to thin. The sun starts to appear more white than yellow. Breathing gets harder.

Razor-thin as it may be, there's energy in that air.

Similarly, while the atmosphere looks immense from the ground, from space it's a different matter. Former shuttle astronaut Vice-Admiral (Ret.) Richard Truly, commander of NASA's Naval Space Command, explains it like this: "When you look at the Earth's horizon, you see an incredibly beautiful, but very, very thin line. You can see a tiny rainbow of color. That thin line is our atmosphere. And the real fragility of our atmosphere is that there is so little of it."[1]

Our atmosphere is a tiny sliver of gas, as thin as a bit of plastic wrapped tightly around a beach ball. Almost all of the atmosphere's mass sits less than 10 miles (16 kilometres) from the ground. Created by life that happened long before us, it acts like a blanket, trapping the sun's heat. It's the atmosphere that makes our sky blue and sun yellow.[2]

This artist's rendering helps to illustrate how the atmosphere is a tiny sliver of gas surrounding the Earth—like a piece of plastic tied tightly around a beach ball. Astronauts report seeing a tiny, beautiful rainbow of color along the horizon.

For centuries, mankind depended on prevailing winds for exploration and commerce. Getting caught in the doldrums—low-pressure areas around the equator—was one of a sailor's worst nightmares. Survival rested in the hands of the wind.

The fact that air actually has mass—that it *weighs* something—may seem odd. I recall a science teacher telling his very dubious students that a full balloon weighs more than an empty one. "But they weigh the same," we scorned, "They're *both* empty, just shaped differently." He was right, of course. When we pulled out the scales, the full balloon *did* weigh more. Thanks to gravity, that thin rainbow of color sticks to the planet—even though stray oxygen molecules are constantly flying off into space.

Razor-thin as it may be, there can be energy in that air when it moves—and lots of it.

Friend to sailors on fine days and enemy on foul ones, bane of cyclists and boon to windsurfers, the winds blow, howl and gust. Hurricanes roar, and the jet streams high above us fly past at hundreds of miles an hour. Capturing all that energy can be a huge benefit to mankind.

The author discovered the power of wind when he cycled across the vast Canadian Prairies—traveling *against* the wind, as was gleefully pointed out by cyclists coming the other way.

Wind vs. Coal

Energy Type	Scale of Power Generation	Capital Costs[3]	Fuel Costs[4]
	Small – a house Medium – a neighborhood Large – a large city	$/watt of capacity	$/kilowatt hour of production
Coal	Large	$1.5 - $4[5]	$0.0175[6]
Wind – Micro	Small	$4 - $7[7]	free
Wind – On Land	Medium	$1.3 - $4[8]	free
Wind - Offshore	Large	$2.5 - $5[9]	free

Comparing wind to coal, with no cost attributed to carbon emissions and using only current economies of scale for wind. This is the picture that exists today—and the picture can only get better for wind. The upper boundary for wind both on land and offshore takes into account the intermittent nature of wind (the capacity factor). A cost to carbon will increase the cost of coal-based production. Wind fuel remains free.

Where Does the Wind Come From?

Wind is really just transformed solar energy—the expansion and contraction of air that has been heated by the sun and then cooled. As gusty and haphazard as wind may appear, large-scale global movements of air currents over land and sea ensure that there are areas where it is quite constant.

Air heats and rises from the equator, shedding moisture as it heads north and south at high altitudes. As it gradually cools, it drops back down to the surface as very dry air. These planet-sized currents are what form deserts, cause trade winds and give us our global weather patterns—patterns that are pretty reliable. That up-across-and-down action at the equator is called a Hadley cell, and a similar process repeats itself two more times between equator and pole.

The planet's spinning means that some of the pole-bound air at the top of the atmosphere shears off in one direction or another. This "Coriolis effect" is what gives us the trade winds, those highly regular currents sailors rely upon—and which almost broke my knees in the Prairies.

Wind is really just solar energy, the result of expanding and contracting air.

An exotic wind is the jet stream, a high-altitude wind that goes fast enough to lengthen or shorten our jet journeys. Jet streams are highly regular, and have been measured at speeds greater than 400 miles per hour (640 kilometres per hour). They're created where two atmospheric zones meet, about six to nine miles (10 to 15 kilometres) up in the subtropics, and about four miles (seven kilometres) up for the polar jet stream. The "troposphere" decreases in temperature with height, but above it is the "stratosphere," where temperature increases with height. That temperature difference conspires with the Coriolis effect to create the fast-moving jet stream.

Air heats and rises from the equator, shedding moisture as it heads north and south at high altitudes. As it gradually cools, it drops back down to the surface as very dry air. This pattern, repeated over and over, is what gives us our global weather patterns.

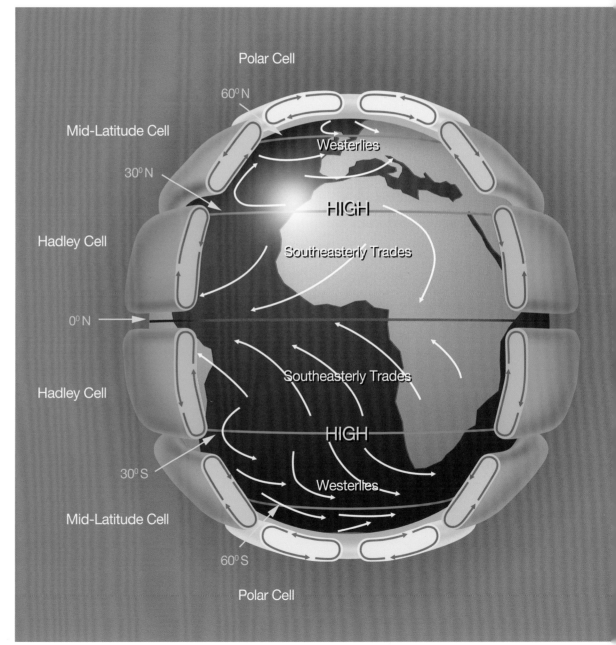

Polar Cell

60° N

Mid-Latitude Cell

Westerlies

30° N

Hadley Cell

HIGH

Southeasterly Trades

Hadley Cell

0° N

Southeasterly Trades

HIGH

30° S

Westerlies

Mid-Latitude Cell

60° S

Polar Cell

For centuries, windmills were prevalent around the world, though few people took better advantage of the wind—both on land and at sea—than the Dutch.

How Does Wind Energy Work?

Any mass that moves has *kinetic* energy, compared to *potential* energy (like a ball ready to roll down a hill) or *chemical* energy (like a charged battery). The trick is to grab the kinetic energy in the air and convert it to another form—usually electricity.

Wind turbines all work pretty much the same way: The wind blows, creating enough force to spin a turbine, which in turn powers a generator. There are subtleties (see "Why Do All the Big Ones Look the Same?" pg. 48), of course, but that's the thrust of it.

Wind energy has been captured by humans for thousands of years, not just for sailing, but also for grinding corn and wheat (hence wind*mill*), and pumping water. The first practical windmills are thought to have appeared in Persia between 500 and 900 AD,

and in northern Europe starting in the 12th century. Before the Industrial Revolution, there were more than 10,000 windmills dotting the British Isles. Throughout the Great Plains of America, windmills pumped

A single wind turbine can power a decent-sized town.

water for irrigation, and for locomotives to produce steam on their early journeys across the continent.

Nowadays, wind is big business, and the energy captured is almost always used to create electricity. We've applied some of the same principles used to power modern aircraft to building the massive blades—some of which are as big as the wings of a jumbo

jet—and these days, a single wind turbine can power a decent-sized town. Turbines three times taller than the Statue of Liberty are to be installed in the harsh conditions of the oceans, and small turbines that look like revolving sculptures are being installed in our urban environments.

Farms of windmills already pepper the landscape, and soon, massive stretches of these farms separated by huge distances will be connected by a supergrid, ensuring that when one region is calm, another can pick up the slack. Eventually, we'll be able to tap the vast and constant energy resource that is the jet stream, with high-altitude generators tethered to the ground miles below.

How Much Wind is Out There?

The fairly easy-to-get stuff can provide *five times* the total amount of electricity generated worldwide,[10] but if we want to get ambitious, the US Department of Energy reckons that wind could generate *15 times the total world energy use*. That's 15 times all the oil, coal, nuclear, electricity, whatever. The sky's the limit!

That's not to say there aren't pitfalls. Getting the power to where it's needed, storing it so that the lights stay on when the wind doesn't blow, even the protestations of those who don't like the way turbines look—these are all obstacles to be overcome.

But even T. Boone Pickens, that irascible American oil magnate, is sold on wind. He

The US Department of Energy reckons that wind could generate 15 times the world's total energy needs.

has called the United States the "Saudi Arabia of wind."

Let's see what that visionary oilman is so excited about.

Across the Great Plains of America, windmills pumped water for irrigation and supplied the steam for locomotives on their early journeys across the continent. This image from a pioneer museum underscores the importance of the windmill to homesteaders.

Farms of windmills already pepper the landscape, and soon, massive stretches of these farms, separated by huge distances, will be connected by a supergrid, ensuring that when one region is calm, another can pick up the slack.

The Big Stuff

Farming the Wind

Denmark is an understated country, not big on grand monuments. One of the most popular tourist sites in the capital, Copenhagen, is a life-sized statue of a mermaid—not exactly showy. We could say the opposite about California. Hollywood, Los Angeles, San Francisco—glamour, color, glitz! Yet, these two unlikely partners ignited the explosion in wind power that continues today.

Back in the 1970s, when OPEC decided to hold the world to ransom by choking off oil supplies, little Denmark felt even more vulnerable than the rest of the world. That's because the country imported nearly all of its energy. Those oil shocks, if they'd continued, would have brought the economy to its knees. In response, Denmark decided to develop wind power—big-time. In the meantime, half a world away in California, some of the most farsighted economic incentives were being put in place to encourage the generation of power from wind. Denmark made the turbines, and California installed them.

Large-scale wind power is the fastest-growing energy source in the world.

Since then, mainland Europe has taken the lead in wind generation, but the rest of the world is catching up fast. Large-scale wind power is the fastest growing energy source in the world, and 94 gigawatts of capacity was installed in 2007—enough to replace 90 coal-fired plants or power almost 90 million homes. The current champion is Germany—it has over 20,000 turbines up and running, generating more than 7% of the country's electricity. But the United States could soon overtake Germany—with Texas leading the pack.

And big industrial players like General Electric are getting into the game, putting considerable resources into developing wind-turbine technology.

The turbines themselves just keep getting bigger. Back in 1980, a decent-sized wind

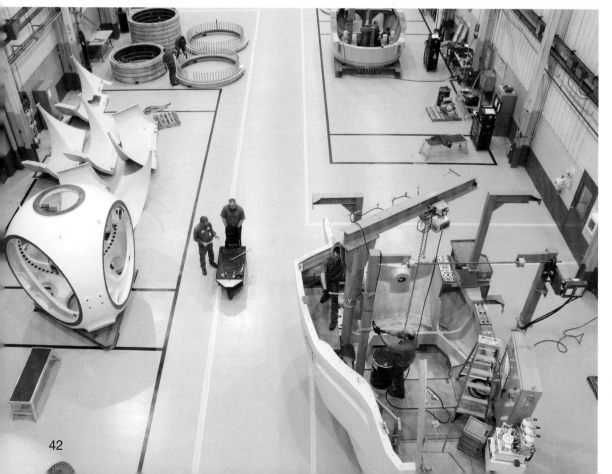

The enormous scale of the latest giant wind turbines becomes evident when you see the components alongside the technicians assembling them. The generator housing shown is for the Liberty turbine from Clipper Windpower.

Installing the mammoth turbines is a precise engineering exercise. To get a sense of just how huge these monsters are, pick out the two workmen standing in the generator housing, waiting to connect the giant rotor to the shaft plate.

turbine stood 50 feet high (15 metres) and could generate enough power for a few homes. Clipper, a California-based company, is now developing a turbine that will be rated somewhere between 7.5 and 10 megawatts—

One large turbine can provide enough electricity for more than 6,000 North American homes.

that's 200 times more power than the older model, or enough to supply a decent-sized town—with a rotor diameter twice the wingspan of a jumbo jet. One large Clipper can provide enough electricity for more than 6,000 North American homes.[11]

A word for the birds

It's untrue that wind turbines are a significant threat to birds. Turbines kill an average of one to two birds per turbine, per year.[12] Compare that to 57 million bird deaths from vehicles; 1.25 million from tall buildings; 97.5 million from plate-glass windows; anywhere between four million and 10 million from telecommunications towers; and 100 million from household cats—and that's in the US alone.

Not to be outdone, the European Union is funding research into a 20-megawatt turbine that will stand almost three times the height of the Statue of Liberty—and they're looking at ways to attach these turbines to the seabed or to floating platforms. They're even working on "smart blades" that change their shape depending on the wind conditions.

Canada is contributing to the evolution of these massive machines. A Canadian company called WhalePower has come up with something called Tubercle Technology. The leading edge of its blades are modeled on—you guessed

These big turbines are generally installed in huge wind farms extending to the horizon. Now *that's* a power plant.

it—the flipper of a humpback whale, making movement through the air more efficient. The technology is sort of like the dimples on a golf ball, creating just the "right kind of turbulence" to minimize drag.

These big turbines are not normally installed one at a time, but in huge wind farms that extend to the horizon. Now *that's* a power plant! These expansive farms can be found on land, on shallow coasts—and soon the deep sea.

The leading edge of this turbine blade uses Tubercle Technology, which dramatically improves the efficiency of its movement through air. The discovery was made when a scientist saw a whale sculpture and thought the fins were on backwards.

On Land

Most of the world's existing wind farms are on land. Obviously, that's the easiest place to start, and it's certainly the most cost-effective. The world's largest wind farm (as of mid-2009) is the Horse Hollow Wind Energy Center in Texas, with more than 400 huge turbines rated between 1.5 and 2.3 megawatts, and covering 47,000 acres. Even this massive farm will soon be overtaken, and right in Texas.

A new project, funded in part by Shell, will try to solve the problem of what to do when the wind doesn't blow, by using underground compressed air to store power and act as a kind of battery.

A project big enough to power three million homes,[13] owned in part by Shell, will blow the Horse Hollow project away, and not only in size. It will try to solve the problem of what to do when the wind doesn't blow, by using underground compressed air to store power and act as a kind of battery. Pump up the reservoir when it's windy, and release the pressure to drive a turbine when it's not.

How much wind is there on land? More than enough to power the US—"North Dakota alone is theoretically capable (if there was adequate transmission capacity) of producing enough wind-generated power to meet more than one-third of US electricity demand," according to the American Wind Energy Association.[14]

T. Boone Pickens certainly views the American Great Plains as a resource ready to exploit, and he's putting his money where his mouth is. The legendary oilman is gearing up to build wind farms all the way from the Texas panhandle to North Dakota, and figures we could generate one-fifth of the US electrical production for $1 trillion.[15] (Oh—and throw in another $200 billion to transmit that energy to where it's needed most.)

The world's largest wind farm, the Horse Hollow Wind Energy Center in Texas, has more than 400 huge turbines rated between 1.5 and 2.3 megawatts, and covers 47,000 acres.

In Shallow Water

Land may be the easiest place to put up a wind farm, but it's open water that's got the really good wind. Today, lots of wind farms

The London Array in the Thames Estuary will be a 1,000-megawatt monster, generating enough power to feed 750,000 homes.

sit in water shallow enough to attach the turbines right to the sea floor. It's not hard to do—just drive a massive steel stake into the seabed and attach the turbine.

In the shallow harbor outside Copenhagen sits the Middelgrunden project, where 20 two-megawatt turbines, each more than 330 feet (100 metres) tall, stand in a gentle curve. They provide some serious competition for that understated little mermaid—they're a tourist attraction in their own right. Generating enough power for 30,000 homes, they stand as a testament to Denmark's early lead in big wind.

However, it's the UK that's emerging as the offshore champ, with a number of existing projects and more in the works. Any wonder for an island nation? The London Array in the Thames Estuary will be a 1,000-megawatt

The UK is emerging as the offshore champ.

monster, generating enough power to feed 750,000 London homes. A slightly smaller farm has been approved for North Wales. Siemens expects Britain to account for half of the company's worldwide offshore turbine sales.[16]

The Middelgrunden project, with 20 wind turbines at two megawatts each, generates enough power for 30,000 homes. It sits in shallow water just outside Copenhagen harbor. The area has restricted access due to its use as a onetime dump site for harbor sludge.

MIT and the National Renewable Energy Laboratory have a vision: huge offshore wind turbines powering hundreds of thousands of homes. The trick? The turbines float on platforms 100 miles out to sea, where the wind is strong and steady—and no one can see them from onshore.

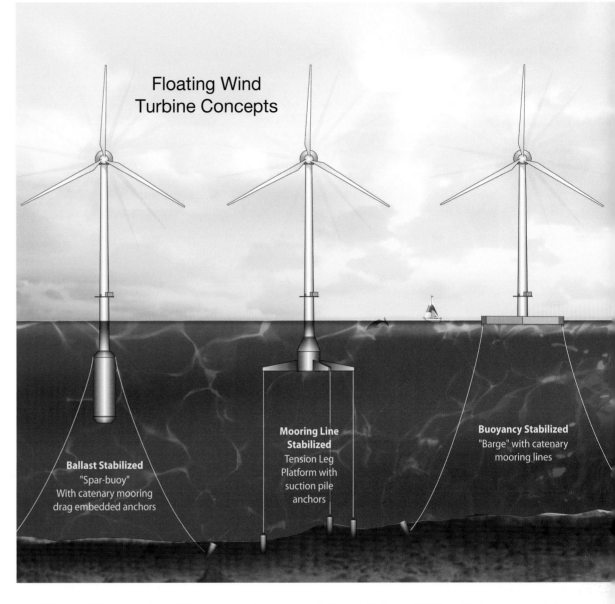

Floating Wind Turbine Concepts

Ballast Stabilized
"Spar-buoy"
With catenary mooring drag embedded anchors

Mooring Line Stabilized
Tension Leg Platform with suction pile anchors

Buoyancy Stabilized
"Barge" with catenary mooring lines

The Deep Sea

If you've ever gone sailing, you'll know that the wind on open water is far stronger than on land. Compare the winds in the Gulf of Maine, for instance, to those in the American Midwest, and you'll find that they're about one-third more powerful. That may not seem like much, but the extra bit more than doubles the amount of energy generated. University of Maine professor Habib Dagher calls it "the largest renewable resource that the US has." And it's a resource that's crying out to be developed.

But turbines on the open water must be able to withstand the vagaries of the ocean: strong gales, massive ocean waves and swells, and saltwater spray. Not only is the sea hard on the turbines themselves, but the horrendous conditions make it all the harder to service them. Plus, there's the added hurdle of getting all that power to land.

The potential payoff is huge, though, so that pretty much guarantees the engineering problems will be solved. Another incentive lies in the fact that almost 80% of the electricity in the US is consumed by people living along the coasts of the Atlantic, Pacific and Great Lakes. "With all due respect to North Dakota and South Dakota, which have also been labeled the Saudi Arabia of wind, people live along our coastlines,"[17] says Raymond Dackerman, general manager of Blue H, a Boston-based company.

Deep-sea test projects are underway in Norway, Denmark and France, and a full-scale wind farm is planned for 2013 in the North Sea. It will be a while before they're commercially ready, though, so it looks like Mr. Pickens might win this race on land.

Why Do All the Big Ones Look the Same?
(A Bit of Physics)

Ever wonder why all large turbines look similar? To be sure, there are almost as many types of turbines as there are cars—one blade, two blades, many blades that form a wheel, wild-looking vertical egg-beaters, and even lovely twirling statues that look like a jazz riff on the helix shape of our DNA (more on that in the next section). But the big ones—the massive turbines that make up the utility-scale wind farms—all look similar, with the same kind of blades, and nearly always three of them. Why? It's all physics.

Intuitively, it seems like the wind *pushes* those blades around to generate power, but that's not the case. Just like a puffed-out sail or the wing of a jet in flight, a different force is at play.

When a jet flies through the air, it uses *lift*—an upward force that counteracts gravity. That lift comes from something called Bernoulli's principle,[18] and it's the same thing that turns the turbine blade, except the wind is slower and the blade is vertical. But it's lift, or suction, that *pulls* the blade, just like the wing of a jet. That's why the blades all look roughly the same—they've been designed to maximize lift and minimize drag (friction) of the blade passing through the air.

Sure, but why always three blades? It's all a matter of efficiency.

Though there are many types of wind turbines, the utility-scale ones nearly all have the same three-blade configuration. It's a matter of efficiency—three blades maximize exposure to the air without overtly increasing drag.

To get the most energy out of the passing air, the rotating blades need to interact with as much of that air as possible. Lots of blades may seem more efficient, since there's more surface area to interact with the wind. But as they rotate, they also interact with each other, by disturbing the airflow. That's a bad thing. So, how about fewer blades? They'd have to rotate faster to interact with all the passing air, creating too much drag. It's a balance: The blades have to turn fast enough to interact with all the air, slow enough that drag isn't an issue, and with few enough of them to ensure they don't interact with each other. It turns out that three blades is pretty much optimal.

There are other shapes and ideas for different purposes, of course. One novel idea was created by a German company: SkySails, a great big sail that's attached to an ocean-going freighter. It helps to pull the boat, and can reduce fuel use by 10% to 35%, according to the company.[19]

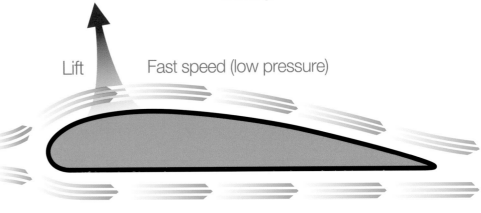

Turbine blades benefit from the same "Bernoulli's principle" that keeps airplanes aloft—the lift created on the front surface pulls the blade through the air, increasing the turning power of the shaft that spins the electrical generator.

Lift

Fast speed (low pressure)

Slow speed (high pressure)

A German company has developed enormous towing kites for ocean freighters, dubbed SkySails, that can reduce annual fuel costs by 10% to 35%. The unique "paraglider" shape of the sail generates five times more propulsion power than a conventional sail.

Helix Wind, based in California, has developed a small-scale turbine that spins on a vertical shaft. It operates well at a wide range of wind velocities, no matter the wind direction. So it works everywhere from the Arctic Circle to marine petroleum platforms to sub-Saharan Africa.

Micro-Wind

Small is Beautiful

As puzzling as it seems, some people just don't find wind turbines beautiful. Though most of our industrial trappings —vehicles, roads, factories, telephone poles— aren't exactly easy on the eyes, wind is often singled out for aesthetic criticism. One solution is to plant wind farms away from urban areas or in the open sea.

Another solution is to make them smaller and more beautiful, designed to integrate right into coastal, mountainous or urban environments.

Micro-wind designs are normally used to provide power in remote locations. They differ only from their larger counterparts in size. Helix Wind has added a twist—literally.

> Micro-wind turbines are normally used to provide power in remote locations. They're similar in operation to the big turbines, just smaller.

Helix, based in San Diego, California, started with a vertical design. The spinning part extends straight upward from a vertical shaft. Vertical designs have been around for a while, and there are advantages: They spin equally well whatever the wind direction, and they stand up to much stronger gusts than their larger, horizontal cousins.

Helix's breakthrough is to develop a visually stunning design, made from an aluminum alloy, that looks like a pulsing piece of modern art. CEO Ian Gardner says: "Why do early-stage technologists become enamored with engineering and forget the aesthetics?

The people buying and using their inventions care about what it looks like and how their neighbors might react."

Based on a double-helix shape similar to

> It is art, of course. It just happens to make electricity.

our DNA, and producing enough power for several homes, Helix's turbines are designed to please the eye. Also used in isolated environments (like cell towers or remote facilities), they are meant to integrate into the modern urban landscape. The first Helix installation, by the side of a highway in urban California, is often mistaken for art.

It *is* art, of course. It just happens to make electricity, too.

The Skystream 3.7 connects to your home's electrical meter. When the wind blows, it powers your house. When it doesn't, you can draw power from your local utility. Some meters even spin backwards when you generate more energy than you use.

The Upper Skies

Mining the Jet Stream

Where might wind power go from here? While some companies are eyeing the deep oceans, others are looking up—waaay up.

The jet stream never stops. Based on the Earth's rotation and some basic atmospheric physics, you can count on it day or night, summer or winter. The problem, of course, is the height. The jet stream sits somewhere between 20,000 and 40,000 feet (6,000 and 12,000 metres) up, running east in the northern hemisphere, at speeds that average from 125 to 160 miles per hour (200 to 260 kilometres per hour).

Mining the jet stream could deliver enormous amounts of power. According to atmospheric scientist Ken Caldeira, at the Carnegie Institution's Department of Global Ecology at Stanford University, "My calculations show

> "My calculations show that if we could just tap into 1% of the energy in high-altitude winds, it would be enough to power all civilization. The whole planet."

that if we could just tap into 1% of the energy in high-altitude winds, it would be enough to power all civilization. The whole planet." We're hunting really big game here. So who's on the prowl?

An American company called Sky Windpower has developed functional prototypes designed to fly in the jet stream, generate power and send it back to Earth through the cables to

which they are tethered. Since these sky-high turbines are portable, they can be packed up and moved when the jet stream shifts around, as it sometimes does.

The folks at Sky WindPower reckon that if these high-flying turbines were deployed en masse, they could generate power at two cents per kilowatt hour—that's way less than coal. *Time Magazine* thinks enough of the company's take on things that it recently named the company's flying electric generator as one of the top 50 inventions of 2008.

This isn't pie-in-the-sky stuff—it's real, it's possible, it's large-scale, and it's on the way.

A slightly less lofty vision comes from a Canadian company called Magenn. Its vision is to enable small-scale, reliable generation by using a helium balloon to get a small turbine up above the unstable winds found at lower heights. They're simple but effective, particularly for areas where the good winds are found above surrounding treetops or buildings. Hoist the balloon and turn the switch!

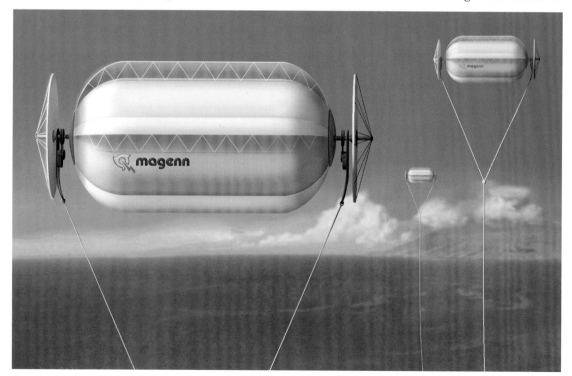

A Canadian company called Magenn plans to use helium-filled balloons deployed at a few hundred feet to tap into the consistent winds found there. Each cylindrical balloon spins on a central axis, powering a generator and feeding electricity down through the tether line.

Sky Windpower has developed giant "spinning kites" designed to fly in the jet stream. They will generate power 24/7 and send it back to Earth through the tether cable. Since they're portable, they can be moved when the jet stream moves, as it sometimes does.

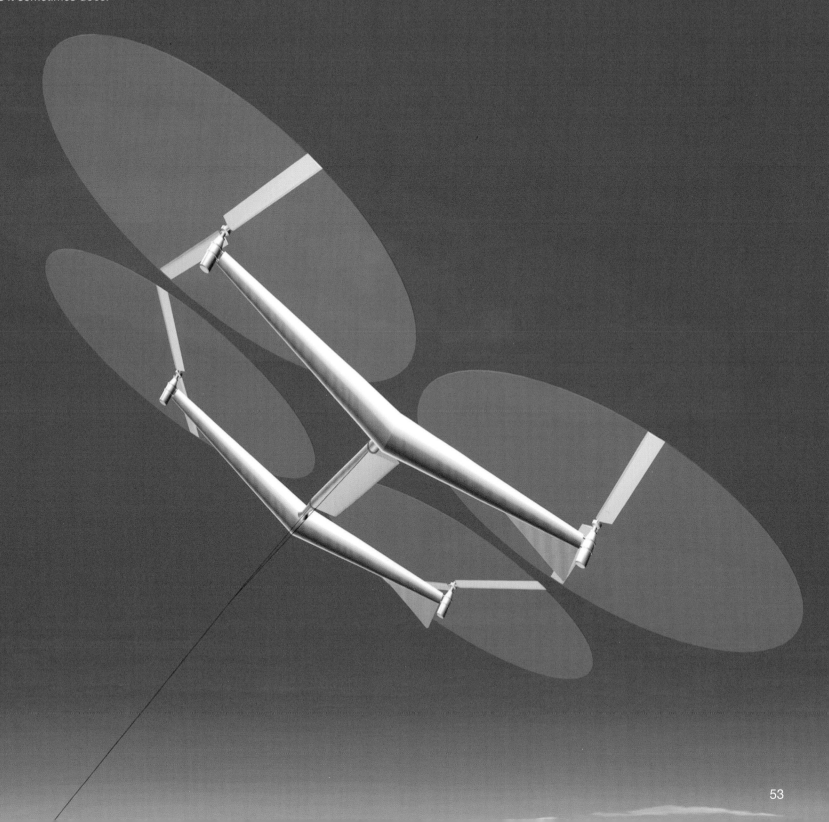

Potential and Pitfalls

We've seen the potential of wind. There's enough harvestable wind out there to provide five times the world's electrical consumption. And that's without any of the futuristic stuff, like mining the jet stream, which I'll ignore for now.

What is wind's potential? Easily 20% of our energy needs, and probably more like 40%, with storage and grid balancing.

As you might suspect, it's not quite that easy. Sometimes, the wind doesn't blow, and it's often far from the cities where it's needed. The distance issue is simple: Build a big grid. The intermittency problem is a bit harder to solve. When we flip a light switch, we want the light to come on, regardless of whether the wind is blowing. It's that simple.

Generally speaking, if the proportion of wind is less than 20% of the total electrical supply, it's not much of a problem. Only Denmark is close to reaching that point; even Germany and Britain have a long way to go. The US is at around 1%, as is the rest of world. So there is *lots* of wind yet to harvest, without any fancy tricks.

And as far as fancy tricks go, there are really just two. First trick: Store the energy. One way to do that is with giant storage—like the compressed air concept they're going to use in Texas—or hydrostorage. Hydrostorage means using wind power to pump water up a hill into a giant reservoir, then using that water for hydroelectricity when the wind stops. There's another way. When the Energy Internet arrives, storage could take place in millions of small batteries—like the ones that will run our electric cars. They could store energy when they're not being used, but that story will have to wait until Chapter 10.

Second trick: Connect lots of wind farms (and other renewable sources) from faraway places to the same grid. When one place is calm, another is windy. Studies from the University of Kassel in Germany show that so-called large-scale grid balancing can increase the percentage of wind's contribution in Europe to 70%.[20] A similar figure

When we flip a light switch, we want the light to come on whether the wind is blowing or not.

could probably be reached in the United States.

What's the potential of wind? Easily 20% of our energy needs, and probably more like 40%, with storage and grid balancing. How fast can we get to 40%? We'd need to install around 1.5 million two-megawatt turbines over the next 10 years or so.[21] That's a massive job, but as Lester Brown of the Earth Policy Institute says: "We build 65 million cars every year, so it's not a big deal. We could produce these wind turbines for the entire world simply by opening the closed automobile assembly plants in the United States."[22]

The Trillion-Dollar Question:

So, what do you get for $1 trillion?
Straight from T. Boone Pickens: You could replace 20% of the US electrical supply (that's almost half of coal-based production), with maybe another $200 billion required to get that energy to where it's needed.

The National Wind Technology Center in Golden, Colorado, is upgrading its blade test facilities to accommodate the behemoths being installed on today's enormous turbines—like this 146-foot (45-metre) blade.

Even without any of the futuristic stuff, there's enough harvestable wind out there to provide five times the world's electrical consumption. For many countries, it's an opportunity to convert unused manufacturing capacity to the production of wind turbines. This is a shot of Vestas's two-megawatt and three-megawatt turbines in Meroicinha, Portugal.

Climate Science I

The Basic Stuff

If something is based on "theory," we can still say we know it!

Anyone watching television or reading the daily paper over the past decade or so could hardly be blamed for thinking climate science a murky affair, rife with disagreement and doubtful claims. One "expert" is pitted against another, the first muttering something about solar flares and the other trying to explain what "peer review" means. But there hasn't been *real* disagreement on climate change for some time—at least in reputable scientific circles. The remaining arguments are about fine details. But it's easy—and comforting—to find a marginal crackpot on television telling us not to worry. That's irresponsible journalism, and it gives an impression of doubt where none exists.

We know that the Earth is warming, we know *our* carbon dioxide emissions are causing it, and we know that, without big reductions in those emissions, the climate will change in ways that are harmful to our way of life.

Those who publicly doubt climate change will say that because it is based on "theory," it can be

Average worldwide temperatures have risen sharply in the last century—the fastest rise in the past 1,000 years.

dismissed as mere conjecture. But that is to mistake what is meant by "theory." It is scientific theory that the Earth is round, and it is theory that the sun will rise in the east tomorrow. For scientists, *all* knowledge is refutable, given the right evidence. There's a degree of doubt associated with every

theory. If one day the sun rose in the west, theories about planetary movement would change. The real issue is—what is the *degree* of doubt?

Climate science is complex. But one of the largest international assemblies of scientists ever formed, the Intergovernmental Panel on

Carbon levels are rising fast, and human activity is responsible. Deforestation and fossil fuel use are what's changing the game.

Climate Change (IPCC), agrees on the basics. Even the *slightest* chance that they're right would warrant serious action, a kind of insurance policy against calamity. But the chances of the IPCC being correct are not slim—you can bet your house on it. Here are some basics.

Carbon dioxide[1] (carbon) in the atmosphere warms the Earth, acting as an insulating blanket. It lets in more energy as sunlight than it lets out as heat, trapping that heat. We've known this since the early 1800s.[2] Without greenhouse gases, the Earth would be inhospitable—but there can be too much of a good thing. More than 100 years ago, scientists began to worry, calculating how much carbon was emitted by burning coal and to what degree it might warm the atmosphere. Emissions then were tiny, and it remained a theoretical curiosity.

Carbon concentrations are linked to temperature over long periods of time.[3] Carbon concentrations—calculated in parts per million—were measured directly starting in the 1950s, and it's possible to track levels going back hundreds of thousands of years, by looking at tiny bubbles trapped in Antarctic ice. The deeper into the ice you go, the further back in time the air was trapped. Temperature is calculated by measuring the ratio of two kinds of molecules—a heavy isotope of oxygen and deuterium—set by the temperature at the time the bubbles were formed. We know that when carbon levels increase, so does temperature.[4] There are other ways to confirm this link, like looking at ancient tree rings or the sediment at the bottom of deep lakes. They all say the same thing.

Carbon levels are rising fast, and human activity is responsible. Deforestation and fossil fuel use

We know the Earth is warming, we know our carbon dioxide is causing it, and we know the changes will be harmful to our way of life.

are what is changing the game. The carbon concentration has risen from pre-industrial levels of 280 parts per million to more than 390, higher than it's been for hundreds of thousands of years. It's still rising by three parts per million each year. We know we're responsible because we know how much carbon we release, and we know how much is absorbed.[5] Roughly, the difference is us. Really dangerous levels of carbon occur around 450 parts per million, so without big changes, we'll be there when today's preschoolers are attending university.

We are causing the latest warming, which is happening alarmingly fast.[6] Average worldwide temperatures have risen by 1.8 F (0.6 C) in the last century—the fastest rise in the past 1,000 years. The rise is directly correlated to the rise in carbon. Temperature cycles in the past that saw ice ages come and go were caused by subtle changes in the Earth's orbit (called Milankovitch cycles), but that's not the case now. Those cycles are regular, we know when they occur—and this isn't one of them.

The future looks bleak if we don't change our behavior.[7] Warming is not a gradual, gentle process that lets Torontonians wear shorts in December and lengthens the golf season in New York State. It disrupts ecosystems, causes violent storms and changes weather patterns. It will render life very difficult. That story continues in "Climate Science III – The Bad Stuff."

Finally, this stuff is coming at us faster than is generally acknowledged in the popular media. The IPCC is authoritative, but conservative.[8] The latest science shows that we've already passed their worst-case scenarios. Stuff that wasn't supposed to happen for decades is happening before our eyes, like the summer melting of Arctic ice and permafrost, and the recent droughts in Australia.

THREE

Geo

hermal

A GIANT THERMOS CALLED EARTH

The main spring at the Roman Baths in Somerset, UK, was originally considered a sacred shrine by the Celts. Today, the soothing waters attract thousands of visitors annually, and remind us of Earth's free and plentiful resource—endless heat.

Geothermal

An Introduction

Humans have a long history of tapping the Earth's heat. It warmed the waters of the spa towns of Britain, where the Roman's came to bathe. Today, natural hot-water spas around the world attract millions of visitors seeking the soothing comfort of that healing heat. Its fury has bewildered humans throughout history, with violent eruptions spewing hot ash and lava from giant pores in the Earth's surface. Less dangerous—but no less impressive—are its displays of contained energy, such as those that entertain tourists in Wyoming's Yellowstone Park, where geysers spout with startling regularity and force. It ranges in temperature from the extreme heat of the Earth's core to the constant (and much more comfortable) temperatures found just a few feet beneath the planet's surface.

The heat in the ground comes from a massive, but very weak, nuclear furnace.

Geothermal energy is one of the only[1] meaningful sources of renewable energy available to us that is not ultimately reliant on the sun.

Although the Earth's core is about 12,000 F (7,000 C), the heat near the surface—the upper crust of rock that's about 60 miles (100 kilometres) thick, and below which we've never explored[2]—has a nearby, nuclear source. Radioactive elements like thorium and uranium are spread throughout the upper crust, and are constantly decaying and releasing heat. Thus, the heat in the ground comes from a massive, but very weak, nuclear furnace.

Generally speaking, the deeper you go, the hotter it gets. There are exceptions, like geysers, hot springs and volcanoes—all examples of Earth's extreme inner heat poking through to the surface via ruptures in the Earth's crust.

Geothermal energy is one of the only meaningful sources of renewable energy available that is not directly reliant on the sun.

Think of geothermal energy as mining the heat in the ground. Today, that energy comes from two kinds of mining operations. We mine *high-temperature heat*—from volcanic activity and hot springs—where it's easy to find, along the Earth's fault lines. We mine *low-temperature heat*[3] where it sits, just a few yards beneath our feet. Think of the high-temperature stuff as digging up a rich vein of gold, and the low-temperature stuff as panning for gold flakes.

Let's call the first kind *hot geothermal*. It's limited to places where the high-temperature stuff is close to the surface, near volcanoes or along cracks in the Earth's crust—where the Romans built their baths. The second kind is often called *geo-exchange*, or ground-source heating. Although it's nowhere near as dramatic as the high-temperature stuff, it has enormous potential for carbon-free energy production. Best of all, you can mine it pretty much anywhere.

Old Faithful, a cone geyser in Wyoming's Yellowstone National Park, erupts roughly every 90 minutes, shooting boiling water to a height of up to 185 feet (56 metres), and lasting between 1.5 and five minutes.

Pamukkale, meaning "cotton castle" in Turkish, is a collection of hot springs in Turkey's River Menderes valley. The mineral-rich waters deposit thick, white layers of limestone and travertine that cascade down the mountain, resembling a frozen waterfall.

Tomorrow's mining will be a hybrid of the two. It's called Enhanced Geothermal Systems (EGS), and it revolves around the simple idea that high-temperature heat can be found pretty much anywhere—if you only drill deep enough. The potential of geothermal energy, once EGS is brought into commercial operation, cannot be overstated—it is simply colossal.

A recent study[4] by the Massachusetts Institute of Technology (MIT) noted that the total geothermal energy available within six miles (10 kilometres) of the Earth's surface is 130,000 times the entire energy needs of the United States. Obviously, not all of it can be tapped, but even conservative estimates of recoverable energy indicate that between 3,000 and 30,000 times the total energy needs of the US are just sitting down there, waiting to be captured. This isn't intermittent power that depends on the sun or wind; this stuff is available all day, every day, year-round.

So, EGS could provide for *all* of our energy needs, all over the world—and it's both constant and reliable. At first glance, geothermal seems to be a bit of a magic bullet. Let's see if that's really the case.

> The potential of geothermal energy, once EGS is brought into commercial operation, cannot be overstated—it is simply colossal.

Geo-exchange

Mining the Heat in Your Own Backyard

Whether we're walking down a city street, strolling through a park or sitting in our own backyard,

Think of the ground as a "heat battery," and think of a "heat pump" as a way to get the heat in and out of that battery.

there's a reliable, clean and renewable energy resource just a few feet below us. Although we've known about it for decades, it's a resource that's scarcely been tapped.

The temperature of the Earth just beneath the surface—starting at about 10 feet (three metres) and continuing down for hundreds of yards—is *roughly constant*, year-round. It stays somewhere between 46 F and 60 F (8 C to 16 C), depending on geography, depth and time of year.[5] Geo-exchange is the art of using that energy to heat and cool buildings throughout the year. Think of the ground as a "heat battery," and think of a "heat pump" as a way to get the heat in and out of that battery.

There are already more than a million geo-exchange installations in North America. The easy installs are in buildings with a big yard, where you can bury the pipes. Where that's not possible, you can always go straight down.

How does it work? Let's look at an example for heating: First, you pump liquid—normally a glycol solution—through a length of pipe[6] (called the "geo loop") that's buried or drilled into the ground.[7] The liquid absorbs heat from the surrounding earth as it travels through the pipe. Let's say the glycol goes in at 46 F (8 C) and comes out at 52 F (11 C). The heart of the system is the heat pump,[8] which acts like a refrigerator in reverse. It takes heat out of the liquid and transfers it to the building. The liquid returns to its original temperature, and the process repeats. The net effect is to mine the heat from the ground and transfer it to the building. How do you cool a building? The same process in reverse.

There are more than a million geothermal installations in North America alone, and we've barely scratched the surface.

Here's the key to energy production: The heat pump can get three to five times more energy out of the ground than it consumes. That means it runs at 300% to 500% efficiency and can lower a building's energy use by up to 75%. Depending on the source of the electricity, the carbon footprint can be almost completely eliminated.[9]

Simply put, geo-exchange is the holy grail of heating and cooling—no other technology can touch it. High-efficiency furnaces, modern air conditioners, baseboard heaters—none of these come close. As a bonus, the entire heating system gets pushed to the electrical grid, which will one day be powered by clean, carbon-free, renewable energy. There's no way a natural-gas furnace can *ever* go carbon-free.

This is a typical installation of a "horizontal loop" for geothermal heating and cooling. It will serve a new building being constructed at Wyggeston and Queen Elizabeth I College in Leicester, U.K.

Heat pumps are used for either heating or cooling by transferring heat between two reservoirs. In the warmer months, they act like an air conditioner, in colder months like a heater. Even a 32 F day (0 C) produces enough heat to warm a home.

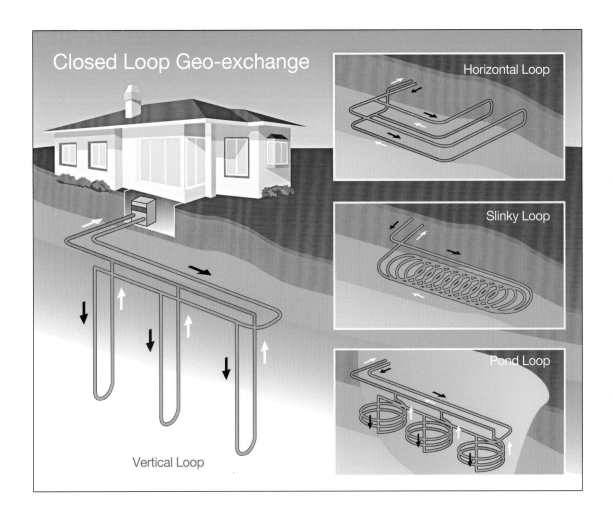

Closed Loop Geo-exchange

Horizontal Loop

Slinky Loop

Pond Loop

Vertical Loop

Sounds great—*so why isn't a geo-exchange system installed in every building?*

Mainly, it costs more. A typical house would face about $10,000 in additional costs, above and beyond the price of a furnace and air conditioner. You've got all those pipes to bury in the ground, and maybe some holes to drill. Why go to all that bother and expense? It does pay for itself over time,[10] but we don't always think long-term.

Plus, there's often a disconnect between paying for the geo-exchange system and getting the savings. A typical condominium or housing developer doesn't pay the ongoing energy bills, and they're motivated to minimize construction costs. Again—why go to the extra expense?

Geo-exchange can change the face of heating and cooling—no other technology can touch it.

Despite these hurdles, geo-exchange is catching on. There are more than a million installations in North America alone, and we've barely scratched the surface. The easy installs are in buildings with a big yard where you can bury the pipes—but now, geo is going downtown.

A building development of my own, called Planet Traveler—a hotel in a dense part of downtown Toronto—has been designed to be the greenest[11] hotel in North America. We wanted to prove that buildings in dense urban cores, with little or no land for the geo-loop, can still use geo. We have literally no ground to bury pipes—the building takes up the entire footprint of the property. So how did we do it?

Toronto's new Planet Traveler Hotel plans to be the greenest hotel in the world. Thanks to the city, an adjacent publicly owned laneway was used to bury geo-loop pipes, which connect to a heat pump to support the building's heating and cooling.

At Toronto's new Planet Traveler Hotel, 10 holes were drilled to bury 4,000 feet (1,200 metres) of geo-loop pipe. Although drilling is tough work, the long-term payback makes the effort worthwhile.

We forged an agreement with Toronto city council that allowed us to bury 4,000 feet (1,200 metres) of pipe in 10 holes drilled into the publicly owned laneway that runs alongside the building. Not only did the city give the go-ahead, but it's now looking at opening up all public lands—parks, laneways, everything—to geo-exchange. That would make Toronto the first city in the world to formalize this kind of relationship, allowing its citizens to be their own geo-exchange utility.

The technology may not be new, but as Paul Mertes, CEO of Canadian geo-exchange provider Clean Energy Developments, puts it: "Geo-exchange makes existing heating and cooling technologies look like an 8-track player." Bring on the iPod!

Hot Geothermal

Mining the Hot Stuff

If geo-exchange is like panning for gold flakes (mining lots of low-temperature heat), then hot geothermal is like finding a rich vein of gold. The heat is more intense—sometimes hot enough to make steam and produce electricity—but it can only be found in a few places. Areas around volcanoes, geysers and other perforations in the Earth's crust are all places the hot stuff—normally buried much deeper underground—has poked its way close to the surface.

Hot aquifers are formed when water seeps close to one of these areas, and some gets sealed under a rock cap. Geysers are examples of that cap being punctured, releasing gasps of the hot steam. Hot geothermal makes use of that heat by tapping into hot aquifers located close to the surface.

Iceland is famous for its hot springs, geysers and volcanic activity. About a quarter of the country's electrical production is geothermal, and almost all of its buildings are heated by geothermal sources. Iceland

> Hot geothermal makes use of heat by tapping into hot aquifers located close to the surface.

has so much of the stuff, they even heat their sidewalks. Paris is a long way from Iceland, but even there, geothermal energy is used to heat entire neighborhoods.

The Blue Lagoon is one of Iceland's most visited attractions. The warm waters, rich in silica and sulfur, flow from a nearby geothermal power plant and are said to have special curative effects for people suffering from skin diseases such as psoriasis.

The Geysers geothermal field in the northern coastal region of California produce more electricity than any other geothermal field in the world—enough to power over 850,000 homes. Two "recharge projects" recycle treated wastewater to extend the life of the steam field.

How does it work? The idea is simple: Drill down to the hot aquifer, pump hot water to the surface, then either use the heat directly or—if it's hot enough to make steam—to generate electricity.

Waters of different temperatures are treated differently. If it's *really* hot—like superheated steam at 575 F (300 C)—it will be under a lot of pressure and can be run directly though a turbine. Tapping that resource at the surface, if exposed to the open air, can sound like a jet engine. Lower temperatures—say, 300 F (150 C)—are still used for electrical production, but it takes an extra step. Heat from the geothermal water is extracted and used to boil a second liquid—butane or pentane—that has a lower boiling point. It's the vaporized second liquid that drives the turbine. Finally, if the temperature is low enough—between 140 F and 160 F (60 C to 70 C)—then the heat can be used directly.

The average geothermal plant is smaller than a coal plant and will produce enough energy to power about 50,000 homes. But several can be scattered over the same geothermal

Geothermal plants are not environmentally pristine, but release far fewer contaminants per unit of power than their fossil-fueled counterparts.

resource. The Mammoth Pacific plant in California, operating since the late '80s, is typical, producing enough power for 40,000 homes. A large plant in Larderello, Italy—the world's first geothermal electrical installation, built back in 1913—now provides 10% of the world's geothermal supply, powering over a million homes.

Geothermal plants are not environmentally pristine, since the geothermal water can contain contaminants—including carbon dioxide. But geothermal plants release far fewer[13] of these

The average geothermal plant will produce enough energy to power about 50,000 homes.

contaminants per unit of power than do their fossil-fueled counterparts.

There are hundreds of geothermal plants worldwide, producing enough electricity to power about 11 million homes. That's actually not much—less than 1% of world electrical production. The problem is geology—there just aren't that many rich veins of hot water near the surface—and production is limited mainly to a few places like the US, Costa Rica, Indonesia, Italy, Japan and Mexico.

If we had to stick to the stuff close to the surface, geothermal would remain a bit player on the world energy stage. But geothermal is ready to hit the big leagues.

Wairakei geothermal field, located in the middle of New Zealand's North Island, has been in production for more than 50 years. The power station, commissioned in 1958, was the world's second large-scale geothermal facility.

Enhanced Geothermal Systems

Mining the Hot Stuff, Anywhere

To get a feel for enhanced geothermal, think geo-exchange, only bigger and deeper, with more complicated pipes—and used for electrical production instead of just heat. In most of the world, the ground six miles (10 kilometres) beneath our feet is dry, but as hot as the hottest aquifer. That heat can be mined, brought to the surface and used to generate electricity.

Enhanced geothermal systems (EGS) represent the great hope of geothermal. If geo-exchange is the holy grail of heating and cooling, EGS

The ground beneath the US could easily provide all its energy needs for the foreseeable future.

is the holy grail of electrical production. Available around the clock, all year long and almost anywhere, it could be the workhorse of the world's electrical system, with a constant baseload supply. It's got colossal potential—the ground beneath the US could easily provide *all* of the country's energy needs for the foreseeable future. EGS is the real deal.

How does it work? Drill down 2.5 to six miles (four to 10 kilometres), until you reach hot rock approaching 400 F (200 C). Drill another hole some distance away. Push water down the first hole at high pressure, creating a network of cracks between the two holes. Essentially, you're creating a big, complex and very deep geo-loop. To mine the heat, pump liquid down one hole, and let it seep through the cracks in the rock and up the other. Grab the heat at the surface and use it to generate electricity. If you ever run out of heat, just move over a mile or two and start again, allowing the first area to heat up again.

To get a sense of how much energy is stored in the ground, imagine a 70,000-metric-ton pile of coal. Extracting enough heat to lower the temperature of a chunk of rock measuring just one-quarter of a cubic mile (one cubic kilometre) by just *one degree* will give you as much energy as burning that pile of coal. It could provide electricity to 14,000 homes for a year.[14] Ten degrees gets you 140,000 homes.

EGS is the holy grail of electrical production— available around the clock, all year long and almost anywhere.

The real magic of EGS is that you can drill for it pretty much anywhere—London, Adelaide, Toronto or New York, it doesn't matter. We're not limited to those few, thin veins of heat close to the surface.

Thanks to experimental projects in the 1970s at Los Alamos National Laboratory in the US, and at Cornwall, in the UK, in the 1980s, researchers developed methods of making fractures in hot, dry rock deep below the surface. A full-scale international collaboration is underway in Soultz, France. Small experimental holes 2.2 miles (3.5 kilometres) deep were drilled back in 1997, and the site has now been expanded into a full-scale pilot project, using three holes 3.1 miles (five kilometres) deep. Water pumped into one hole emerges from the other at about 400 F (200 C). A power plant big enough to power 1,500 homes is currently in operation.[15]

Unlike conventional hot geothermal, which captures the relatively shallow heat found in fissures in the Earth's surface, so-called enhanced geothermal reaches down several miles to tap into the mammoth and unlimited heat reserves that reside there.

How Enhanced Geothermal Works

1. Drill an "injection well" 2.5 to six miles deep (four to 10 kilometres), until you reach hot rock approaching 400 F (200 C). Pump down cold water at high pressure, creating fissures in the low-permeability basement rock.

2. The water flowing into the fissures of the hot, dry rock creates a reservoir of very hot geothermal fluid. This essentially creates a massive, complex and very deep geo-loop.

3. Drill a nearby production well to roughly the same depth and pump the heated fluid back to the surface. As it rises, the pressure decreases and it turns into steam.

4. At the surface, the steam is captured and runs a series of turbines to generate electricity. At various steps in the process, excess water is captured and returned to a reservoir, creating a "closed loop" system.

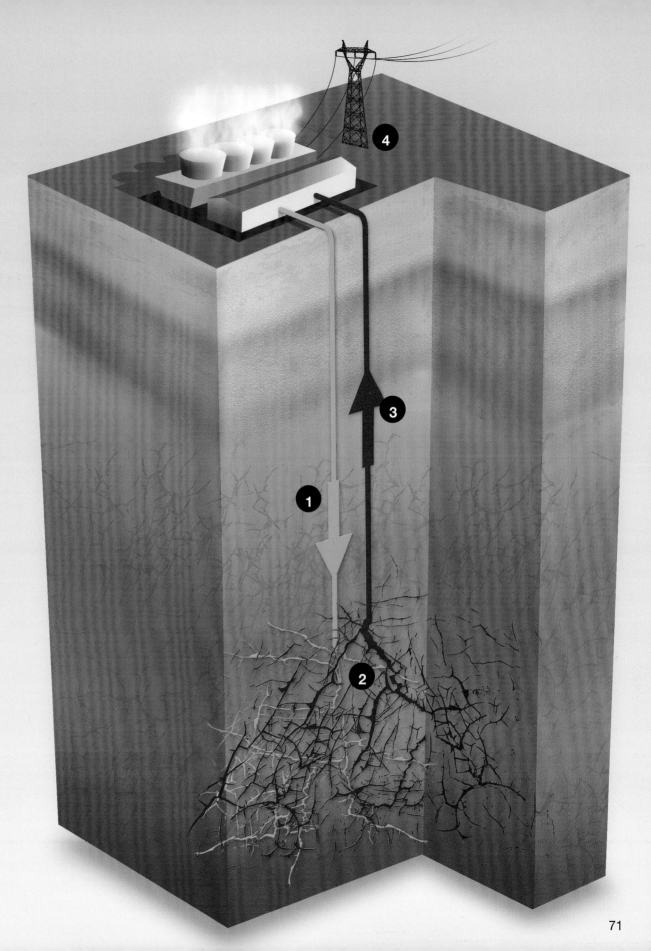

Enhanced geothermal, also called the "hot fractured rock" method, is being perfected in Australia's Cooper Basin, which is said to have the hottest granites on Earth. In January 2008, Geodynamics's Habanero 3 well reached its target depth of 13,850 feet (4,221 metres).

Soultz is not the only project on the way. Drilling has started at two locations in Australia—one at Paralana, and a massive second project at Cooper Basin. There has been an operational plant in Landau, Germany, since 2007 that produces enough power for more than 6,000 homes. Sweden

When a plant runs out of heat, you simply drill new holes a few miles away. The Earth will gradually reheat the original area.

and Japan are also in on the action. And the first commercial plant in the US, partly funded by the US Department of Energy, is planned for Desert Peak, Nevada.

MIT estimates that an EGS plant capable of powering 100,000 homes would take up less than a square mile (two square kilometres), and use a 1.2-cubic-mile (five-cubic-kilometre) underground reservoir of rock. When that plant runs out of heat—every six years or so—you simply drill new holes a few miles away. The Earth will gradually reheat the original area. This is truly renewable energy.

An MIT report established that there is more than enough accessible EGS energy to power the entire planet for thousands of years.

EGS is still in the early stages of commercial development, and there remain technical uncertainties related to the geophysics of deep-earth rock fracturing, water flow and loss rates. Plus, all sorts of engineering

issues are sure to pop up. But these are mere engineering problems—the sort of challenges engineers face all the time.

Bob Potter is one of those engineers. Mr. Potter, now 88, was a cofounder of EGS while working at Los Alamos National Laboratories back in the 1950s. Not one to hang up his hat, just five years ago, Mr. Potter founded Potter Drilling. Now, backed by money from Google, he's working on (literally) cutting-edge technology to lower the cost of drilling those deep holes. He and his son have invented a new type of drilling technology that fractures the rock by spraying super-heated 1,500 F (800 C) water out of a nozzle,

instead of using traditional drill bits. They figure they can bring the cost of drilling down by half and get it done faster. Drilling is a big part of the cost of EGS, and proving that it can be done cheaply would go a long way to establishing the commercial viability of the technology.

There's no real question about the long-term potential of EGS. That MIT report clearly established that there's more than enough accessible EGS energy to power the entire planet for thousands of years.

The drilling of a deep geothermal test well in Basel, Switzerland, had to be temporarily halted in 2006 after it triggered a 3.4-magnitude tremor. Here, the technology is called "hot dry rock" energy extraction.

Potential and Pitfalls

There's not much downside to geo-exchange—it really is one of the lowest-hanging fruits on the carbon-reduction tree. It can cut heating and cooling energy

We need a new, well-funded utility—a geo-exchange utility.

use in all our buildings—office towers, hospitals, houses—by between 50% and 75%.

Buildings account for more than half of greenhouse gas emissions in large urban areas, so geo-exchange can take a really big bite out of city emissions—easily one-quarter. There are no real impediments to large-scale geo-exchange, either. It takes no high-tech factories or long-term planning—just simple commodities like pipes and compressors, and some local labor.

Geothermal serves nature, too. The mountains of Nagano, Japan—site of the 1996 Winter Games—contain a series of geothermal hot springs that help to keep the Japanese Macaques, known as snow monkeys, warm through the cold winters.

Iceland's unique geological makeup gives it an abundance of hot geothermal energy. Five major power plants produce over 26% of the country's electricity, plus 87% of the heating and hot water requirements for its buildings.

Yellowstone National Park in Wyoming contains the world's largest assemblage of hot springs, geysers and mud pots. The mineral-rich waters of some hot springs support beds of brilliantly colored bacteria and algae that thrive in the heat.

It does take capital, however, and as long as building developers don't have a stake in the energy costs of a building, they'll continue to avoid the added expense.

So how do we get there? We need a new, well-funded utility—a geo-exchange utility—that pays for geo-exchange systems (for both new buildings and retrofits) in return for the right to charge for the energy delivered. Everybody wins. Developers win, since they deliver state-of-the-art buildings at no extra cost. Condo owners win, since they pay less for their heating bills. The new utility wins, since it generates a long-term, stable return on capital. The rest of us win because we lower our collective carbon footprint.

The big stuff, the real promise of geothermal, is EGS. All the energy we need is there—we just need to get at it.

Hot geothermal, the easy-to-reach stuff, is limited and will remain a marginal contributor to world energy production.

The big stuff, the real promise of geothermal, is EGS. As noted earlier, conservative estimates of the accessible geothermal energy in the US is *3,000 to 30,000 times* the total energy needs of the US. Similar abundance exists everywhere in the world. The energy is there—we just need to get at it.

MIT estimates that what EGS needs is a $1-billion R&D kickstart (spread over 15 years) to establish the engineering know-how. At that point, market forces would take over. They estimate that by 2050, enough EGS systems would exist in America to satisfy 100 million homes, or 10% of the total expected US electrical demand.

That's a conservative estimate of the potential, since it relies heavily on market forces and a natural rate of uptake. I saw nothing in the MIT report that talked about what will happen when there's a hard price—or cap—on carbon, other

A not-so-modest proposal: Start drilling EGS holes beside every existing coal plant. Replace the furnace with a heat-exchanger, and keep the rest of the infrastructure, including turbines and transmission lines.

than to note that EGS will "gain an economic advantage." You bet it will—the installation rate would be even higher. What's the total

upside for EGS? It's truly open-ended, since more energy than we need is right there and—unlike other renewables—there are no constraints on when or if it's available. EGS plants could replace, one-for-one, existing and planned coal plants.

There are pitfalls, of course. In order to exploit this resource effectively and economically, we need to know a lot more about using and expanding the natural fissures in deep rock formations. We must also learn more about how that structure will respond to having large amounts of heat extracted over time. In other words, we need to know more geology. In Basel, Switzerland, there were reports of seismic disturbances when an EGS system was activated, so we certainly need to be aware of potential earthquakes or other possible disturbances.

But these are the sorts of challenges the

engineering and scientific communities solve all the time. The real barrier to widespread deployment is economic incentives. What EGS really needs is a market signal that says: Ready, set—go!

These are the sorts of challenges the engineering and scientific communities solve all the time.

A not-so-modest proposal: Start drilling EGS holes beside every existing coal plant. Replace the furnace with a heat-exchanger, and keep the rest of the infrastructure, including turbines and transmission lines.

The Trillion-Dollar Question:

So, what do you get for $1 trillion?
That kind of money invested in geo-exchange could provide heating and cooling for 80% of US households,[16] lowering total residential energy use by more than 40%[17] and generating the energy equivalent of more than 1.5 billion barrels of oil[18]—every year.

And for $1 trillion worth of EGS? Around 400 gigawatts of capacity,[19] enough to fill three-quarters[20] of US electrical requirements.

In 1913, the world's first geothermal power plant was built in Lardarello, Italy, a region of Tuscany known since ancient times for its geothermal properties. It currently delivers 10% of the world's supply of geothermal electricity, powering over a million homes.

By July 2008, a deep geothermal test well called
Jolokia 1 had been drilled to a depth of 12,526 feet
(3,818 metres) in Australia's Cooper Basin. The
developer, Geodynamics, hopes to be generating
geothermal power at its nearby Habanero wells in
2009.

Climate Science II

The Complex Stuff

Just because it's complex doesn't mean we can't make good predictions!

Hundreds of millions of years ago, tiny creatures and swampy plants breathed in vast quantities of carbon dioxide, storing it in their bodies. They stored enough carbon to perform a sort of global air-conditioning service for us, turning the Earth's inhospitable atmosphere into one in which mammals like us could thrive. Over millions of years, the remains of these organisms became the coal and oil that now power our cars, iPods and air conditioners.

As power plants burn this fuel and release all that stored-up carbon, it sets off a complicated chain of events. The Earth's climate may be one of the most complex systems ever studied, but the endgame is simple: Releasing that carbon into the atmosphere will eventually undo what that ancient life did. That story begins in "Climate Science III – The Bad Stuff."

Complex as it is, the role of carbon dioxide in our evolving climate is well understood. The question is not whether we understand the mechanisms—we do—but how accurately we can predict the future. The climate system is "chaotic," meaning there are ways it is stable, but also ways it can change rapidly into something quite different.

Predicting chaotic systems is like predicting hurricanes. You know one is coming—and soon—but you can't say exactly when. Not being able to give a precise day and time doesn't mean you don't understand hurricanes, and it doesn't mean you can't give meaningful predictions. No one in Florida doubts the prediction that more hurricanes are coming or the advice that they should fortify their homes, even though no one can say exactly when it will happen. The same goes for predictions about climate change.

People sometimes think that since we can't predict the weather two weeks from now, we can't predict the climate 20 years down the road. But that assumes that weather and climate are the same thing. They're not. For example, we have no idea what the weather will be like on Dec. 10, 2030, in New York City. But we do know that the average temperature in December of that year will be lower than the average temperature in June. Climate predictions are not about particular events; they're about trends and probabilities. We're pretty good at those predictions.

The ice at the poles reflects sunlight and heat back into space. As the ice disappears, the dark water that replaces it will absorb heat.

What makes climate so complicated? Everything is interlinked: Carbon affects temperature, temperature affects carbon, and temperature affects temperature. This is called "feedback." Positive feedback means a change causes more of the same—things speed up. Negative feedback means a change causes less of the same—a braking system. Positive feedback is a pencil balanced on the tip—any tipping causes more tipping, because it's unstable. Negative feedback is a marble in a bowl—any rolling causes it to roll back, because it's stable. Our climate is a mix of positive and negative feedbacks.

What worries scientists are positive feedbacks, which accelerate climate change. We can't predict exactly *when* positive feedbacks will occur, but we can predict that they *will* occur, and we know what will happen when they do. Two basic positive feedbacks look like this:

Higher carbon levels increase temperature, which increases carbon levels (which increases temperature...).

Right now, the oceans absorb between one-third and half of the carbon we emit. Water and plankton act as a carbon *sink*. When temperatures rise, they'll flip into being a carbon *source*. Climate change will cause itself to speed up. Why? Warm air causes warmer oceans, and just like a can of pop fizzing in the sun, they'll release stored carbon.

Same goes for our great rainforests. The Amazon is a giant carbon storehouse. But rising temperatures cause desertification, and eventually the Amazon will stop absorbing carbon and release it all in one great gasp. Even our soil will flip from a sink to a source. Warmer soil means microbes get more active, releasing stored carbon. That's already happening.[1] It is predicted that by 2040,[2] living systems will begin to release more carbon than they absorb.

There's an elephant in the room—a bigger, badder feedback than either of these. The Arctic permafrost holds huge amounts of methane, a potent greenhouse gas. Were it to be released, it would effectively[3] *triple* the amount of carbon in the atmosphere. It's already happening—lakes in

Oceans and rainforests act as a carbon sink. When temperatures rise, they'll flip into being a carbon source.

Russia are bubbling with the stuff.

Higher temperatures cause higher temperatures (which cause higher temperatures...).

The ice at the poles reflects sunlight and heat back into space, acting as a giant mirror. As the ice disappears, the dark water that replaces it will absorb heat. As temperatures increase enough to melt the ice, it will cause temperatures to increase. Again, this is already happening.

There are all sorts of other feedback effects, but you get the idea. Climate science tries to predict which of these changes will occur at what temperatures and what levels of carbon. It is entirely up to us when (and if) we reach those levels.

The bottom line? It's thought that the really bad stuff—all those positive feedback mechanisms—start to kick in around 450 parts per million, and 500 parts per million is a "no-go zone," where all bets are off and the system might be yanked out of our control. We're at 380 now.

FOUR

Biofu

els

FILL'ER UP WITH NATURE

BIOFUELS

An Introduction

The Hummer, king of SUVs and preeminent symbol of extravagant energy consumption, is properly vilified for the prodigious amount of carbon dioxide that blows out of its tailpipe as it roars about town. Carbon dioxide, the main contributor to global warming,[1] is now about as popular as ants at a picnic.

Yet, we humans breathe out an average of about two pounds (one kilogram) of carbon dioxide a day. That adds up. With six billion of us, our breathing accounts for more than 4.4 trillion pounds (two trillion kilograms) of CO_2 a year!

The answer to the problem of the Hummer lies in biofuels—fuels that are derived from plants.

The more effort we exert, the more carbon dioxide we exhale. That means America's favorite high-calorie burner, Michael Phelps,[2] is exhaling vast quantities compared to a couch potato who sits watching reruns of *Jerry Springer* all day. Does this make Phelps the equivalent of a horrible Hummer, and the couch potato a pious Prius? Should we curtail our exercise and hit the couch to become better stewards of our planet?

Absolutely not! Human exhalations aren't the same as a car's exhaust, and there's a good reason for that: The carbon dioxide we breathe out has been captured from the atmosphere by the food we eat. It's a closed

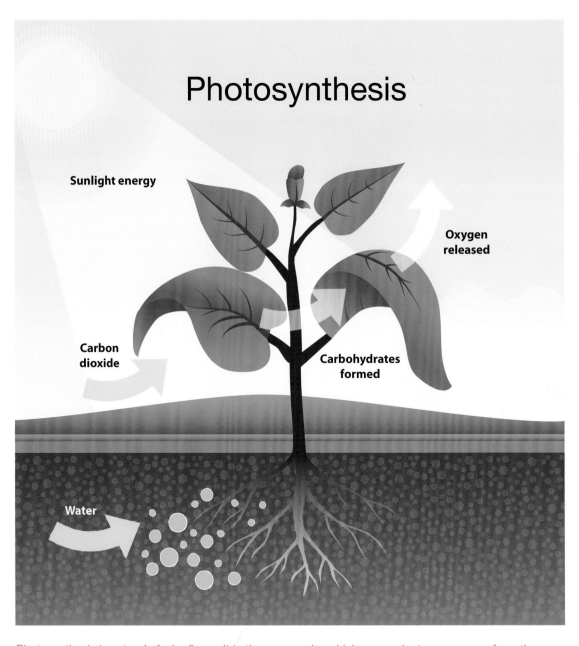

Photosynthesis

Sunlight energy

Oxygen released

Carbon dioxide

Carbohydrates formed

Water

Photosynthesis is nature's fuel refinery. It is the process by which green plants use energy from the sun to convert carbon dioxide and water into oxygen. The resulting creation of plant sugars is like storing power from the sun in a chemical battery.

The Hummer, preeminent symbol of extravagant energy consumption, does not have an EPA gas mileage rating because it falls under the class of "heavy vehicles" (similar to shuttle buses and ambulances).

circle. The Hummer, on the other hand, releases carbon dioxide that was locked away long ago in fossil fuels. It's not the same thing as far as our atmosphere is concerned. Our breathing is *carbon neutral*; the Hummer's exhaust is not.

Could we make the Hummer more like us? Could we make cars breathe carbon dioxide like we do? There's already a similarity—we both *combust* our fuel. The energy we get from food is stored sunlight. When sunlight hits a plant, it is stored as chemical energy in the form of sugars—think of the plant as a chemical battery. When we eat it (or eat the animal that eats it), those sugars react with oxygen—they get *oxidized*—releasing the energy.[4] The fuel the Hummer burns is

Our breathing is carbon neutral; the Hummer's exhaust is not.

being oxidized as well, releasing solar energy that was stored up millions of years ago.

Humans and Hummers are both *oxidizing* something, both *combusting* or *burning* fuel. The answer to the problem of the Hummer lies in biofuels—fuels that are derived from plants. Biofuels can produce both heat and electricity, but their unique promise is as a replacement for liquid fuels—petrol, gasoline and diesel—powering the engines of our cars, trucks, trains and planes. Biofuels are a sunlight battery for the common engine. It's not quite that easy, though—two problems must be resolved.

Front Range Energy, based in Windsor, Colorado, began ethanol production in June 2006. The plant processes approximately 40 million gallons of ethanol and 396,000 tons of wet distiller's grain each year.

First, where does biofuel come from? We can eat almost anything—from pizza to pop to liver and onions—and convert it to energy. Engines can't. We need to convert—"predigest"—plants (biomass) before they can go in the tank. But the easiest plants to convert happen to be the ones that *we* eat,

Ethanol from corn is a bad idea. Not only does it eat up a food crop, but it can take more energy to make than it produces.

too. The last thing we want in a crowded world is to be competing with our engines for food. Driving a Hummer with biodiesel in the tank is not so virtuous if someone in the developing world goes hungry as a result.

Second, do we get more energy out of the biofuel than we put in? It takes energy and often fossil fuel–based fertilizers to produce the biomass and transform it into fuel. Biofuels only make sense if we get more out than we put in.

Existing biofuels—the first generation—come from waste and easy-to-convert crops like corn, sugar and soy beans. None of these will ever contribute much to long-term energy supply, since they don't solve either of these two problems. Ethanol from corn, for example, is a bad idea. Not only does it eat up a food crop, but it can take more energy to make than it produces.

Future-generation biofuels hold more promise. The biotech industry is racing to engineer microbes that will predigest wood chips and the inedible parts of our crops. Strange fungi are being discovered that actually breathe out diesel fuel. Scientists are

The last thing we want in a crowded world is to be competing with our engines for food.

engineering plants that digest themselves, along with strange machines that can rip apart material and put it back together in new forms. New kinds of plants that grow in the desert and drink saltwater will replace the crops we need to feed our kids, and algae factories will pump out fuel for our jets.

First-Generation Fuels

They're Here Today

When I first became aware of the climate change problem, I had an immediate (and quite selfish) reaction: Can't I enjoy a campfire under the stars anymore? Perhaps, if the wood comes from a forest that isn't being degraded, there's no real carbon problem.

Wood pellets can, in theory, be used to replace coal in coal-fired electrical plants.

Just like that campfire, one way to use biomass is to burn it and use the heat directly. Wood for cooking and heating is renewable biomass—as long as the forest isn't stripped bare. In developing countries, this basic form of energy is still a big contributor: about 20% in China and 40% in India.[5] In developed countries like Sweden and the UK, there are crops grown for this purpose, like fast-growing willow.

Wood pellets can, in theory, be used to replace coal in coal-fired electrical plants. Ontario Power Generation, in Canada, has fired the massive Atikokan Generating Station with wood pellets and is studying what's involved in converting all of the province's coal-fired plants.

Incinerating municipal, industrial and farm waste is another potential source of heat. Municipal waste is just a fancy word for garbage. Industrial waste is stuff like wood chips, and farm waste is crop residue, like inedible stalks. These aren't exactly renewable, but if we're producing it anyway, we might as well use it. Denmark gets almost 5% of its electricity from burning municipal waste, and Sweden and Finland get about 20% of their energy from basic biomass.

The people of Burlington, Vermont, were pioneers in renewable energy. In 1978, they voted 73% in favor of replacing their coal-fired power plant with the McNeil Generating Station. It employs wood gasification to generate low-cost electricity from wood chips.

Biogas

President Ronald Reagan once derisively dismissed global warming as just a "bunch of cow farts" (he was referring, of course, to methane). Ironically, methane is a greenhouse gas,[6] and capturing any form of it to use for energy is a win-win. It's easy—let wastes naturally decompose into methane (called anaerobic digestion) and use it for heat or electricity. Landfills—great big piles of garbage buried under a layer of dirt—leak methane over many years.

Animal waste is a perfect candidate for so-called biogas. Decomposition is sped up by adding water and controlling the temperature. There's a farm in Ontario, Canada, doing just that. Each cow in the herd produces enough energy to keep three 50-watt lightbulbs lit constantly.[7]

What's the potential? Not much—there's enough animal waste in the UK, for example, to power about 400,000 homes. That's less than 1% of capacity.[8] And it would be about the same in other countries.

> Methane is a greenhouse gas, and capturing any form of it to use for energy is a win-win.

We're producing these wastes anyway, so we might as well use them. But there's not enough to really change the game.

This production plant in South Dakota produces ethanol from corn. As a first-generation biofuel, it's a bad idea. Not only does it use a food crop, but it can take more energy to make than it will give back as fuel.

Ethanol and Methanol

Brewmasters everywhere know how to make fuel: Start with a starchy (sugar-filled) food and ferment it to produce alcohol.[9] The same idea runs through the winemaker's art, the finest Scotch whisky and ethanol from corn. While wine and whisky are great ideas, ethanol from corn is not.

Our cars can certainly run on ethanol. But corn is something we need to eat. Converting all the corn grown in the US to ethanol would barely make a dent in energy consumption—but it would surely cripple the food supply. Even worse, it takes almost as much energy to produce ethanol as we get from the fuel[10]—its "energy balance" is low. Energy is needed to produce and transport the corn, and fossil fuel–based fertilizers are required to grow it. We need to drop "corn-to-ethanol"—it's a pipe dream.

Brazil has a slightly better idea. Sugar cane has a higher energy content than corn, so that's what they convert to ethanol. Their PRO-ALCOOL program is the biggest commercial biofuel project in the world, and it's estimated to have saved over $40 billion in imported energy over its first 25

> Converting all the corn grown in the US to ethanol would barely make a dent in energy consumption—but it would surely cripple the food supply.

years. Many cars in Brazil are modified to run on 100% ethanol, and those that aren't can run on an ethanol blend. "Flexifuel" is the real deal in Brazil.

The largest ethanol plant in Europe is operated by CropEnergies in Zeitz, Germany. Its process utilizes cereals—mainly wheat, but also barley, triticale and maize—as well as sugar syrups.

This shot of a field in Alberta, Canada, shows the dichotomy between renewable and fossil fuels. The pump jack is pulling up crude, while the surrounding crop of canola, a derivative of rapeseed, is a staple in the production of biodiesel.

Biodiesel

Diesel engines are more efficient than gasoline engines, and it's diesel that powers our trucks, ships and trains. Finding a replacement for diesel would be a real coup. Well, look no further than your local supermarket or deep fryer. When Dr. Rudolph Diesel invented

"The world food supply is heading into a perfect storm, and the key element that is pushing the system into crisis is biofuels."

his engine back in the 1890s, he envisioned it running on vegetable oil, which almost any diesel engine can do. Biodiesel is easy to make—just squeeze the right seed. Many seeds, like soy or mustard, contain oils that can be readily converted to biodiesel. The question is, what's the best seed?

Just like corn-based ethanol, many biodiesels compete with our food supply. There's only so much that existing cropland and deep fryers can contribute. In the US, waste grease could replace less than 1%[11] of US diesel use. If all current US soy production were used to make biodiesel—and we'd be giving up a huge slice of our food production to do that—it would replace less than 5% of US diesel.[12] There are slightly better choices—like mustard seed and rapeseed (also known as canola) that produce more oil per acre[13]—but the general lesson remains: *There is nowhere near enough land to make both food and fuel using existing crops.*

According to Canadian historian Gwynne Dyer, "The world food supply is heading into a perfect storm, and the key element that is pushing the system into crisis is biofuels...To be more precise, it is the first-generation biofuels, based on converting corn or sugar cane into ethanol,

If all current US soy production were used to make biodiesel— and we'd be giving up a huge slice of our food production to do that—it would replace less than 5% of US diesel use.

and soy or palm oil into biodiesel."[14] The long-term solution to biodiesel lies in next-generation sources[15]—like cellulose, algae and halophytes— that don't compete with our food sources.

Second-Generation Fuels

From cellulose

"The fuel of the future is going to come from fruit like that sumach out by the road, or from apples, weeds, sawdust—almost anything...There is fuel in every bit of vegetable matter that can be fermented." That was Henry Ford way back in 1925—and he was right.

Forget food sources—the next generation of liquid fuels will come from inedible things like wood chips, the stalks and leaves

> ## Converting cellulose to ethanol is considered by many to be the Holy Grail of biofuel production.

of corn, switchgrass, and other indigestible goodies. To make this switch, we need to figure out how to produce ethanol from something called cellulose. Cellulose is the most abundant organic molecule on Earth,

> ## Forget food sources—the next generation of liquid fuels will come from inedible things like wood chips, the stalks and leaves of corn, switchgrass, and other indigestible goodies.

since it's found in nearly all plant life. It's the fibrous stuff that forms 50% to 90% of a plant's structure. But locked away in that hard-to-digest material is sugar. Converting cellulose to ethanol is "considered by many

as the Holy Grail of biofuel production,"[16] according to Phil McKenna of *New Scientist* magazine.

The key? Finding a way to break down the cellulose. Companies around the world are in a race to genetically engineer new proteins

and bugs that do the job, plants that digest themselves, and even a fungus that breathes out diesel fumes. Cutting-edge science is designing new ways to break down the complex molecules, rip apart the material and put it back together in new ways.

Cellulose is contained in nearly every natural, free-growing plant, tree and bush the world over—no agricultural effort required. Wood chips from forestry waste are a perfect feedstock for biofuel production.

Massachusetts-based Qteros uses the Q microbe to eliminate the intensive pretreatment step normally required to break down non-food biomass for ethanol production. The Q microbe performs just like yeast and an enzyme all in one.

Building a New Molecule

One way to get at those sugars is to build an "enzyme" to do the job. That's a complicated molecule made by living organisms like bacteria. Enzymes are usually proteins, and they act as a *catalyst*—meaning they speed up a chemical reaction. The trick is to find an enzyme that speeds up the breakdown of cellulose into sugars.

How do we find (or engineer[17]) the right bacteria? That's the hard work done in labs run by companies like Iogen, based in Ottawa, Canada. Once they've found the right bacteria, the idea is to mass-produce it in a giant "bioreactor," unleash the enzymes on the cellulose and voilà—out pop the sugars. The next step is to add yeast to brew a kind of beer. That "beer" is refined into ethanol. Iogen has a demonstration plant up and running, and it's working to overcome at least two problems—energy and money. The company can't use much of either if the plant is to go commercial.

Building a New Bug

Other companies, like Qteros, based in Hadley, Massachusetts, are skipping the enzyme altogether. Qteros wants to develop a bacteria than does the job directly. Its bacterium is called the Q microbe.[18] Shaped like a lollipop, the tiny bug can be engineered for different plant sources, producing the "beer" for refinement to ethanol. The Q microbe is, according to the company, like the "yeast...plus the enzyme...all in one."

One of Qteros's competitors, Boston-based Mascoma, has produced a similar bacterium. Founded by professors from Dartmouth College at the University of California, Mascoma has a pilot plant up and running that converts wood chips and other cellulose sources into almost 250,000 gallons of ethanol a year. A full-scale commercial plant in Michigan is expected to be operational by 2012.

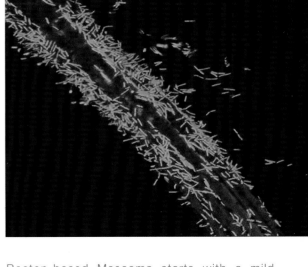

Boston-based Mascoma starts with a mild pretreatment of the biomass, then introduces microbes that both hydrolyze and ferment the sugars into ethanol. This image shows how a microorganism is attracted to cellulose.

A Diesel-Breathing Fungus

Lurking in a tree in Patagonia is a fungus that grows on cellulose and breathes out the components of diesel. Forget the enzymes, forget the bacteria, forget the yeast. This little fungus goes straight to the juice—cellulose to diesel! Not only can it skip the steps from cellulose to fuel, but its discovery also means that microbial agents may be able to produce oil directly—even though conventional wisdom says that oil is only produced by geological processes involving intense heat and pressure over long periods of time.

Gary Strobel, of Montana State University, discovered the fungus. "There's no other known organism on the planet that does this," he says. "We'll do some scale-up and fermentation, then get enough to run a little engine."[19] Transforming this fungus into a large-scale commercial operation will come with a host of problems, but it's an elegant concept.

Lurking in a tree in Patagonia is a fungus that grows on cellulose and breathes out the components of diesel. Forget the enzymes, forget the bacteria, forget the yeast. This little fungus goes straight to the juice—cellulose to diesel!

Researchers at Michigan State University have spliced three new genes into a corn called Spartan Corn, which in turn produces three enzymes that break down cellulose. "Our corn is a green bioreactor using free energy from the sun," says Dr. Mariam Sticklen.

Corn that Eats Itself

Here's a wacky idea: Build a corn stalk that produces enzymes that can break down its own cellulose. Make sure it only does it to stems and stalks, and only when you tell it to—by grinding it up, not when it's growing in the field. A corn stalk that turns itself, on demand, into the goop that others work so hard to produce—sound far-fetched?

At Michigan State University, researchers have spliced three new genes into a corn called Spartan Corn, which in turn produces three enzymes that break down cellulose. Each gene produces an enzyme to perform a step in the process.[20] Further tweaking limits enzyme production to leaves and stalks, and

A corn stalk that turns itself, on demand, into the goop that others work so hard to produce—sound far-fetched?

only within a sort of storage area in each cell. That means that the enzymes aren't released until the stalks are ground up into little pieces. Pretty crazy stuff.

What the Michigan State team has built is corn that acts as its own breakdown bacteria. "This is basically a shortcut; you don't need to put this gene in other microbes," says MSU researcher Mariam Sticklen. "Our corn is a green bioreactor using free energy from the sun."[21] It's early days, however, and the corn needs to demonstrate productivity and resistance. In other words, that clever bioreactor must also show that it's good at being regular old corn.

Pulling it Apart and Putting it Together

Lego—kids love it because they can put all those bits and pieces together in so many ways. Take apart a spaceship and build a robot. Could the same principle apply to

The converters are designed to be small and modular, so you can bring the plant right to the feedstock.

cellulose? Could you take it apart and put it back together again in a different form—just like making a robot from a spaceship? Range Fuels, based in Colorado, makes a device that does just that. The company's converter breaks biomass into little bits, and then puts those bits back together in a more useful form—like ethanol.

Range Fuels has fed more than 30 different kinds of non-food feedstock into its demonstration plant, including switchgrass, hog manure and lots of Colorado pine killed by the ubiquitous Pine Beetle. The converters are designed to be small and modular, so you can bring the plant to the feedstock, rather than shipping the feedstock to the plant. Smart.

The first plant in the US to commercially produce biofuels from biomass is currently being built by Range Fuels in Soperton, Georgia—it will be completed in 2010. At full scale, it's expected to produce 100 million gallons of ethanol and methanol each year.

A company called Range Fuels has developed a converter that pulls apart various kinds of non-food biomass and puts them together again as fuel—like ethanol. Its development plant in Colorado has proven that the process is commercially viable.

In Indonesia, rain forests were hacked down to make room for palm oil plantations. The plan backfired because deforestation causes a massive spike in greenhouse gases. The net result was an increase in carbon emissions, not a reduction.

Third-Generation Fuels

Thinking About Limits

Why go to third-generation? Second-generation sounds pretty good, as long as it doesn't compete with our food supply. Is there really a need to go further? Sure there is. According to Dennis Bushnell, chief scientist at NASA Langley Research, "there's just not enough fresh water and arable land to produce enough biofuels to replace the petroleum."[22]

If we were to replace all US petroleum with first- or second-generation biofuels from conventional crops like soy, it would require the use of more[23] than the entire US land mass. Even palm oil, which generates 20 times the amount of biofuel per acre than other biofuel-based crops, would require more than one-third of the arable land—and palms don't even grow in Kansas!

> "There's just not enough fresh water and arable land to produce enough biofuels to replace the petroleum."

When the European Union first mandated that a percentage of all diesel fuel be biodiesel, it ignited a surge of deforestation in Indonesia. Rain forests were being hacked down to make room for plantations of palm for palm oil production. Needless to say, the plan backfired. The net result was an *increase* in carbon emissions, not a reduction, since deforestation causes a massive spike in greenhouse gases.

In early 2008, billionaire adventurer Richard Branson, the founder of Virgin Atlantic, flew one of his planes on a mix

In early 2008, Richard Branson, the founder of Virgin Atlantic, flew one of his planes on a mix of regular fuel and the oil from 150,000 coconuts. It was touted as a sustainable flight. Branson is now looking into producing fuel from algae.

of regular fuel and the oil from 150,000 coconuts. It was touted as a sustainable

> If we were to replace all US petroleum with first- or second-generation biofuels from conventional crops like soy, it would require the use of more than the entire US land mass.

flight. The problem comes when you count the coconuts. Analysts pointed out that

there aren't enough coconuts in the world to fuel all the planes flying in and out of Heathrow alone. To be fair, though, Branson *did* demonstrate the possibility of alternative fuels, and he's now looking into something even more far out: producing fuel from algae.

Algae is one of three new sources of biofuel that look promising. Algae can be cultivated in tanks and farmed from seaweed in our oceans. Halophytes—plants that drink saltwater and can grow in unproductive deserts like the Sahara—won't compete with food. Jatropha, a plant that can grow on marginal land and on top of regular crops without reducing yields, also holds promise.

Algae, the Truly "Green" Fuel

Pond scum, seaweed, green goop—the unappetizing slippery stuff is one of the most promising sources of biofuel. It's possible to squeeze the oil out of algae to produce biodiesel, and break down the rest to produce ethanol. John Sheehan, at the US National Renewable Energy Laboratory, says: "There is no other resource that comes even close in magnitude to the potential for making oil."[24]

Harvested from the ocean or grown in tanks on non-fertile land, algae can be fed wastewater or even the emissions from smokestacks. These little balls of[25] oil are harvested on a continual basis, and can produce more than 40 *times more fuel per acre than any other plant*—up to 20,000 gallons per acre, per year. In the right conditions, algae can double its volume overnight. The trick is to get the growing conditions just right, and to do it on a big scale.

How big? Solix, in Fort Collins, Colorado, has been dabbling in algae-based fuels for years. The company's CEO, Douglas Henston, says: "If we were to replace all of the diesel that we use in the United States with an algae derivative, we could do it on an area of land that's about one-half of 1% of the current farm land that we use now." No doublt it's promising, but that's one big pond—and we're not talking about a regular old turtle-and-tadpole pond here. These are high-tech, triangular-shaped aquariums called "photobioreactors."

Algae can pack a double punch: Since it can eat high concentrations of carbon dioxide, it can be fed straight from a conventional power plant. You can create one of these bioreactors by fine-tuning the algae to the CO_2 and the surrounding enviroment using selective culture growth. By feeding in water and emissions samples, you can grow just the right algae to optimize production. The idea is to surround power plants with thousands of bioreactors that gobble up CO_2 *and* produce oil at the same time.

Algae can also be grown in the dark. California-based Solazyme feeds its algae plant sugars like wood chips, rather than sunlight. Solazyme's challenge will be the same as other biomass users: securing a big enough supply of plant sugars to produce fuel on a commercial scale.

"There is no other resource that comes even close in magnitude to the potential for making oil."

Algae-based fuels are just beginning to hit the big-time, and we don't yet know who the winners will be. One thing is certain: Big money is starting to flow to algae, much of it in California. San Diego-based Sapphire Energy has raised more than $100 million for algae production. Another San Diego company, Prize Capital, has announced a $10-million "X-prize" to encourage critical breakthroughs.

Algae can pack a double punch: Since it can eat high concentrations of carbon dioxide, it can be fed straight from a conventional power plant. The idea is to surround power plants with thousands of bioreactors to gobble up CO_2.

Harvested from the ocean or grown in tanks on non-fertile land, algae can be fed wastewater or even the emissions from smokestacks. These little balls of oil are harvested on a continual basis, and can produce more than 40 times more fuel per acre than any other plant.

97

Farming the Desert

Halophytes are plants that love saltwater. So here's an idea: Irrigate vast swaths of desert with saltwater, and grow plants for biofuel. This may not be happening on a commercial

The Sahara Desert alone could provide 94% of the world's power if it were converted to halophyte biofuel production.

scale yet, but the idea is sound, and some high-powered thinkers are getting behind it. Dennis Bushnell, chief scientist at NASA's Langley Research Center, says: "This is a revolution for agriculture as well as for energy."[26]

What's the potential of halophytes? Well, according to Bushnell, the Sahara Desert alone could provide 94% of the world's power[27] if it were converted to halophyte biofuel production. This may sound crazy—but these

"This is a revolution for agriculture as well as for energy."

are the sorts of ideas that we need to take a really close look at. It was once thought absurd to cross the ocean or split the atom or go to the moon!

The inedible nut of the Jatropha plant can yield up to 40% oil, which makes it one of the best candidates for future biofuel production. It can be grown along with existing crops without lowering their yield, which makes it a kind of "fuel for free."

Between the Cracks

Jatropha is a plant that grows an inedible seed that's ideal for producing biodiesel. What makes the plant *really* promising is that it can be grown on crummy land that's no good for crops, or nestled among existing crops, without lowering the yield. That means it's a kind of "fuel for free" when mixed with other crops. It's promising enough that the government of India has singled the plant out for a national biofuels push.

Halophytes, like this salt marsh grass, are plants that thrive in salt-laden environments. The best species for producing biofuels, *salicornia bigelovii*, or pickleweed, may someday turn the wastelands of the world into a valuable source of fuel.

Potential and Pitfalls

Clearly, biofuel has a role to play in the clean-energy future. Some European countries already generate up to 20% of their energy needs from biomass, mainly from burning waste for heat and electricity.

To completely eradicate the need for petroleum, biofuels must come from the sorts of third-generation fuels outlined—mainly algae and halophytes.

Its biggest contribution will be to replace our liquid fuels, primarily those used for transportation. To replace more than a small fraction of our petroleum use, biofuels must stop competing with our food crops for arable land, water and fertilizer. To get *really* serious, we have to get more sophisticated than using wood, inedible farm waste and other cellulosic sources.

Existing biofuels, like from this plant in Zeitz, Germany, come from waste and easy-to-convert crops like corn, sugar and soy beans. None of these will ever contribute much to our long-term energy supply—but third-generation fuels, like algae and halophytes, have way more potential.

The Trillion-Dollar Question:

So, what do you get for $1 trillion?

Say we were to use that money to irrigate the Sahara for halophyte farming and build biodiesel factories to process the plants. In that case, we'd be able to irrigate enough land[28] and bring online enough processing capacity to replace about half of the total world oil supply.

The problems associated with cellulosic ethanol are twofold: limited biomass supply and the dangers associated with the required genetic engineering. There just aren't enough wood chips and plant stalks, and even if there were, engineering those tiny little self-reproducing microbes, like bacteria, is risky. There's always the danger of introducing new bugs that upset our delicately balanced ecology.

To completely eradicate the need for petroleum, biofuels must come from the sorts of third-generation fuels outlined above—mainly algae and halophytes. Biofuel is no magic bullet. Biofuels will only change the game if we spend as much money building vast fields of bioreactors and irrigating deserts

To replace more than a small fraction of our petroleum use, biofuels must stop competing with our food crops for arable land, water and fertilizer.

with saltwater as we do finding and defending our sources of oil.

Climate Science III

The Bad Stuff

Just because we can't predict "when" doesn't mean we can't predict "what."

This is a book about hope. It is a celebration of what's possible. We can kick the fossil fuel habit and live in a world supplied with clean, renewable energy. So why this negative bit—food shortages, geopolitical upheaval, an end to much of the world that we take for granted? To put it bluntly, to spur the effort it will take to reset our energy economy. That job *is* possible—albeit difficult—and it's important to understand why it's worth the effort. So bear with me for just a moment.

An image in the March 2009 issue of *New Scientist* magazine would have seemed alarmist in its vision of the Earth later this century—if it hadn't been reflective of current science. In it, a sort of "superdesert" occupies much of the planet, a desert much hotter than anything that exists today. Canada looks just fine, but China, Africa, Central and South America, the United States, Australia and much of Asia—what used to be the world's breadbasket—are now incapable of growing crops. Hospitable land is limited mainly to small, crowded bits near the poles. Much of what used to be coastal land is underwater or headed there. New Orleans, Mumbai—gone. The image is a nightmare.

Our problem is that this nightmare scenario isn't science fiction—it's based on the predictions of some of the smartest people in the world. Even more terrifying is that it's based on a mere seven degrees Fahrenheit (four degrees Celcius) of warming. Without a full reset of how we produce our energy, that level of warming could occur as early

as 2050 and will almost certainly be here by the end of the century.

Seven degrees may not seem like much. It's less than the swing in temperature from dawn to midmorning, or early to late spring. But a global average temperature change is not the same animal, and those seven degrees are the difference between a planet that supports what we have and one that does not. The single biggest problem? Food. A seven-degree rise puts Mother Nature firmly back in charge. What might it look like?

"We have just a small window of opportunity and it is closing rather rapidly. There is not a moment to lose...We are risking the ability of the human race to survive."

—Dr. Rajendra Pachauri, chair of the Intergovernmental Panel on Climate Change, 2005

Most of Asia, including Japan and China, will become inhospitable desert. So will much of the United States, Mexico and Africa.

Most of the world's glaciers will be gone. While mountain-lovers may be upset at the news, the problem has nothing to do with the incredible beauty or deep sense of history glaciers provide. The problem is food. Glaciers store water during the winter and release it during the summer, and their spring runoff irrigates much of the world's crops. Parts of the American Plains, China and

India will suffer. So will Pakistan, which is really just a big desert with a river running through it. The Indus river system supplies water to the largest irrigated land system in the world. No Indus runoff, no crops. At present melting rates, this will happen by the early 2030s.

The deserts will grow and get even hotter. The increased energy of the Hadley cells that form our deserts (see Chapter 2) will cause those deserts to expand. Most of Asia, including Japan and China, will become inhospitable desert. So will much of the United States, Mexico and Africa. The Amazon will disappear. None of these deserts will be suitable for food production. Average temperatures will exceed the hottest days on record now—they'll be off the charts.

Global grain markets may no longer exist. Since deserts will take over what used to be our breadbaskets, global output will diminish so much that little is for sale. Countries that can grow grain (like Russia and Canada) will feed only themselves and their closest friends.

The oceans won't be able to feed us anymore. Higher temperatures and increased acidity from carbon absorption will take out key life-supporting species, like plankton—which means the oceans will no longer be much of a food source.

Storms will get increasingly more powerful. Hurricane Katrina was just a hint of how storms will change. As bodies of water warm up, hurricanes gather more energy, since it's the water that fuels their fury.

Many of the world's great cities will be drowning. Sea levels will have risen by three to six feet (one to two metres), and will keep rising for many centuries, no matter what we do. Cities like Mumbai and New Orleans will already be underwater. The world's ice takes a long time to melt—probably a century or more—but when it does, the total rise in sea levels will be near 320 feet (100 metres).

Our problem is that this nightmare scenario isn't science fiction—it's based on the predictions of some of the smartest people in the world.

Our population will have severely shrunk or have been displaced from where we live now, or both. Only a fraction of the planet will still be productive—mostly Russia and Canada—so we'll all learn to live very efficiently on that land, or not.

So, how fast do we need to decarbon? We can't do it fast enough. If we want to buy some insurance against this scenario, then we should fully decarbon—that means no fossil fuel use at all—by 2050, and hit 80% reductions by 2030.

"We are getting almost to the point of irreversible meltdown, and will pass it soon if we are not careful."
—Sir John Houghton,
Former co-chair of the IPCC, 2006

FIVE

Hydro

power

HOLDING UP THE FLOW

The Hoover Dam, originally known as Boulder Dam, straddles the Colorado River on the Nevada-Arizona border, just an hour's drive from Las Vegas. This concrete "arch-gravity" wonder was completed in 1936 and now provides enough power for more than two million homes.

Hydropower

An Introduction

Watch a shallow puddle on a sunny day, and it can disappear right before your eyes. Sunlight hitting the surface gives the water molecules a little burst of energy—enough for some of them to break the bonds with their neighbors—and they venture forth in a new, gaseous form. About a quarter of all solar energy that hits the Earth is used up giving water molecules that little bump, mainly in the oceans. That means water vapor in the atmosphere represents an enormous store of converted solar energy.

Almost all of that energy is released into the air, mainly as heat, as the water condenses into clouds. But a tiny fraction remains. Clouds eventually fall as rain (or snow), of course, watering our crops, ruining our picnics, filling our lakes and swelling our rivers. The weight of that water is potential energy. Sounds all very

> ## Sunlight lifts vast amounts of water up into the sky, to later fall on our fields, rivers and lakes. The weight of that water is potential energy.

abstract—evaporating water, molecules being lifted into the sky, converted solar and potential energy. How does it all add up to power?

The Hoover Dam, an immense structure built in the 1930s—partly as a cure for the last big economic hangover—stands less than an hour's drive from the razzle-dazzle that is Las Vegas. Straddling the Colorado River on the Arizona-Nevada border, the plaques that adorn it stand as testament to a time when engineers—not bankers—were almost heroic figures in the economy. Peering over and down the slowly curving 726-foot-high (220-metre) concrete wall on top of the dam, you can't help but feel a sense of awe—and vertigo. Far below, powerful currents come and go, as gates controlling the flow of water open and close.

The Hoover Dam's job? To capture a few of those previously evaporated water molecules as they make their way back to the ocean, interrupting their flow just long enough to convert some of their movement into electricity. Built at a time when engineers used slide-rules, not computers, and a pencil and paper stood in for design software, the dam continues to produce enough power for more than two million homes. Those evaporated molecules sure can add up.

About a quarter of all solar energy hitting the Earth is used up evaporating water, mainly in the oceans. This vapor condenses into clouds, with some falling back to Earth as rain, watering our crops, ruining our picnics, filling our lakes and swelling our rivers.

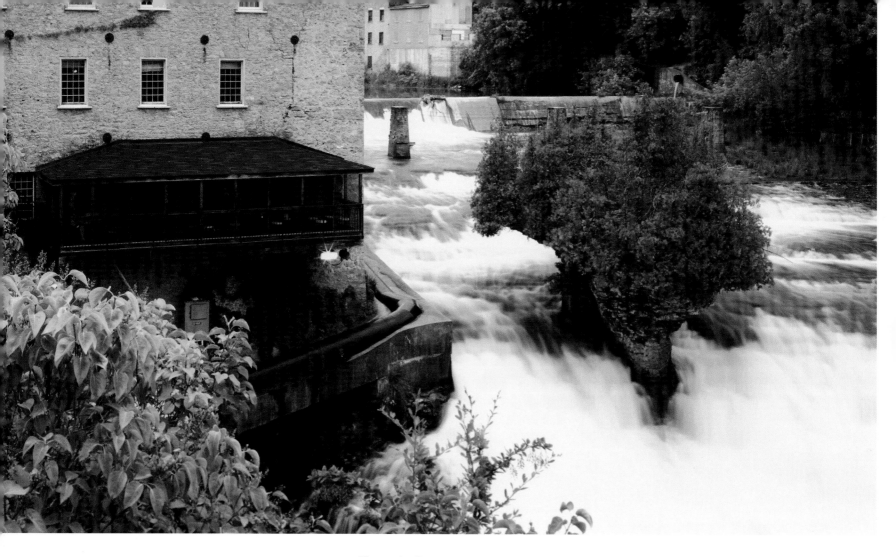

The quaint Elora Mill Inn, in rural Ontario, Canada, produces its own power from the rushing waters of the Grand River. A meter on the wall allows patrons to see when excess power is being pumped to the grid.

A Bit of History

Hydropower has been used for thousands of years, starting with powered irrigation systems, as well as for milling and other industrial processes. Waterwheels appear in ancient Middle Eastern texts and were also used by the Roman Empire, and in ancient China and Greece. The United Kingdom alone once had more than 20,000 waterwheels turning in streams and rivers. As time went by, hydropower began to be used almost exclusively to produce electricity, and by the beginning of the 20th century, hydro was responsible for the bulk of electrical production. But as fossil fuels and then nuclear came online, its portion dropped to what it is today—somewhere around 20%.

Hydropower has been used for thousands of years, starting with powered irrigation systems.

The Elora Mill, a quaint inn near Toronto, Canada, went through that evolution, as did countless other mills that used to dot our landscape. The mill was built in the 19th century, on the banks of the Grand River, and was one of the area's great industrial grist mills. As the world changed, so too did the Elora Mill, and that same water flow now produces electric power, both for the Inn and—when the lights are low—to sell back to the local grid. Inside the mill's bar, patrons can watch a little power meter on the wall that proudly displays the excess power pumped back to the grid.

Humans have been harnessing hydropower for centuries, first for irrigation, and later for milling and industrial uses. The Glade Creek Grist Mill in Babcock State Park, West Virginia, is a replica made from the original parts of three mills located nearby.

The Grand Coulee dam on the Columbia River in Washington State is the largest power-producing facility in the US and the fifth-largest producer of hydroelectricity in the world. The dam is almost a mile long and, at a height of 550 feet (168 metres), it's taller than the Great Pyramid of Giza.

Hydropower Today

A Renewable Workhorse

Hydro is now the modern workhorse of renewable energy, responsible for 90% of worldwide renewable energy production. Waterwheels have been replaced by highly efficient turbines, and massive dams are built to store and generate quantities of

Norway generates almost all its electrical power from hydro.

power so vast, they make a nuclear plant look small by comparison. Pumped hydro, where water is pumped uphill to large reservoirs for later use, is the only currently viable option[1] for utility-scale grid storage. Without hydropower, our energy landscape would look very different.

Today, it's the big and bold (and sometimes famous) sites that produce the lion's share of hydroelectricity. Some places—like Niagara Falls and Churchill Falls in Labrador, Canada—take advantage of the same landscape that creates such dramatic scenes of falling water. Other places create artificial falls by

Only one-fifth of the hydropower that is technically feasible has been harnessed.

building a dam, like the Grand Coulee dam in Washington State and the controversial Three Gorges Dam in China.

China has, by far, the most installed hydroelectric capacity and is responsible for four of the five largest projects under construction, followed by Brazil, Canada and the US. Canada gets more than half of its electrical power from hydro, and

The Churchill Falls hydroelectric power station in Labrador, Canada, provides the second-largest hydroelectric generating capacity in North America. And with its 11 giant turbines, it's the second-largest "underground" powerhouse in the world.

Norway—though it has relatively small production levels—generates almost all of its electrical power from hydro. The upside of hydropower is well known. Once the plant has been built, you have a reliable, clean and cheap source of power.

It's uncertain how much *more* energy could be produced by these sorts of massive projects. There is certainly more energy to be had—it's estimated that only one-fifth of the hydropower that is technically feasible has been harnessed— but big dams make big lakes, displace people and flood what might otherwise be scenes of great natural beauty. Public opposition to large-scale hydro will probably be the strongest constraint on growth.

Expansion of hydro energy will likely happen with smaller and more subtle projects that don't change a river's flow. "Run-of-river" hydro is a way of generating power while following the natural flow of a river—no flooding required. There's also a more far out technology on the horizon,

Hydro is now the modern workhorse of renewable energy, responsible for 90% of worldwide renewable energy production.

where a well-controlled meeting of river and sea can yield some surprising results.

Natural Falls

The Beautiful

Big Becky, the largest tunnel-boring machine ever built, is digging a third hydro tunnel under the city of Niagara Falls to bring more water to the Sir Adam Beck hydroelectricity stations. With a diameter of 47 feet (14.4 metres), it's 67% larger than the English Channel Tunnel.

Most visitors to Niagara Falls have no idea that more than half of the mighty Niagara River's flow never makes it over the dramatic cliffs that are the Falls. Instead, it's diverted from upriver, flowing underground to power plants on both the American and Canadian sides of the border. At night, when the tourists aren't watching, up to *three-quarters* of the river's flow is diverted for power production.

The Americans were the first to produce hydropower from the Niagara River, back in 1881. By 1896, that power was being transmitted as far as Buffalo, New York. Canadians soon followed suit, building the Sir Adam Beck I generating plant in 1922, with a second, Beck II, operational by 1954. Today, a giant underground boring machine—nicknamed Big Becky—is drilling a new tunnel

Modern turbines are very efficient, turning up to 95% of the water's potential energy into movement.

under the city that will be more than six miles (10 kilometres) long and 46 feet (14 metres) wide, and will feed more water to Beck II. Together, the two sides produce enough power for four million homes, and both have reservoirs for storage. That means they can pump water uphill when power demand is low, store it and release it when it's high.

How does it work? The basic idea behind all hydropower is quite simple: The weight of a column of water builds up pressure at the bottom (that's why your ears hurt when you dive to the bottom of a pool). That pressure is exerted on a turbine blade,[2] which spins a generator to make electricity. The *potential* energy of the water—its mass that can fall—converts to *kinetic* energy as it is captured by the turbine wheel and passed to the generator.

Both power plants have reservoirs for storage. They can pump water uphill when power demand is low and release it when it's high.

Modern turbines are very efficient, turning up to 95% of the water's potential energy into movement, so the water flows out very slowly. The rate of spin of the turbine is tuned to meet the rate of alternating current on the grid.[3] Total power out depends on how much water flows and from what height (called the "head"). The size of the reservoir—really an artificial lake—indicates how much power sits in storage.

Like Niagara Falls, many stations can pump water uphill into the reservoir when electrical demand is low. "Hydro storage" is the only grid-sized storage method in commercial use today. Since grids are large and interconnected, power from anywhere on the grid can be used to pump the water. There's no reason the electrons from a wind farm hundreds of miles away can't do the work!

Niagara Falls, one of the world's major tourist attractions, is also home to mammoth hydroelectric generating stations. Tourists are often unaware that more than half of the mighty Niagara River's flow has been diverted to serve the array of massive turbines.

111

The world's largest hydroelectricity plant, the Three Gorges Dam, on China's Yangtze River, should be fully operational by 2011, after a decade of construction. Although an enormous source of renewable power, it is deeply controversial in China and abroad due to the amount of land sacrificed and the number of people displaced—about 1.25 million.

Building a Dam

The Bold

Niagara Falls and a few other spots like it are ideal for hydropower. What's needed is a lot of two things: flowing water and height. A natural waterfall clearly has both. When there is no natural head, or height from which the water can fall, one can be created by building a dam.

But many of these dams have a downside. The reservoirs are not always a center of watery recreation in the middle of a desert.

The biggest hydroelectric plant in the world is the enormous Three Gorges Dam, on China's Yangtze River. Though it's already generating some electricity, when it's fully complete it will be able to deliver an astounding 22.5 gigawatts. The dam is more than 600 feet (185 metres) high and will serve 26 generators. To put that in perspective, it has 22 times the power of a medium-sized coal or nuclear plant. Most of the big hydro projects under construction are in China.

How does it work? As a kid, I used to build a dam on the creek that ran through our farm. When I was done, the water would rise on the upstream side of the dam. The same idea applies to large hydro: Dam up a river and let the water rise on one side. The result is a giant artificial lake or reservoir, which stores energy. The height from which the water can now fall is measured from the top of that lake. The rest of the story is the same: Spin a turbine[4] and generate electricity.

Lake Mead, which was created as the reservoir for the Hoover Dam, takes advantage of its surrounding natural geography—the flooded area is a high, narrow canyon. As the water levels rose, the area of land flooded was relatively small.

In the case of the Hoover Dam, a technical marvel of its time, the reservoir is the lovely Lake Mead, which stores energy and is enjoyed for recreation at the same time. Hoover Dam takes advantage of the

To put that in perspective, China's Three Gorges Dam has 22 times the power of a medium-sized coal or nuclear plant.

surrounding natural geography, and the flooded area is a high, narrow canyon. This means that as the water rose, the area of land that was flooded was relatively small.

But many of these dams have a downside. The reservoirs are not always a center of watery recreation in the middle of a desert. In the case of the Three Gorges Dam, more than 400 square miles (1,000 square kilometres[5]) were flooded in order to generate a good-sized "head" and build a large reservoir of stored power. Slowly and inexorably, as the waters rose, whole villages, forests and even archaeological sites were flooded. Three Gorges has displaced about 1.25 million people. That's a lot of new homes to be built—not to mention a lot of human misery.

And that's not the only downside—all those drowned trees will eventually rot, releasing methane, a potent greenhouse gas.

Run-of-River

The Subtle

A few summers ago, while cycling up my favorite hill in Newfoundland—it climbs away from the Atlantic Ocean and through the town of Petty Harbour—I saw a curious sight: an enormous, old wooden pipe that followed the road down to the harbor. The pipe, which was taller than me, sprayed water from small leaks that had formed between the slats comprising the exterior shell. It looked like a long, leaky barrel. Climbing the same hill the next summer, I saw that it had been replaced by a modern steel version. It turns out that pipe carries water from a river at the top of the road and delivers it, under pressure, to a small generating station at the bottom. I didn't realize it then, but that leaky wooden pipe was part of an old "run-of-river" power station.

Run-of-river hydro roughly means relying on a river's natural flow to generate power, without disrupting it with large dams and reservoirs.[5] The central point is to minimize the impact on the local ecosystem and to avoid the creation of a large, artificial lake.

How does it work? There are two ways to do it. The first is to dam the river, forcing all of the water to flow through turbines—but at low speeds and without building up the level of the river. In this case, the turbines are usually more propeller-shaped,[6] to be efficient at the lower flow speeds. The second way is to build a pipe that diverts some of the river's water downstream beside the river to a turbine. Because the water is trapped in the pipe—like a giant straw blocked at the bottom—the same pressure is built up at the turbine just as if it were a vertical drop. The pipe creates the head in the same way a vertical dam does—minus the dam.

As you might expect, the system isn't perfect. Run-of-river projects are generally thought to have minimal impact on the environment, but it's not zero. Roads and power lines sometimes

> Run-of-river hydro roughly means relying on a river's natural flow to generate power, without disrupting it with large dams and reservoirs.

need to be built if the river is in a wilderness area, and the amount of diverted water can be large enough to change the river's natural ecosystem. These are valid concerns. British Columbia recently opened up huge wilderness areas for private run-of-river development, and debate about ecological impact is fierce. Also, since run-of-river projects don't build any significant storage capacity in a reservoir, they're completely reliant on natural precipitation patterns. Droughts mean blackouts!

Finer points aside, there's no doubt that run-of-river, developed with care, has a role in our renewable energy future. There are thousands of potential sites, ranging from the small off-the-grid building beside a little creek, to commercial-scale projects churning out renewable energy along the world's major rivers.

Run-of-river hydropower is best suited to rivers with consistent and steady flow. Rivers with seasonal fluctuations require a reservoir at the head of the river to regulate the amount of water being diverted into the buried penstock to feed the turbine downriver.

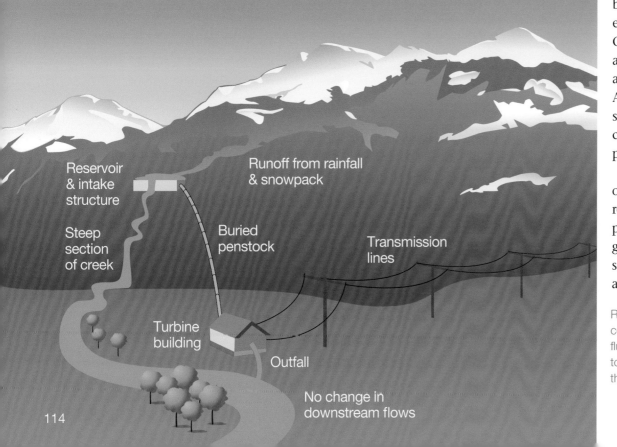

Reservoir & intake structure

Runoff from rainfall & snowpack

Steep section of creek

Buried penstock

Transmission lines

Turbine building

Outfall

No change in downstream flows

There are thousands of potential sites for run-of-river hydropower, ranging from the small off-the-grid building beside a little creek, to commercial-scale projects churning out renewable energy along the world's major rivers.

115

A company called Statkraft is building a small osmosis saltwater generator on a fjord near Oslo, Norway. It's a pilot project for a 25-megwatt power plant, to be completed by 2015, that will generate enough power for 2,500 homes.

Where the River Meets the Sea

A Saltwater Generator

All the hydropower we've seen so far is based on the potential energy water gains when it's evaporated by the sun

Osmosis raises the pressure of the saltwater section as the freshwater flows in, and that increased pressure can be used to spin a turbine.

and carried into the sky. Water leaves the salty oceans and flows back to the sea as freshwater rivers. Now there's another way to use the stored-up solar energy in all that evaporated water—this time by exploiting the *chemical* difference between freshwater and saltwater. There are two competing visions of how to do it.

The Norwegian power company Statkraft is building a small saltwater generator on a fjord near Oslo. Freshwater flows into one chamber and saltwater into another; the end result is enough electric current to power several homes. This pilot project generates only four kilowatts, but the hope is that it's the first step toward building a 25-megawatt power plant—enough for 2,500 homes—by 2015. The only exhaust is a briny mix of fresh and saltwater, which can be dumped into the sea.

How does it work? Osmosis is the principle that freshwater will spontaneously flow into saltwater if the two are separated by a special membrane. Osmosis in reverse is how we squeeze drinking water from seawater in desalination plants. Osmosis raises the pressure of the saltwater section as the freshwater flows in, and that increased pressure can be used to spin a turbine.

A laboratory-sized saltwater battery that employs a technique dubbed "Blue Energy" has sparked a competing technology that could give Statkraft a run for its money. Creator Westus has teamed up with a company called Redstack

Another way to use the energy the sun puts into the evaporated water is by exploiting the chemical difference between freshwater and saltwater.

to take that coffee-mug-sized contraption and build a pilot project in the Netherlands on the same scale as Statkraft's. Salty wastewater from a salt mine is pumped into one pipe, freshwater from a local river is pumped into another, and the result is electrical current. This time, no turbine is needed, since the current is created directly—like a battery.

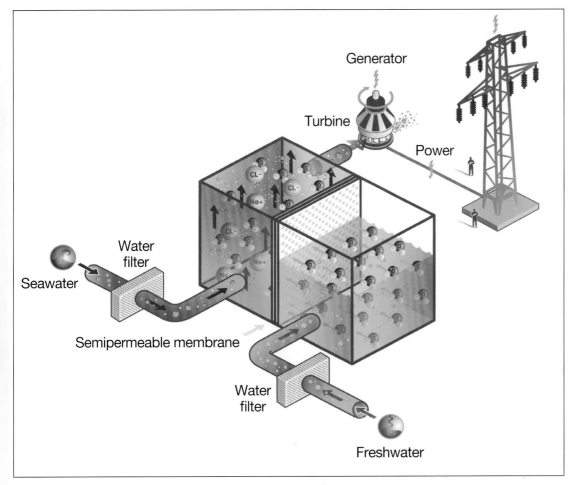

The saltwater generator works on the principle that freshwater will flow into saltwater when separated by a semipermeable membrane. Osmosis raises the pressure of the saltwater section as the freshwater flows in, and that increased pressure is used to spin a turbine.

Generator

Turbine

Power

Water filter

Seawater

Semipermeable membrane

Water filter

Freshwater

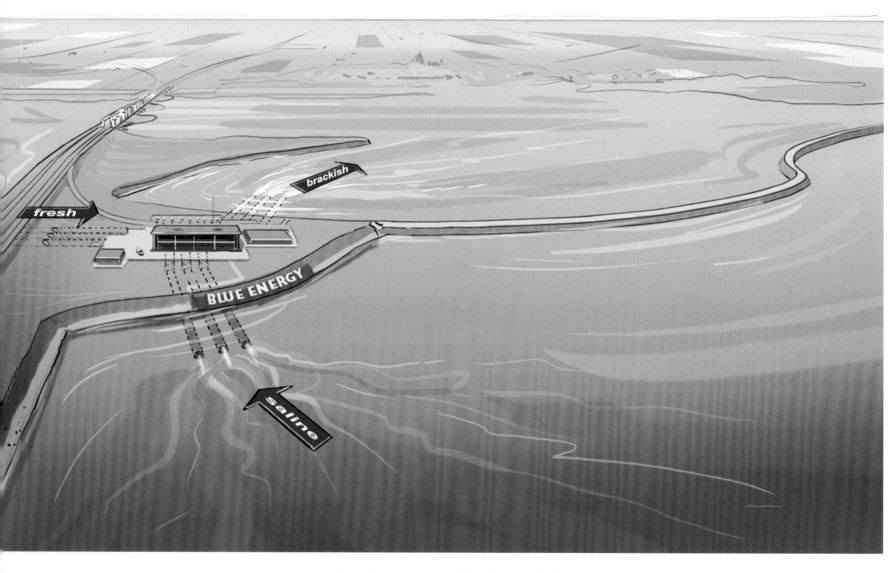

fresh

brackish

BLUE ENERGY

saline

Wetsus has teamed up with Redstack to build a "Blue Energy" generating station in the Netherlands, where wastewater from a salt mine and freshwater from a local river are pumped together—as the different concentrations meet, they create an electrical current.

How does it work? Saltwater contains lots of charged particles; freshwater does not. When salt, or sodium chloride, is dissolved in water, it splits into positively charged sodium ions and negatively charged chloride ions. Freshwater and saltwater flows into a series of chambers, which are separated by membranes that allow only one type of ion to pass through. The membranes allow the different ions to separate, generating a current. Positive ions flow one way and negative ones flow the other, resulting in a saltwater battery.

That's fine for pilot projects, but how well will this idea scale to commercial-sized operations? Technical problems remain—like how to keep the membranes from getting clogged with silt. Good engineers can figure that out. A deeper question is: How much energy can be generated by our river systems without wrecking the rivers? The Blue Energy folks estimate that half the river flows of the world could generate 7% of world energy needs. That's pretty significant. Statkraft's technology isn't quite as efficient—a similar amount of diverted water would meet

only 1% of the planet's energy needs.

That seems like a lot of diverted water, but it's diverted at the mouth of the river, then dumped into the sea. That's where it was headed anyway, so running it through some big batteries on the way doesn't seem so bad.

Potential and Pitfalls

There's no question that both large- and small-scale hydro are viable (we'll forget about the "river meets the sea" stuff for now). Hydro is the single largest and most reliable source of renewable energy, rivaling coal and nuclear for sheer scale of production. Hydro not only provides vast quantities of power, but that power is also *responsive*—which means production can be ramped up (or down) very quickly to react to grid demands. Hydro proved its worth long before carbon was an issue. How big hydro grows from here is a matter of debate. There's a tradeoff between protection of land and mitigation of carbon.

Concerns about projects like the Three Gorges Dam and its effects on both people and the landscape are valid. The criticism that rotting, flooded forests produce methane can be addressed with smart forestry practices prior to flooding, and even deepwater forestry afterward. Other concerns aren't so easy to address. Flooding from the Three Gorges has displaced entire villages, and a lot of beautiful land, valuable archaeology and ecosystems have disappeared.

The sun rises on China's Yangtze River, at the mouth of the Three Gorges. Although plagued with controversy, the Three Gorges Dam, the world's largest hydropower project, will replace massive quantities of fossil fuel normally used to produce electricity.

The Shipshaw Dam on Quebec's Saguenay River was one of Canada's proud contributions to the Second World War. The power plant was rapidly constructed between 1941 and 1943 to supply power for the energy-intensive manufacturing of aluminum, a vital component of modern aircraft.

But if we're going to ask China to stop building coal plants—and we plan to do the same in the west—we must find other ways of producing power. The Three Gorges Dam will prevent more than 100 million tons of carbon

Hydro is a present-day, viable and large-scale renewable alternative to coal, so we should proceed as fast as we can put up the dams.

dioxide from entering the atmosphere[7]— that's almost *twice* the emissions of all[8] the cars on Canada's roads. These projects are so massive, and displace so much fossil fuel, that it's hard to argue, given intelligent management, that there's no net benefit.

Run-of-river projects are not ecologically neutral, although some come pretty darn close. They can affect fish populations, sometimes require transmission lines and roads to be built in what are often pristine wilderness areas, and they do alter the natural flow of the river, at least to some extent. What we need is balance. Not all run-of-river projects bring severe ecological interference. That pipe flowing along my favorite cycling hill in Newfoundland hardly seems problematic.

Hydro is a present-day, viable and large-scale renewable alternative to coal. Given what's at stake if carbon levels get too high (see "Climate Science III"), all else being equal, large-scale hydro should proceed as fast as we can put up the dams.

There is, however, another problem that could be very hard to deal with. If precipitation patterns change as predicted, there may not be much in the way of flowing water to keep those plants going. But our eggs are all in one basket anyway—we need to act to stop that scenario from happening, regardless—so that hardly seems a reason not to proceed apace.

The potential? The world has already harnessed one-fifth of what's technically feasible, and it's reasonable to think we could double that figure, using both large-scale hydro and run-of-river. If electrical consumption were to remain constant, that would raise hydro's share to one-third. But since consumption will double—at least—by 2050, hydro's share would remain the same, at about one-sixth.

The Trillion-Dollar Question:

So, what do you get for $1 trillion? Accounting for a mix of large- and small-scale hydro, $1 trillion would build about 250 gigawatts[9] of electrical generating capacity, or enough to replace more than two-thirds of American coal-based or nuclear electrical production.

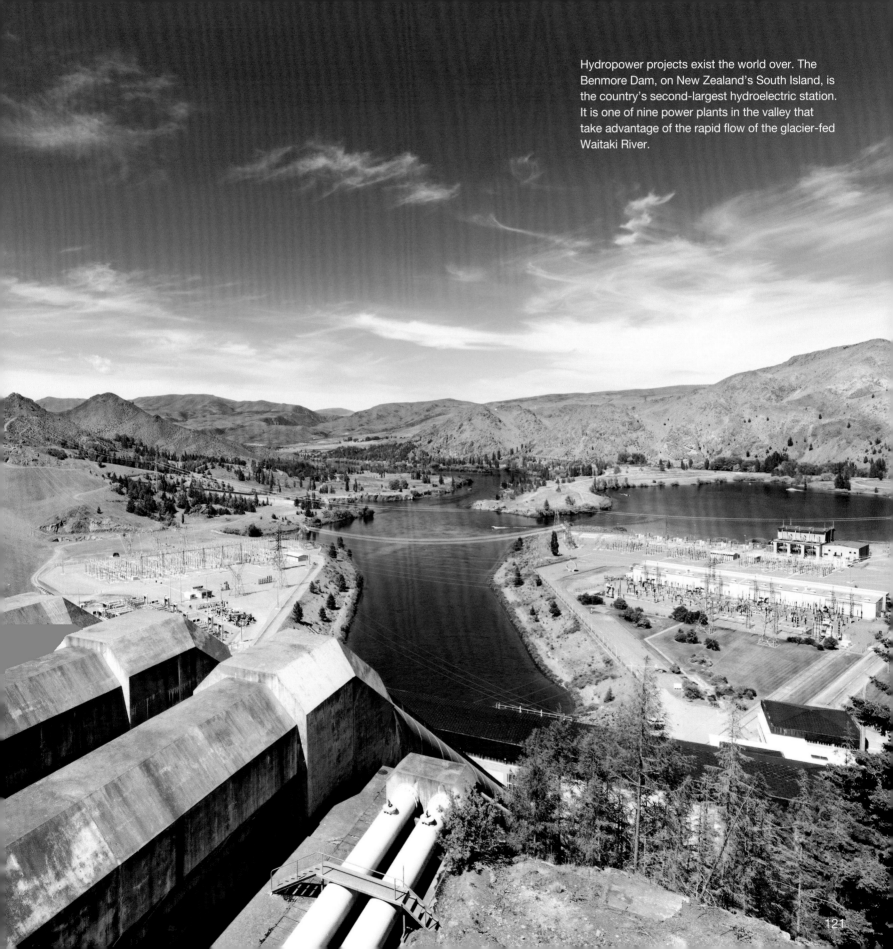

Hydropower projects exist the world over. The Benmore Dam, on New Zealand's South Island, is the country's second-largest hydroelectric station. It is one of nine power plants in the valley that take advantage of the rapid flow of the glacier-fed Waitaki River.

Cheap Money

Enter the Green Bond

Before I tell you about Green Bonds, let's start with three questions.

What does it cost to produce renewable energy? There are lots of different estimates. Funny thing is, you don't have to pay to make the wind blow or the sun shine. So where's the cost? Almost all[1] of the cost associated with renewable energy is the cost of borrowing the money it takes to put up the turbine or build the plant. So cheaper money equals cheaper energy.

Who borrows for the lowest cost? The government (in the form of government-issued bonds). Governments are the safest place for your money, so they pay the lowest interest.

Who is willing to lend money cheaply? Well, if it was backed by the government, and it went toward renewable energy production, the answer could very well be—*most of us!*[2]

It empowers citizens, rather than scaring them, and generates the popular support needed to further tackle the climate change problem.

So, what's a Green Bond? A Green Bond is like a Victory Bond for the environment. Citizens buy a bond, backed by their national government. The money raised is lent out at low rates for renewable energy projects. The energy produced by those projects pays the interest on the bonds. The result is to accelerate our transformation away from fossil fuels and enable people to participate in that transformation.

A Green Bond is like a Victory Bond for the environment.

In the heat of the credit crisis, Green Bonds are even more relevant. All companies are starving for credit, and the last ones we want to see fail are those responsible for leading the charge away from fossil fuels. At the same time, people are desperate for a safe place to put their money.

It's no magic bullet, and it can't replace a long-term price on carbon (see "A New Economics"), but Green Bonds are an important policy tool.

Why engage the public in this way? Green Bonds offer the public the chance to join in a nation-building project. It gives us something more meaningful to do than just changing a lightbulb. Green Bonds give people some "skin in the game" and provide an important step in changing our psychology toward climate change. It empowers citizens, rather than scaring them, and generates the popular support needed to further tackle the climate change problem.

Government plays a limited, creative role: guaranteeing some portion of the bond to ensure that a green investment is a safe investment. The only cost to government comes in the form of defaulted loans. That cost sits on their books (in accounting terms) as a contingent liability.

I worked on just such a proposal for the Canadian government. My team and I built a detailed policy backed by sound economic analysis. We showed that the policy will not break the bank. In fact, we estimate that the cost to government will be a mere $1 to $13 per ton of carbon reduced. That's remarkably cheap as these things go.

We recommended that the private sector should manage investments so that the government would not be picking winners. In our view, private oversight maximizes bang per buck by leveraging their existing expertise, incentives and efficiencies. That's not the only way to do it of course, and any government can tailor-make management to suit their own political and economic context.

Ordinary citizens will help transform the country's energy economy by shifting their savings from banks to turbines.

To be sure though, at a minimum, the government should provide a broad investment mandate. The fund's efficiency would be judged by the cost per ton of carbon reduced, and its overall success by the total amount of carbon reduced.

This is not a kooky idea. The Europeans already issued a Climate Awareness Bond in 2007 to support their sustainable energy sector and the bond sold out in three months. The World Bank followed suit in 2008. This is a policy that could be adopted by every country around the world, designed to engage their own citizens and support their own transition to the new low-carbon economy.

We recommended that the private sector manage the investments.

Build the bond and buyers will come. In the process, ordinary citizens will help transform the country's energy economy by shifting their savings from banks to turbines.

SIX

The C

cean

HARVESTING THE HIGHS AND LOWS

A company called Wavegen, on the Scottish Island of Islay, generates electricity for the grid with its LIMPET shoreline energy converter. It translates the up-and-down movement of waves into a stream of compressed air that spins a turbine.

The Ocean

An Introduction

There is a phenomenon on Newfoundland's East Coast Trail that is a wonder to behold. It's called the Spout, and it's visible for miles around, though accessible only by boat or daylong hike along the dramatic coastline. Every minute or so, a huge gasp of watery spray jets out of a hole in the ground and shoots into the air. The eruption looks like the spout of a giant whale coming to the surface to breathe. That jet of water packs quite a punch—I've seen it up close. In fact, I once threw a small tree down the Spout; seconds later, I watched it shoot into the air high over my head.

At the Spout, nature has conspired to create an underground cavern, shaped just right to concentrate the up-and-down action of waves over a large area into that single watery jet. It doesn't take much—waves only a few feet high cause a spout[1] 100 feet or so (30 metres) above sea level. I've stared at the Spout for hours, wondering how on Earth it

The oceans were formed over millions of years as the continents shifted, and they remain largely unexplored.

works—and whether we could duplicate that underground geometry to create a new kind of power plant.

The answer is yes—but the Scots beat me to it long ago. Their LIMPET design, on the Scottish Island of Islay, translates the up-and-down movement of waves into a stream of compressed air that spins a turbine, creating electricity. Wave power is just one way of getting energy from the ocean.

The world's oceans are actually one massive, interconnected body of water. Covering more than 70% of the Earth's surface, they're the source of the world's freshwater, as the sun evaporates water at the surface, leaving the salt behind. The five

Wave power is just one way of getting energy from the ocean.

oceans (the Atlantic, Pacific, Arctic, Indian and Southern) were formed over millions of years, as the continents shifted, and they remain largely unexplored. The deepest point on the planet is the Marianas Trench, almost seven miles (11 kilometres) down. A two-man team from the US Navy reached the Marianas Trench back in 1960. Since then, only a robotic vehicle called Nereus has managed to reach it, in June 2009. No working craft remains that can take humans so deep under the sea.[2]

The Spout, on Newfoundland's East Coast Trail, shoots an incandescent spray of water high into the air each time a wave crashes into the underground chamber. The eruption looks like the spout of a giant whale coming to the surface to breathe.

Great Ocean Conveyor Belt

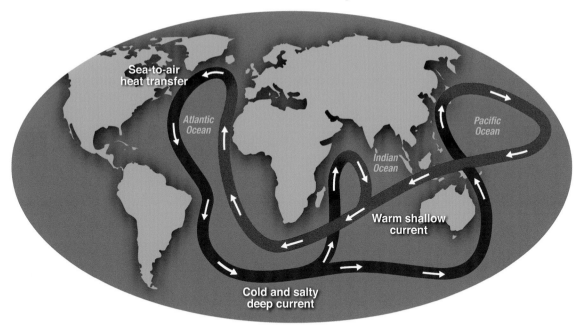

Ocean currents are driven by changes in the density of seawater. The Conveyor Belt transfers warm water from the Pacific to the Atlantic as a shallow current and returns cold water from the Atlantic to the Pacific as a deep current that flows farther south.

Oceans play a starring role in global climate patterns. They moderate coastal temperatures, ensuring that coastal cities are cooler in the summer and warmer in the winter than their landlocked cousins. Ocean currents like La Niña and El Niño, the Gulf Stream, and the Great Ocean Conveyor Belt[3] move huge amounts of heat around the globe. The Ocean Conveyor and Gulf Stream are responsible for Europe's moderate climate; without it, places like the UK would be as chilly as Labrador, on Canada's east coast. Oceans also help moderate global warming,

Oceans play a starring role in global climate patterns.

absorbing as much as one-third of our carbon emissions.

As the Earth warms, the oceans' contribution to our climate will change in a number of ways. Instead of being a carbon *sink* (absorbing carbon dioxide from the air), they could flip into a carbon *source*. Just like an open bottle of pop left in the sun, all that absorbed carbon dioxide could bubble out, causing a huge jump in global warming. The Ocean Conveyor might slow[4] or even stop, moving Europe's climate closer to that of Canada. Hurricanes will get stronger as the oceans warm, since it's the heat from tropical waters that fuel them. It's already happening.

Oceans also contain energy that's useful to us, of course, and it can be captured in three ways. First off, there are all sorts of funny-looking contraptions, with names like the Clam, the Whale and the Anaconda, that ride the waves and convert their movement into electricity. Then there are fields of underwater turbines that can be installed in tidal currents, spinning as the tides rise and fall, much like wind turbines. Finally, giant vertical tubes can plumb the ocean depths, exploiting the difference in temperature between the surface and deep water, and creating enough energy to spin a turbine.

All three forms of renewable energy work, but it's tidal power that will likely be the easiest to exploit in a big way. There are some tricky engineering and reliability issues

Oceans help moderate global warming, absorbing as much as one-third of our carbon emissions.

to solve when it comes to wave power, but it too has potential. As for those vertical tubes, they're still more curiosity than utility. There is, however, an audacious plan for a different kind of tube—one that uses wave power to promote vast algae growth, translating wave power into carbon sequestration.

Sea ice melting at the poles is global warming's canary in the coal mine. Average temperatures at the poles are rising twice as fast as they are elsewhere in the world. There is now a serious risk that oceans could flip from "carbon sink" to "carbon source."

Although waves appear to be water moving horizontally along the surface, that's an illusion. Instead, they move up and down in a circular motion as the force of the wave passes by—until it breaks onshore.

Riding the Waves

Waves are the ocean's way of storing wind power. Wind passes over the water's surface, causing ripples that are then amplified by more wind. By the time large swells reach the coast, they've often traveled thousands of miles, with the storms responsible for creating them long gone. Although waves appear to be water moving horizontally along the surface, that's

Waves are the ocean's way of storing wind power.

an illusion. Much like the human "wave" at sporting events, where each person stands up and sits down in turn, no single particle actually follows the wave along the water's surface. Instead, they move up and down in a circular motion[5] as the force of the wave passes by—until it breaks onshore.

Harnessing the power of waves isn't easy—but it can be done. There are almost as many

The trick is to build something that translates all that motion—random and regular—into movement uniform enough to produce power.

ways to do it as there are people who have tried. The trick is to build a machine that translates all that motion—random and regular—into movement uniform enough to produce power. The *really* hard part is making sure it can stand up to the harsh ocean environment.

Onshore systems take advantage of waves' energy as they hit the coast. One trick, an

oscillating water column, works much like the Spout. Imagine an open pop bottle, with its bottom cut off, sitting in the water. As the water level goes up and down with passing waves, air moves through the opening and spins a turbine.[6] The key to generating power is to perfect the geometry of the chamber to maximize the force of air for a given size of wave.

Another way to tame the waves for onshore production is to build a tapered, uphill ramp leading to a reservoir. As waves hit the ramp, they get narrower, converting their energy

to height.[7] It's like pumping water up a hill using wave physics. Once the water is in the reservoir, electrical production is the same as conventional hydropower.

As for offshore production, there are dozens of tricks, with one constant: One part of the machine stays roughly still relative to the surface of the water (or what would be the surface, were it calm). Another part moves with the waves, either pumping liquid or moving air to spin a turbine.

Wavegen of Scotland uses "Wells Turbines" in its shoreline power generator. Waves create an oscillating column of water, forcing air back and forth through the turbine. The turbine always rotates in the same direction, regardless of the direction of airflow.

The aptly named Clam is a large, 12-sided floating device that pushes air between 12 separate chambers. So far, it's only a prototype.

Wave energy is tricky business, not just because of the unique way waves deliver their energy, but also because the ocean is such a harsh environment.

But when it's built to full scale, the Clam will be more than 180 feet (60 metres) in diameter, with chambers big enough to hold a conventional hallway. Another protoype, the Whale, is shaped like a giant whale tail that oscillates with oncoming waves.

The only commercial-scale project to date is the Agucadoura Wave Park, off the coast of Portugal. It's based on a Scottish-made machine called the Pelamis—a 500-foot-long (150-metre) snake-like system that bends and flexes with the waves. Unfortunately, it has been plagued with problems: A few months after it was deployed in 2009, it was hauled back to shore with technical difficulties. Then the project's financing fell through. For now, the giant Pelamis sits in a harbor, awaiting a second chance.

The Anaconda, a similar device made by UK-based Checkmate Sea Energy, is made of rubber and fabric. Checkmate is betting that its simpler design will get past the trial stage, and the company hopes to one day produce

So far, the only commercial-scale project is the Agucadoura Wave Park, off the coast of Portugal.

commercial-sized Anacondas 650 feet (200 metres) long. The dream is for hundreds of these serpentine power plants to be anchored offshore, each of them delivering enough power for 1,000 homes.

Wave energy is a tricky business, not just because of the unique way waves deliver their energy, but also because the ocean is such a harsh environment. There are lots of wonderful devices and original ideas, and the wave-energy industry is probably only a decade or so away from delivering utility-scale power.

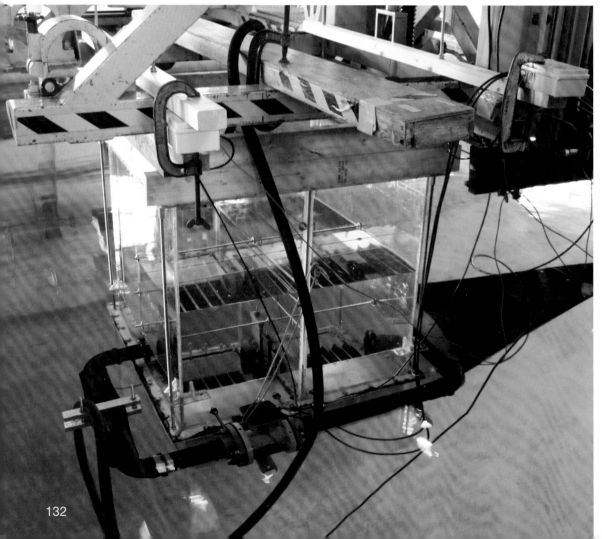

UK-based Checkmate Sea Energy used a massive wave pool to test its snake-like "Anaconda" wave energy converter. When tethered to the seabed facing into the waves, enough pressure is created by the waves traveling through the snake to generate hydraulic power.

There is another way to use wave energy

Influential thinker and scientist James Lovelock, originator of the Gaia hypothesis,[8] has proposed a simple and elegant way to suck carbon out of the air and store it in the ocean.

How does it work? Lovelock's idea is to install a bunch of tubes, 650 feet (200 metres) in length and 65 feet (10 metres) in diameter, that go from surface to bottom, with a one-way valve on the lower end. As the tubes move up and down with the waves, the cold, nutrient-rich water close to the ocean floor rises to the surface. When the sun hits that water, algae grows and sucks carbon dioxide out of the air. When it dies, some of that algae will drop to the ocean bottom. Voilà—cheap carbon capture.

The Scottish-made Pelamis is a snake-like system that bends and flexes with the waves. The wave-induced motion is resisted by hydraulic rams that pump fluid through hydraulic motors, driving electrical generators.

The Bay of Fundy, in eastern Canada, is home to some of the world's most dramatic tides. The rise of the water is more than 50 feet (15 metres) when the tidal currents are forced through the Minas Passage.

Tidal Flows

Ever wish your days could last a few hours longer? Wait a few hundred million years and they will. The tides—that great sloshing-around of the oceans as they are pulled one way and then another by the moon's[9] gravity—dissipate enough of the Earth's rotational energy to slow down the rate of spin. About 600 million years ago, one day—one spin of the Earth on its vertical axis—lasted only 22 hours, not 24.

Sir Isaac Newton laid the foundation for our understanding of gravitational forces back in 1687, when he famously explained that the moon and sun exert a force on the Earth similar to the one that pulls apples to the ground. A century later, another great mathematician, Pierre Simon Laplace, came up with differential equations[10] describing how water moves horizontally given a tug upward from the moon. That horizontal movement translates into tidal currents.

The French brought tidal power into modern times in 1966, building a generator in the Rance Estuary that delivers enough power for 240,000 homes.

In places where that moving water is forced though a channel, very strong currents result. Anyone who has battled tidal flows in a kayak knows firsthand how quickly they can arise and how powerfully they flow. The Bay of Fundy, in eastern Canada, is home to some of the most dramatic tides on the planet. The rise of the water is more than 50 feet (15 metres), and when the tidal currents are forced through the Minas Passage, the water flows at speeds of up to 8.7 miles per hour (14 kilometres per hour). At its peak, that flow

Anyone who has battled tidal flows in a kayak knows firsthand how quickly they can arise and how powerfully they flow.

has a volume of more than all the world's rivers and streams put together! Converting that moving water to electricity is what tidal power is all about.

The Romans were probably the first to build mills that made use of tidal currents, near what is now London, and they remained in operation throughout the Middle Ages (to see one in action, check out the reconstructed Woodbridge Tide Mill, originally dating from the 12th century, near Suffolk). The French brought tidal power into modern times in 1966, building a 240-megawatt generator—enough to power 240,000 homes—in the Rance Estuary. An early Canadian effort was the much smaller 20-megawatt generator in Annapolis, Nova Scotia.

The Woodbridge Tide Mill in Suffolk, UK, was originally built on this site in 1170. The present building is relatively modern, dating from 1793. It was the last working Tide Mill in the UK—in 1957, the square, 22-inch oak main shaft broke, and the wheel came to a halt.

How does it work? There are two ways to do it. The first is with a tidal barrage—a kind of dam that traps water as it rises with the tide, then drains it through a turbine. In reverse, the barrage stops the water from

Since water is about 800 times denser than air, it contains much more kinetic energy than air moving at the same speed.

rising before releasing it through the turbine. The process is similar to conventional hydropower, except tidal barrages build potential energy in the water by exploiting the moon's gravitational pull. That's how older systems, like the one in Rance, work.

A more modern method is to place turbines right in the tidal current, letting the moving water turn the blades directly. These turbines can work in both directions. Since water is about 800 times denser than air, it contains much more kinetic energy than air moving at the same speed. Water flowing at eight knots (15 kilometres per hour), for instance, contains as much kinetic energy[11] as a 263-mile-per-hour (424-kilometre-per-hour) gale!

It's not easy tapping that power. Much like offshore wind farms, these turbines need to withstand the corrosive effects of saltwater and be maintained on the open sea. To be economical, they need to work reliably for years. But tidal power is well on its way to commercial viability.

Marine Current Turbines (MCT), based in the UK, was a pioneer of the tidal-current turbine, and it's now a world leader. Peter Fraenkel, the company's technical director, first proved the concept in 1994 with a 15-kilowatt turbine (enough for 15 homes) in Lock Linnhe, Scotland. MCT's latest model is the SeaGen, a giant, 1.2-megawatt generator (enough for about 1,000 homes) that costs around $14 million. Two separate turbines hang off a central tower, which is driven into the ocean floor. Both sets of blades can be

Tidal barrages are similar to conventional hydropower, except they build potential energy in the water by exploiting the moon's gravitational pull.

hauled out of the water for maintenance. A 10-megawatt tidal farm in Wales, the Anglesey Skerries, is set to begin construction in 2011. It will grow to an industrially respectable size of 100 megawatts—enough for a good-sized town—if fully commissioned.

It's most effective to place turbines right in the tidal current, with the moving water turning the blades directly—in either direction. They're quite efficient, but they do face some challenges, like withstanding the corrosive effects of saltwater and allowing for easy maintenance in open water.

Verdant Power's free-flow tidal hydropower project in New York's East River was the world's first grid-connected array of tidal turbines. With the demonstration phase now complete, plans are proceeding for the full 30-turbine array.

Alderney Renewable Energy, in the Channel Islands of Guernsey, plans to use "Open-Centre" turbines to farm the tidal power around the island. They could generate somewhere between one and three gigawatts of power for the French and UK grids.

MCT is not the only game in town. Verdant Power, based in New York, has a 10-megawatt project in the works in the East River, and a 15-megawatt farm of turbines is planned for Canada's St. Lawrence River (Verdant's

The amount of tidal power available is significant.

M.O. is a mix of tidal and river current flows). Yet another player, Clean Current Power Systems, operates a small pilot project on Canada's west coast, which is considered to have a total tidal potential of around 4,000 megawatts, or the equivalent of four medium-sized coal plants.

The biggest project currently on the table stems from a deal between the UK's Lunar Energy and a contingent of South Korean

partners. Their plan is to build a 300-megawatt tidal farm off the Korean coast, at a cost of roughly $750 million. That power is comparable to about half a medium-sized coal plant. Similar in size to the SeaGen, the consortium's Rotech Tidal Turbine also works in both directions, but has the added twist of a "venturi" opening: Water enters a duct with a diameter of 49 feet (15 metres) and is compressed into a smaller channel before hitting the 38-foot (11.5-metre) turbine. This accelerates the water flow and straightens it, too, eliminating the need for complicated blade-pitch adjustments.

There are more plans afoot. The tiny Channel Islands of Guernsey have the potential to generate the equivalent of 25 medium-sized coal plants, and it should all start around the island of Alderney. Alderney Renewable Energy was formed in 2008 to farm the tidal

power around the island, and the company could generate somewhere between one and three gigawatts of power, which will be sold into the French and UK grids.

Is this the start of something big? Time will

The tiny Channel Islands of Guernsey have the potential to generate the equivalent of 25 medium-sized coal plants.

tell, but the amount of the resource available is significant. Total worldwide capacity is estimated to be around one billion kilowatts, or two trillion to three trillion kilowatt hours of output annually. That's about six times Canada's electrical generation, or about the same as all American coal-based electrical production.

Plumbing the Ocean Depths

There is another way. Heat pumps, like the ones used to harness geothermal energy, can also be applied to the ocean. As the sun warms the ocean's surface, it creates a temperature difference between that water and the water deep below. That differential can be used to drive a heat engine and generate electricity. Ocean thermal energy conversion (OTEC), as it's called, is sort of like geothermal—but in this case, you're diving deep to get the cold stuff, not the hot stuff. The idea behind OTEC is simple; scaling it up to utility-sized production isn't.

How does it work? The most common method is to use the heat from the warm surface waters of southern oceans to evaporate a liquid with a low boiling point, like ammonia. (That liquid is contained in a "closed system," which means it doesn't mix with the ocean water.) The expanding

> OTEC is destined to remain a niche technology. Not only is it extremely expensive, but the structures need to be built in a hostile environment.

gas spins a turbine, much like a steam generator. Pipes going deep into the ocean bring up cold water, which condenses the evaporated ammonia back to liquid, and the process repeats.

So far, a few pilot plants have been built, but they've all been far too tiny to be viable—one generated enough electricity to power the lights and computers on the barge the plant sat on. Other OTEC plans have run into major technical difficulties. In 2003, Indian engineers twice tried to lower a 2,600-foot-long (800-metre) tube into the ocean as part

> Heat pumps, like the ones used to harness geothermal energy, can also be applied to the ocean.

of a one-megawatt plant, only to have the pipe drop to the ocean floor both times.

Believers haven't given up, though. Giant defence contractor Lockheed Martin is set to

The Net Power Producing Experiment was the first open-cycle OTEC system ever developed and tested—it converted warm seawater into low-pressure steam for power generation. The research project operated in Kona, Hawaii, from 1993 to 1999.

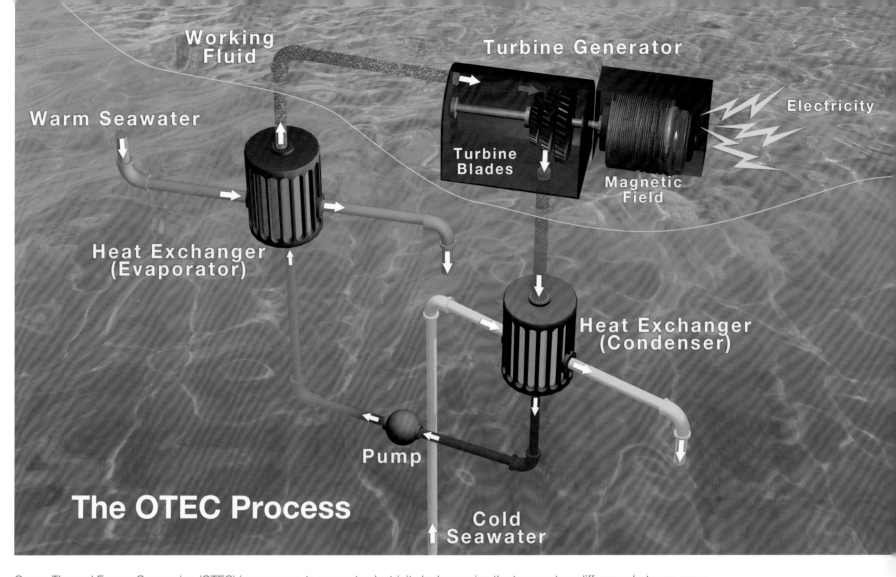

The OTEC Process

Working Fluid

Turbine Generator

Electricity

Warm Seawater

Turbine Blades

Magnetic Field

Heat Exchanger (Evaporator)

Heat Exchanger (Condenser)

Pump

Cold Seawater

Ocean Thermal Energy Conversion (OTEC) is a process to generate electricity by leveraging the temperature difference between warm surface water and cold deep water. The temperature differential drives a "steam" cycle to turn a turbine and produce power.

build a 10- to 20-megawatt plant (enough for up to 2,000 homes) in Hawaii. The plan calls for a 3,300-foot-long (one-kilometre) pipe with a diameter of 88 feet (27 metres) plumbing the ocean's depths. Another company, OCEES International, based in Hawaii, intends to build an OTEC plant for the island of Diego Garcia, home to a US military base.

Enthusiastic proponents of OTEC claim the technology could produce limitless energy, and many dream of massive floating barges harvesting the ocean's energy bounty. But OTEC is destined to remain a niche technology. It might take root in an isolated,

highly valued property like the Diego Garcia military base, or reach small commercial scale in Hawaii, but it won't make much of a splash anywhere else. Not only is it extremely expensive, but the structures required for utility-scale generation are huge and need to be built in an environment that's hostile to grand engineering experiments (to say nothing of algae and barnacles).

Lockheed Martin has plans to build a utility-scale OTEC plant in Hawaii. The concept calls for a 3,300-foot-long (one-kilometre) pipe with a diameter of 88 feet (27 metres) to harvest cold water from the ocean's depths.

Agucadoura Wave Park, off the coast of Portugal, is the only commercial-scale wave energy project to date. It utilizes the 500-foot-long (150-metre) Scottish-made Pelamis articulated power generation system, which bends and flexes with the waves.

Potential and Pitfalls

So, with OTEC relegated to the fringes, where does that leave us? Wave energy can emerge as a major energy contributor (exploiting *all* the technically available power for an island nation like the UK would amount to 20%[12] of total electrical use), but it needs to move from prototype to commercial scale fast.

Utilities value reliable power, and the tides are as reliable as a good watch.

Although they haven't yet been tested on any significant scale, farms of carbon-capturing, wave-powered pumps could provide some much-needed relief for our carbon-ridden atmosphere.

Tidal energy holds the most promise, and we're well on our way to developing utility-sized tidal power plants that will probably end up producing the same amount of energy as conventional geothermal does now.

Tidal power has its drawbacks, though, including big capital costs and limited geography. Plus, it's intermittent, since tidal generators operate only when the tides flow, generating power about 10 hours a day (twice

Tidal energy holds the most promise, with future power plants producing the same amount of energy as geothermal does now.

that, if the turbines are bidirectional). And since tides are dominated by the lunar cycle, which is out of sync with our 24-hour clock

by about 50 minutes, the times when tidal plants generate power change day to day. Inconvenient, but not a deal-breaker. Utilities value *reliable* power, and the tides are as reliable as a good watch.

The bottom line is that it's too good to pass up: Worldwide tides could deliver enough energy to match US coal-based electrical production. In countries like Canada, with its small population and lots of coastline, tidal power could be a major player.

The Trillion-Dollar Question:

So, what do you get for $1 trillion?
For $1 trillion, we could develop all of the world's potential tidal power. That's equivalent to all American coal-based or nuclear electrical production.

UK-based Lunar Energy and South Korea's Korean Midland Power are developing the world's largest tidal power project off the south coast of South Korea. The giant 300-turbine field is expected to be providing 300 megawatts of renewable energy by 2015.

143

Hydrogen

A Piece of the Puzzle

Hydrogen is the most abundant element in our universe, making up about 75% of its mass. When fossil fuels, a.k.a. hydrocarbons, combust—whether it's natural gas or coal in a power plant, or gasoline or diesel in a vehicle—it's the hydrogen molecule that powers the engine. The element, which puts the "H" in H_2O, combines with oxygen to form water, releasing energy in the process. Hydrogen can be burned on its own in a car, or provide the fuel for fuel cells, which produce clean electricity for buildings and electric vehicles.

BMW's sleek and powerful Hydrogen 7 runs solely on hydrogen, and instead of coughing out fumes from its exhaust pipe, the only thing this car produces is water. And it's on the road today. When hydrogen is fed into a fuel cell

Hydrogen isn't a source of energy; it's a way of storing it. Hydrogen doesn't compete with fossil fuels; it competes with batteries.

(see Chapter 10), it combines with oxygen to produce an electrical current, which can be used to power a building or car—electrical production, with water as exhaust. It's no wonder hydrogen is often touted as a kind of wonder fuel: clean-burning and so abundant, our oceans are *made* of the stuff. So, why aren't all our cars and power plants running on hydrogen already?

It's not quite that easy. Hydrogen may be the most common element on the planet, but the problem is that it's always attached to some other element—oxygen to form water, for instance, or carbon to form fossil fuels. In the sugars that can make ethanol, it's bound up with both oxygen *and* carbon. And there's the rub: To split the hydrogen away from the atoms to which it's attached takes energy—more energy than you'll ever get from combusting the stuff or putting it in a fuel cell. That reflects the second law of thermodynamics, which says: "There's no such thing as free energy."

So, hydrogen isn't really a fuel source, like coal or oil—we can't mine the stuff and dump it into our engines. Instead, think of it as a kind of energy carrier, a way of transforming one kind of energy into another, or as a way of storing energy. The ability to store energy is a key component of the Energy Internet.

There are two common ways of producing hydrogen: electrolysis and reformation. Electrolysis means running an electric current through water to split the water molecules into hydrogen and oxygen. To make the whole process more efficient, you can add heat—and if you use only clean sources of energy, like solar PV or solar thermal, hydrogen becomes a truly clean fuel.

Reformation means stripping a fossil fuel—say, natural gas—of the carbon it contains. But since the process releases carbon dioxide, it's not a carbon-free source of energy (unless you bury the CO_2). It's also possible to produce hydrogen directly, using algae. If deprived of sulfur, some strains of the stuff will actually breathe out hydrogen. The key to biological production is scale—making enough of it at a low enough cost to make it worth the effort.

But even if we could produce hydrogen on a commercial scale, there's still the problem of how to store it. Not so much an issue for stationary fuel cells, but certainly a barrier for hydrogen-powered cars or trucks. Hydrogen contains a lot of energy by weight, but not so much by volume. That means you'd need several enormous storage tanks of hydrogen just to replace the diesel tank of one truck. One solution might be creating special metals that can hold large amounts of hydrogen with chemical bonds, packing lots of power into a small volume.

Hydrogen may be the most common element on the planet, but the problem is that it's always attached to some other element.

Until the storage problem is solved, hydrogen's most promising application is in stationary fuel cells. Fuel cells are like electrolysis in reverse: They combine hydrogen and oxygen to produce electricity. Some fuel cells even work both ways, using electricity to make hydrogen in one direction, and using hydrogen to make electricity in the other.

Eventually, I envision a nationwide network of fuel cells that will replace the diesel generators now used in most large buildings to provide backup emergency power. At night, when power is cheap, the fuel cells will fill giant tanks with hydrogen. During the day, they'll use that hydrogen to power the building. The whole system will pay for itself with the difference in cost.

Since hydrogen isn't a source of energy, but rather a way of *storing* it, the element doesn't compete directly with fossil fuels; it competes with batteries. Only when hydrogen fuel cells are more cost-effective than big batteries, like the giant sodium sulfur ones used now for large-scale storage, will they succeed. The problem: Batteries are very efficient, returning almost 80% of the energy put into them. As for fuel cells, right now they return less than one-third. Their sole advantage is that the storage tanks cost almost nothing, so they can store huge amounts of energy with little additional capital cost.

The hydrogen economy has a wonderful ring to it: clean, renewable power used to make a fuel that emits nothing but water. Dig a bit deeper, though, and hydrogen emerges as part of the puzzle, not a solution all by itself.

SEVEN

Smart

Buildings

PERFECTLY SEPARATING INSIDE AND OUT

Smart Buildings

An Introduction

I live in downtown Toronto—a country kid in an urban landscape. In the spirit of embracing city life, I moved into a condo. The place was hip, with a great view, and besides, what could be more energy-friendly? Shared walls, each unit surrounded on five sides by other units—surely it would take less energy to heat and cool than a house.

It was not to be. When I first walked into the hallway, my hair was literally blown back. A local bylaw dictates that a certain amount of air move through shared spaces, and the hallway was nothing but a warm-air tunnel: In winter, cold air got sucked in, heated up and blown out again. In summer, warm air got cooled by an air conditioner and blown out. There wasn't even a decent heat-exchanger to save that energy. My share of the energy bills was more than what I'd paid at my drafty old house. That's a dumb building.

So, what's a smart building? Is it a place with lots of high-tech lighting that turns on when you enter a room, has silent air-conditioning and automatic doors? Maybe it has a refrigerator that knows when you're out of butter and walls incorporating digital art that changes with the mood. Sure, that'd be great, but those are toys. A smart building is designed to do one thing really well: Keep the outside *out* and the inside *in*.

We've already covered solar panels and geothermal heating and cooling systems, and in the last few chapters, we'll look at low-energy LED and compact fluorescent lighting, and electrical systems that are hooked up to the Energy Internet. But these are systems *within* the building. The building itself is an envelope, keeping the elements one step away and the environment inside to your taste. How well it does that tells us how smart it is. My condo building was dumb, its envelope torn open to make the halls breezy.

> ## A smart building is designed to do one thing really well— keep the outside *out* and the inside *in*.

A smart building can act like a thermos, locking heat in (or out). It can interact with the sun and Earth to take advantage of the energy on offer. It amplifies and stores heat in winter or diminishes it in summer. A smart building integrates with the environment around it, in a way that makes it a lovely place to live. It is *not* a warm-air tunnel.

Buildings suck up more than half the energy used in major urban centers, and 40% overall. How we build new structures—and change the face of ones that already exist—will be a key battle in the fight to kick our fossil fuel habit.

Most of the ideas that follow aren't new—they just haven't been widely adopted yet. There are buildings dug into the Earth and open to the sun. Some are built like a thermos. The very best need no heating or cooling at all. And Net Zero buildings go one step further, generating as much energy as they consume. There's even a way to "re-skin" existing structures, letting us re-imagine entire cityscapes.

Many modern buildings are stacked with rows of rooftop air conditioners churning out so much cold air that the occupants below need to wear sweaters. A smart building envelope not only saves massive amounts of energy, but it also delivers optimum comfort.

A smart building acts like a thermos when it needs to. It can interact with the sun—and the ground—to take advantage of the energy on offer. It amplifies and stores heat in winter, and diminishes it in summer.

149

"Passivhaus" is a voluntary standard for ultra-low-energy buildings—over 15,000 have been built, primarily in Germany and Scandinavia. Although they cost about 10% more to build, that money can be recouped quickly thanks to lower energy costs.

Earthships and Passivhauses

A community in Taos, New Mexico, is sculpted from some very beautiful and unusual buildings. These "Earthships" look like a cross between the creations of Spanish architect Gaudi and something a Hobbit might occupy. The force behind the Earthship project is Michael Reynolds. His mission? To build the most energy-self-sufficient buildings in the world—and to persuade people all over the planet to do the same.

They only cost 10% more to build than a regular house—and you can recoup that in no time with the money you save on energy bills.

Each Earthship is as unique as its owner, but they're all constructed from recycled materials—old tires, bales of straw, recycled glass. To get around the need for active heating and cooling systems, Earthships are dug into the ground on one side, with lots of windows on the other. The ground moderates temperature, and dense material like rock or cement store the heat of the sun, making the structures comfortable through long winter nights—no high-tech insulation required. Of course, they're not for everybody—Earthships are as much a reflection of the community members' need to live outside conventional suburban norms as they are a bold comment on how we might better integrate with our environment. Earthships go where no building has gone before.

The "Passivhaus," a new kind of home that appeared in Germany in 1990, is like an Earthship for the rest of us. Like Mr. Reynolds's creations, the Passivhaus requires no active heating or cooling.[1] Instead, it relies

"Earthships," an unusual community in Taos, New Mexico, features buildings sculpted from recycled materials, like old tires filled with mud and straw. The mission of founder Michael Reynolds is to build the most energy-self-sufficient buildings in the world.

on the sun and heat from the bodies of the people living there. Think of it as a giant thermos—but one disguised as a regular-looking house. The only way to know it's a Passivhaus is to take a look at the energy bill.

The Passivhaus requires no active heating or cooling.

How does it work? Triple-glazed windows face the equator, capturing solar heat. The windows are small enough not to leak heat at night, yet big enough to capture as much as possible during the day. The sunlight streaming through the glass hits a material with lots of so-called thermal mass—say, concrete—which stores heat during the day and releases it at night. The building breathes through a heat-exchanger, which can capture 80% of the heat before it vents.

Even through Germany's cold winter months, the homes stay comfortably room-temperature. Here's the best part: They only cost 10% more to build than a regular house—and you recoup that in no time, thanks to all the money you save on energy bills.

This ultra-energy-efficient home in rural Ontario, Canada, was designed by Toronto-based Solares. The architects chose advanced building materials and technology to provide comfortable year-round living—without the need for conventional heating and cooling systems.

A German institute dedicated to promoting the Passivhaus cause—and certifying buildings that meet the standard—was formed in 1996, and similar institutions are popping up around the world. Now, even office buildings and schools are being built on the same principle. No heating and cooling—does it get any better than that?

Even if you don't reach the Passivhaus standard, you can get pretty close. The husband-and-wife team behind tiny Solares, in Toronto, Canada, has put up some pretty smart homes. They use heating, but not much. A Solares house stayed a comfortable 64 F (18 C) during a –13 F (–25 C) cold snap —and that was *before* they installed the

> "We've never built a structure that needed air-conditioning. In my view, a building that needs it is badly designed."

heating unit. And air-conditioning? Forget about it. "We've never built a structure that needed air-conditioning. In my view, a building that needs it is badly designed," says Solares cofounder Christine Lolley.

It's not hard. Why don't we do it all the time? A mix of momentum, education and lax building codes. These buildings cost a tiny bit more to build, and they take more time to design. Unless customers demand it, why would a developer bother? That's how we ended up with the typical North American suburb—thousands of square miles of ill-designed, cheaply built structures.

Net Zero Buildings

Once you've got a smart envelope, you're just a few short steps away from becoming a "Net Zero building"—generating the same amount of energy as you consume (and sometimes even more), by putting solar panels on the roof, building a wind turbine or two, even constructing a neighborhood biomass plant using tree waste from a local forest. The Earthships are probably the original Net Zero homes—but you don't have to be off the grid to be Net Zero. In fact, it's actually easier if you're plugged in—that way, you can give back any extra energy that you produce.

The idea is gaining traction in cities and towns worldwide. Z-Home, a small community in Issaquah, Washington, will use photovoltaic solar panels to power the lights, appliances and geo-exchange heating units. That, along with a program of conserving energy, will mean the community breaks even on power use. In the London borough

To really catch on, Net Zero buildings need a government push.

of Sutton, the UK's first Net Zero community, BedZed will use a biomass electrical plant to bring its net energy use to nil. Even frigid Canada will soon see 12 Net Zero buildings, supported by the Canada Mortgage and Housing Corp.

To really catch on, though, Net Zero buildings need a government push. The UK is leading the way: The government has announced that, as of 2016, all new homes built will be Net Zero. The US Department of Energy is putting some serious money behind a similar effort for the US.

Once the Energy Internet (see Chapter 10) comes online, and people get paid cold, hard cash to produce power, we'll go past Net Zero. Our homes will become a net *source* of power.

The UK's first Net Zero house, in Watford, meets the new "Level 6" standard that will be required for all new homes by 2016. It utilizes solar panels, rainwater harvesting, heavy thermal insulation, biomass boilers, and passive cooling and ventilation to achieve a Net Zero rating.

Re-skinning

Getting smart is easy when there's lots of space, and sunshine pours in through the windows. But what about all the existing condos and apartments the rest of us live in? We're not ready to tear them down and build a billion Earthships in the desert. What do we do?

How about building a brand new envelope around the entire building? It's been done,

and it works. The benefits are twofold: The building gets an aesthetic facelift, and a modern and efficient envelope that brings it closer to that Passivhaus ideal. The new skin is usually a layer of glass on a metal framework. It can even incorporate modern solar PV cells, like on the Co-operative Insurance Co.'s 25-story headquarters in Manchester, UK. Even better, install geo-exchange at the same

time, and hide the pipes like veins under the new skin.

A developer can be motivated by the facelift alone. A 12-level building on the infamous K Street in Washington, DC, was a drab and sorry-looking affair when a private equity firm bought it in 2005. Architects Skidmore, Owings & Merrill suggested re-skinning the building, and it's now a beautiful, modern, floor-to-ceiling glass structure. The top two floors rent for 40% more than they did before the renovation. Smart, and fast: Re-skinning an office tower can take only a day or two, once the exterior structure is up. Gensler, an architectural firm in Indiana, is working to build the entire prefab exterior shell in a day, so eventually, you'll be able to re-skin a living, working building.

How about building a brand new envelope around the entire building? It's been done, and it works.

Re-skinning holds enough promise that Toronto-based Zerofootprint is offering a $1-million prize to the company that comes up with the best way to do it. That's the largest architectural prize in the world, and for good reason. Buildings in urban areas are responsible for more than half our energy use; in New York City it's almost 80%. Re-skinning what we've got could cut that in half.

The CIS Tower in Manchester, UK, was re-skinned in 2005 with 7,000 blue photovoltaic panels. As the largest solar array in the UK, it generates enough energy to power 10,000 computers for a year. The actual energy is fed back into the power grid.

Built in 1971 as a medical office building with small windows, 1801 K Street NW in Washington, DC, has been dramatically re-skinned with a sleek glass wall.
It not only saves energy, but it also offers increased value to tenants, with more natural light thanks to floor-to-ceiling windows.

An interesting challenge to building codes, the Phoenix Earthship is a New Mexico desert landmark. Its unique design separates living areas from the outside with several layers of recycled materials—providing much greater climate control than a single wall.

Building Codes

Subsection 5.c, with reference to bylaw 41, indicating a thermal conversion requirement of...Regulation 32.1 dictates an extension of capacity...Zzzzz, snore! Nothing

Here's a bold idea: Change the building codes.

puts me to sleep faster than reading bylaws and building codes. But they're the bedrock on which developers build. Meet them, they must; exceed them, they rarely do. Change them, and you change the world.

How do you motivate condo developers to install more expensive heat-exchangers, geo-exchange heating and cooling, and triple-glazed windows? The problem is that developers don't pay the energy costs on a building—tenants do. Why invest upfront for down-the-road savings if you're not the one doing the saving? It makes no sense from a business perspective, where only the bottom line matters. From a carbon-reduction standpoint, however, it's a frustrating failure of the free market.

Here's a bold idea: Change the building codes. If the codes were to demand geo-exchange, developers would have no choice but to comply. Same goes for efficient heat-exchangers, better-

insulated windows and even solar thermal. Imagine if the Passivhaus became the standard model for new suburban development, or if re-skinning apartment blocks were mandatory. No developer would have an advantage over the others, because it'd be a level playing field. As for homeowners, the extra costs would be buried in their mortgage payments, and monthly costs would actually go down, thanks to energy savings. It's a no-brainer.

Buildings codes aren't technology. But they *drive* technology—and they can sometimes get in the way.

Potential and Pitfalls

We could easily cut our buildings' energy use in half. Since buildings consume around 40% of our power, that means smart buildings could lower our total energy use by one-fifth.

There are pitfalls, however. The vast majority of the buildings we'll be occupying in 20 years have already been built. So, retrofitting and re-skinning will be the backbone of this effort. Retrofits can be inconvenient; re-skinning, not so much.

Still, developers are slapping up new office towers, condo blocks and subdivisions all the time, from Chicago to Beijing. And chances are good that most of those buildings are dumb. New building codes would encourage those developers to smarten up. But changing

Smart buildings are worth more, and they cost less to operate.

codes is tortuous. Because they're normally regional in scope, each jurisdiction must be cajoled, inspired—or forced—to evolve. After all, people like to do what they know, and engineers, developers and bureaucrats are no exception.

But smart buildings are worth more, and they cost less to operate. So here's another idea: Make re-skinning the law and, at the same time, give developers and building owners access to lots of

We could easily cut our buildings' energy use in half.

low-cost money, via massive bonds or through pension funds. The energy savings, along with higher rents, will pay back the bonds. It's already happening. The Clinton Climate Initiative is putting $5 billion toward building retrofits.

The vast majority of the buildings we'll be occupying in 20 years have already been built. Smart buildings are worth more, and they cost less to operate, so retrofitting and re-skinning these buildings will be vital to achieving energy self-sufficiency.

The Trillion-Dollar Question:

So, what do you get for $1 trillion?
You could re-skin both the condo buildings and office blocks that support a total population of 50 million people.[2] That's a city twice the size of New York, or a country almost twice the size of Canada. For $5 trillion, you could re-skin the entire US.

Nuclear

Fusion and Fission

Nuclear energy is controversial. Although it produces massive quantities of (almost) carbon-free[1] energy, mention it at a gathering of green energy fans and you might as well have set off a stink bomb. It's considered rude.

For some, including eco-luminaries like James Lovelock and Geoffrey Ballard, nuclear is necessary. For others, it is a dangerous example of technology gone wrong. As for me, I think it's an expensive and time-wasting distraction from more promising technologies. Even so, at the risk of seeming to favor the home team, I think there is a role for Canadian-built CANDU reactors in the fight against fossil fuels.

There are two kinds of nuclear energy: fusion and fission.

Fusion, which powers the sun, is often held up as a dream energy—and rightly so. Fusion reactors force two light atoms together, which fuse to form a heavier one. This releases energy according to Einstein's famous formula ($e = mc^2$). Mass turns into energy. The hard part is overcoming the electromagnetic repulsion that keeps the light atoms apart—it's done with powerful lasers or magnetic fields. The best part about nuclear fusion is that, when something goes wrong, the entire reaction stops. That means fusion reactors can't melt down or blow sky high. Plus, they're usually powered by hydrogen, which can be derived from seawater, and the output is harmless helium.

Seawater as fuel, no[2] radioactive waste, no fodder for nuclear bombs and no uncontrolled meltdowns? Sounds too good to be true. It's not. The problem is that fusion is still probably 50 years away (so far, it's only been proven in small-scale experimental reactors). And since we have to solve our carbon problem in the next 20 or 30 years, fusion simply isn't an option for us. Our grandchildren's generation perhaps, but not ours.

Fission means splitting heavier atoms, normally uranium, into smaller bits. Most of the world's 400-odd reactors are so-called light-water reactors that use an enriched form of uranium (U-238) as fuel. U-238 is fissile—it's the stuff bombs are made of. A few reactors, like the CANDU, are heavy-water reactors. They're able to use natural uranium (U-235) almost right out of the ground (along with thorium[3]). Even better, the CANDU gets between one and a half and two times as much energy from the same amount of fuel as its light-water competitors. It can also act as a recycler, reusing spent fuel from the world's light-water reactors.

Deploying the CANDU would let us squeeze more out of an industry we already have, without adding to its problems.

The problems with nuclear are well known. Spent fuel remains radioactive for hundreds of thousands of years, and finding a way to store it safely isn't easy—not to mention persuading some place to actually play host to a nuclear waste site. (Today, most spent fuel sits in pools of water at reactor sites.) There are occasionally accidents—though to be fair, far fewer people get hurt in nuclear accidents than, say, mining coal. And, of course, reactors can be used to refine

fuel to produce weapons-grade uranium and plutonium. Nuclear energy isn't exactly unsafe, but there are definitely long-term liabilities in spent fuel and possible weapons proliferation.

The problems increase along with nuclear production. It took decades to cement a deal to store US waste at the Yucca Mountain site, near Las Vegas, and even that long-awaited decision is being reconsidered. The site is large enough to hold 10 years' worth[4] of the world's nuclear waste. If we want nuclear to contribute significantly to carbon reduction and step up to one-third of electrical supply by, say, 2030, we'd need to increase world production by 800%.[5] That means finding the equivalent of a Yucca almost every year.

Are these problems worth the massive, constant stream of energy? Perhaps.

Nuclear takes a long time to come online. It takes at least five years to build a plant—and that's with no public consultation or safety assessment. Realistically, it's more like 10 or 15 years. We don't have that much time. In a decade, we could cover the deserts with solar, dig for deep geothermal, construct massive offshore wind farms and pipe the power across the country with HVDC lines. We can't wait for nuclear.

But the biggest problem is cost. Nuclear energy is expensive (though the price is always understated by its fans). No nuclear plants attract enough private money to stand on their own merits—state guarantees and subsidies almost always come into play. Jon Wellinghoff, the head of the US Federal Energy Regulatory Commission, stated the obvious: "They're too expensive. The last price

I saw for a nuke was north of $7,000 a kilowatt. That's more expensive than a solar system."[6]

Nuclear seems to comfort big industry, maybe because it reflects big industry itself—huge, centralized, high-tech and complicated. When the Canadian province of Ontario committed

Fusion is still probably 50 years away. We've got to solve our carbon problem in the next 20 or 30 years, so it's not an option.

itself to a big renewable energy push, it also renewed its promise to nuclear—probably to ease the fears of big industry, which seems to be the only group that trusts nuclear.

I'll suggest a compromise. We already have a nuclear industry; the last thing we should do is turn it off. But it's hard to argue that the technology can save the day. So let's use the CANDU as a nuclear-waste recycler. Put one up next to every existing light-water reactor, take its waste fuel, rejig it a bit, and feed it in.

We'd double our nuclear output, with no net increase in nuclear waste. The risk of proliferation would not increase, since you'd have to guard the initial waste anyway. One design could be used worldwide, so it would be well understood and less risky. Pardon my patriotism, but the CANDU is a gem. Love or hate nukes, deploying the CANDU would let us squeeze more out of an industry we already have, without adding to its problems.

EIGHT

Transp

ortation

LEAVING A SMALL FOOTPRINT

Transportation

An Introduction

The contrast couldn't have been greater. Having pedaled from Toronto to Vancouver, fighting ancient hills in Ontario, headwinds in the Prairies and mountains in British Columbia, I was headed home. In a jet. Peering down on the wheat fields of Saskatchewan, I absorbed in minutes a landscape that had taken days to cross by bicycle. Never before had I so appreciated the power of the modern engine and the fossil fuels that fired it. The bicycle is probably the most efficient form of human transport and the modern jet, the least. The bike is slow enough that you can see every rock along the way, and the jet so fast I could miss entire provinces while eating dinner.

Whatever new forms of transport appear, we need to slow the flow.

Transportation, like communication, ties us together. Our world depends on a vast, constant flow of people and the stuff we buy. Boats, planes and trucks move more frequently over ever-longer distances. Our TVs are made with components from at least a dozen countries. Cars made anywhere use parts from almost everywhere. We commute, go on vacation and business trips, and visit friends. All that movement takes liquid fuel—mostly gasoline, diesel and kerosene.

If we could make enough biofuel to power all these vehicles, the story would end here. But we can't—at least not sustainably.[1] Some modes of transport, like planes and boats,[2] will probably *always* require liquid fuel. Unfortunately, even producing that much biofuel would put a strain on the food supply (see Chapter 4), and switching to electric cars and fuel-cell-powered trucks means more than doubling our electrical production.

So, what's the most important thing we can do? Whatever new forms of transport appear, we need to *slow the flow*.

There are new inventions on the horizon: Life-like holographs will one day nullify the need for business trips, and floating airships will carry us across oceans. But clean transport is already here.

Electric cars cruise our streets. Floating trains that reach 300 miles per hour (500 kilometres per hour) hustle tourists into Shanghai. Only slightly slower versions tie Europe together. First-rate public transit lures people out of cars, and smart metering can charge those cars for every mile they drive. And as for the bicycle—that most humble of vehicles that took me across Canada—it already gives commuters the freedom car owners seek, but rarely find.

Transportation, like communication, ties us together, but all that movement takes liquid fuel—mostly gasoline, diesel and kerosene. We could switch to biofuel, but producing enough of it would put a strain on the world's food supply.

The modern jet is probably the least efficient form of human transport, so airlines worldwide are scrambling to lessen their environmental impact. Southwest Airlines plans to save $42 million in fuel this year by flying a little slower and extending each flight by one to three minutes.

Amsterdam is one of the most bike-friendly cities in the world, with about 600,000 bicycles in use. Driving a car is discouraged, so extensive facilities are provided for cyclists, including abundant bike paths and racks—like these ones outside Central Station.

Paris launched the Velib (or bicycle freedom) rental program in 2007. It was an astounding success and now includes 20,000 bicycles at 1,500 stations throughout the city center—roughly one station every 1,000 feet (300 metres).

The Humble Bicycle

I've always loved Amsterdam, with its quiet streets and canals lined with narrow buildings—not to mention the city's deep sense of history and famously tolerant culture. But there was something else about Amsterdam that I could never put my finger on. Then one day, as I sat in a café watching a steady stream of bicycles whiz by, I finally figured it out: There were very few cars. The streets were quiet and clean, and everyone was part of the scene. Here in North America, cars so dominate our cities that we forget what a downtown core could be like without them. It's magical.

Worldwide, bicycles outnumber cars two to one. In China and India, they're especially common—but that's changing fast. The burgeoning middle class demands cars, and that's a problem. If all those cyclists ditch their bikes and climb into cars instead—even electric ones—we're sunk.[3] Instead of the poor aspiring to the car, the rich should be getting in the saddle. The humble bicycle is one of our best bets for clean, livable cities.

In Copenhagen, more than one-third of people bike to work. In Amsterdam, more than half of commuters who travel five miles (7.5 kilometres) or less travel by bike. The city's Central Station is surrounded by a sea of bicycles. In fact, roads all over the Netherlands include bike lanes, and everyone, from kids to grandmothers, enjoys a ride. Specially designed bikes with luggage compartments are even used to deliver goods.

In the US and Canada, bicycles are an afterthought, although that's beginning to change. It's part culture—North Americans have an unmatched love affair with the car—and part urban planning. Our cities are made for cars, and our sprawling suburbs mean that long commutes are the norm, not the exception.[4]

But bikes can be a pleasure to ride, even from the suburbs. What do we need to make it happen? More bike lanes on our roads. Showers at work. More bicycle parking at train stations and room for two-wheelers on commuter transit would help, too. Perhaps more importantly, drivers need to learn to respect cyclists on the road. Without bike lanes, you often put your life on the line—just try cycling in London, UK.

US federal funding now supports cycling to the tune of almost $1 billion a year, and plans are afoot in the country's 50 largest cities to double the number of bike routes. By 2030, New York City plans to quadruple its bike lanes, to 1,800 miles (2,900 kilometres). In France, Paris's Velib scheme lets you rent a bike, ride it, and drop it off at one of 1,500 spots around town. As for London, it's making amends[5] with $1 billion for cycling over 10 years. It's a start.

But cycling isn't just clean and green. I whiz by cars sitting in traffic on my way to work in downtown Toronto. Not only do the drivers I pass look stressed and impatient, but they're also completely cut off from the city and the people around them. They face a daily search for parking and the fees that go with it. Me? I'm getting fit, saving my money for an after-work drink, and grinning from ear to ear.

Trains

I attended a conference recently at Stanford University, in California. Instead of staying in Palo Alto, I got a hotel in downtown San Francisco. Each morning, I hopped on the Caltrain, which runs between San Francisco and the Silicon Valley corridor. My days began with 40 relaxing minutes spent reading the paper, sipping coffee and watching the city roll by. Each time I got off the train, I was surrounded by a horde of cyclists—Caltrain has a separate car to accommodate those who choose to use two wheels to cover the last mile or two. Why anyone would choose to make that journey by car every day was beyond me.

What Caltrain does for Silicon Valley, high-speed trains do for much of Europe: downtown London to Paris in a couple of hours, Paris to Amsterdam or the south of France in a few more. France was one of the first countries to tie its cities together with high-speed rail. The TGV (Train à Grande Vitesse) averages 120 miles an hour (200 kilometres per hour) and has reached top speeds of almost three times that. And the tracks cost as little as $20 million per mile ($12 million per kilometre)—that's one-tenth of what more exotic tracks, like the maglev (see below), cost.

The TGV experience is one of fast, convenient luxury: Have a drink in the bar,

A network of high-speed trains linking North American cities would be expensive, but it would do wonders.

get some work done on your laptop and arrive downtown, on time. These trains are serious competitors to short-haul flights and make driving seem primitive. A network of high-speed trains linking North American cities would be expensive, but it would do wonders. We'd lower our fuel use by getting cars off the road and planes out of the sky, and, even better, we'd finally have the kind of civilized, relaxing travel most Europeans take for granted.

President Obama gets it, and he has urged Americans to imagine "whisking through towns at speeds over 100 miles an hour, walking only a few steps to public transportation, and ending up just blocks from your destination."[6]

In Shanghai, there's a faster, more exotic kind of travel. The maglev (magnetic levitation) train travels at breathtaking speeds, and it's so smooth, it's eerie. Floating just above the rails that guide it, the maglev zips passengers from the Shanghai airport into the city at speeds of up to 430 miles per hour (almost 700 kilometres per hour). What a dream: maglev trains almost as fast as airplanes connecting our cities and running on clean electricity. Sadly, the tracks are so expensive that it might just stay a dream. The proposed 300-mile (500-kilometre) maglev track between Osaka and Tokyo, in Japan, is expected to cost almost $100 billion, or $300 million a mile ($200 million a kilometre)—although part of that cost is due to the 60 miles (100 kilometres) of tunnels that need to be built along the way.

There's another problem with high-speed rail: The faster trains go, the more fuel they use. Increasing speed from 140 miles an hour (225 kilometres per hour) to 220 miles an hour (350 kilometres) doubles[7] energy consumption for the same trip. If that train ran on diesel, or on electricity produced from coal, it would emit more[8] carbon per passenger than a jet over the same distance. So these trains *must* be powered by clean electricity.

Japan's Shinkansen, the world's first high-speed rail network, opened in 1964—in time for the Tokyo Olympics. The 320-mile (515-kilometre) trip between Tokyo and Osaka takes two hours and 26 minutes on the fastest "Nozomi" ("hope" or "wish") train).

France's TGV high-speed rail service started in 1981 and now connects cities across France and in adjacent countries. It holds the record for the fastest scheduled rail journey, with a start-to-stop average speed of 173 miles per hour (279 kilometres per hour).

The all-electric Tesla Roadster is sleek, powerful and fast—zero to 60 in less than four seconds. It's the first production automobile to use lithium-ion battery cells and can travel 244 miles (393 kilometres) on a single four-hour charge.

The two-seater ZENN (Zero Emission, No Noise) epitomizes the emerging neighborhood electric vehicle category. It charges in four to eight hours, travels up to 50 miles (80 kilometres) and does not exceed 25 miles per hour (40 kilometres per hour).

Electric Cars

Our love affair with the car just won't end, even though they never deliver what the ads promise. We don't take our SUVs cross-country. The top is not down, and the wind is not in our hair. Instead, we

Electric cars don't solve the energy problem. But by pushing consumption away from fossil fuels and onto the grid, they give us a clean option.

spend most of our time stuck in traffic and fuming mad, moving along at about the same speed as a horse and carriage. And cars cost US owners more than $9,000[9] a year to operate. What are we doing? It's a *bad habit*.

But love them we do. So here's some good news for car lovers everywhere: Electric vehicles aren't the glorified golf carts they once were.

The Tesla Roadster, backed by big money in Silicon Valley, is everything American cars were meant to be: sleek, powerful and fast—zero to 60 in less than four seconds. That's as fast as it gets. It's also electric. The Tesla's motor produces torque a gas-powered engine can't match, and it's powered by batteries[10] that sit in the trunk.

If you don't have a hundred grand to shell out for a Tesla, there are other options. Canada's ZENN Cars (Zero-Emission, No Noise) has an electric car that's perfect for commuters, and now builds electric drive trains. General Motors will launch the Chevy Volt in 2010. The Obama Administration has made it clear that the electric car—or a hybrid mix—is a top priority. Even the Oracle of Omaha, famed investor Warren Buffett, is getting in on the action, backing Chinese carmaker BYD.

Electric vehicles aren't the glorified golf carts they once were.

Electric cars don't *solve* the energy problem. But by pushing consumption away from fossil fuels and onto the grid, they give us a clean option. Great—as long as the grid can handle it and is powered by clean electrons. Burning coal to make electricity to power a car is worse[11] than running a car on today's fuels.

We've become hooked on moving things around—from food to goods to people. Much of it is unnecessary and, if eliminated, could save millions in fuel costs—plus countless billions for future generations who will be stuck with the cost of saving the environment.

Slowing the Flow

People and goods[12] will always flow—traveling and trading with our economic partners is part of what makes us human. But it can be absurd. People in downtown Manhattan sip bottled water from Fiji. In my hometown, near Niagara Falls, Canada, they ship peaches to California, even as California ships peaches right back to us. We travel thousands of miles just to make a sales call, and commute vast distances every year, by ourselves, in vehicles that weigh several tons.

Thinking about *why* we travel or ship goods is just as important as *how* we do it. Whatever else we do, one thing is for sure: We need to slow the flow—of the stuff we buy, the incessant overnight business trips and the cars that clog our streets. Less is more.

The Virtual Trip

The business trip is standard fare for us suit-wearing folk. Cab to the airport. Fly across the country. Check into a crappy hotel. Wake up. Shake someone's hand, chat for an hour, then fly home. For a bit of "face time," we put up with a lot. And we use a lot of energy.

With Cisco's TelePresence, you can avoid the whole miserable experience. TelePresence is to video-conferencing what Mark Phelps is to swimming—so life-like that people on the other side of the planet look like they're sitting right in front of you. Life-sized high-definition video and three-dimensional sound bring them to life, but little details bring them even closer. The desks in one TelePresence room seem to be an extension of the desks in the other, and the rooms have identical décor. It's so real that when I tried out the technology at Cisco's headquarters in Silicon Valley, I couldn't help but turn around to look when someone entered the *other* room.

Thinking about *why* we travel or ship goods is just as important as *how* we do it.

If that's not enough, just wait for the holographic version of TelePresence. It'll allow you to replicate all the elements of face time—body language, a handshake—that make developing rapport so much easier. Why fly when you can send your holographic twin?

Cisco's TelePresence creates a live, face-to-face communication experience. Now firms can nurture interpersonal relationships without the need for travel—and their people spend less time away from home and family.

Smart Cities

Smart cities build density, not sprawl. They're designed so that residents don't have to get in the car to buy a carton of milk, and they include public transit that people actually want to ride. Good transit is not demeaning and slow, and only on offer for people who can't afford cars; it's faster and cheaper than driving. Decent transit is the only way to slow the flow of cars in our cities.

But as long as drivers don't have to pay for road access, our cities will continue to choke on cars. Electric cars alone aren't the answer—they still bring most transit to a crawl, and they won't stop traffic jams.

The most basic rule of the free market says: If something is scarce—like space on downtown roads—make people pay for it. When London's mayor, Ken Livingstone, installed cameras

Skymeter can make our roads just like any other commodity—subject to market forces.

around the city to identify cars and charge them a fee for entering downtown, there were howls of protest. But it worked. Cars and buses moved faster, emissions[13] went down, and London's air cleared up. The same goes for similar programs in Singapore and Milan.

Canada's Skymeter has a solution that makes London's system look archaic. The company makes smart meters for cars—a GPS system that can track any car, anywhere. Governments could charge different amounts depending on the street and time of day. Cities can use the technology to change traffic flow, and insurance companies can use to charge by the mile. It can even charge for parking. What Skymeter can do is make our roads just like any other commodity—subject to market forces.

Singapore, the second most densely populated city-state in the world, is perfect for public transit. Its Mass Rapid Transit system opened in 1987 and now spans the entire island, with 70 stations and 1.5 million riders daily. It's the smart way to get around.

Airships

Here's something far out—or rather, high up. Imagine crossing the ocean or touring Africa from the air, floating along in the lap of luxury as you watch the ground pass by. An airship is a giant structure held aloft by a gas lighter than air—like helium or hydrogen—with a range of up to 6,000 miles (10,000 kilometres). Even using a traditional engine for power, airships cut the energy needed to travel by air by up to 90%.[14]

It's still hypothetical. Although airships have been in use for almost a century, for everything from military surveillance to sky-high advertising during sporting events, no one's offering commercial, long-distance tours—yet. There's no reason to think we won't soon be taking trips above the treetops.

The downside is that airship passengers have to be patient. Current speeds are about 80 miles an hour (130 kilometres per hour), which means Paris to Toronto in a couple of days. But really, is that so bad? Why are we always in such a hurry? Traveling by airship, we'd arrive home from our overseas vacations relaxed—and ready to hop on a bike.

> Why are we always in such a hurry? Traveling by airship, we'd arrive home relaxed—and ready to hop on a bike.

Millennium Air Ship is developing the Skyfreighter, a maneuverable, lighter-than-air "heavy-lift" vehicle that can deliver massive cargo loads worldwide. Vertical takeoff and landing will allow it to serve remote areas that have no airport facilities—and it's even amphibious.

The Taiwan High Speed Rail network opened in 2007 and spans the west coast of the island from Taipei to Kaohsiung. An express train now covers the 208-mile (335-kilometre) journey in 90 minutes, compared to the four and a half hours it took before.

NINE

Efficiency &

Incorporating carbon capture into coal plants means tacking on an additional 50% to 90% to the cost of producing electricity.

CCS is unproven on a commercial scale, and it's decades away from widespread adoption.

And there's no incentive to pay that cost. Why pay to bury carbon when it's free to emit? The only exception is using CCS to squeeze more oil out of old fields—but then we're just using one batch of carbon to unearth another. There's no net gain.

Putting a price on carbon would help. Adding CCS to a coal plant becomes economical when carbon costs between $30 and $60 a metric ton[5] to emit. But that requires a robust and enforceable international agreement. It was hard enough to negotiate the relatively toothless Kyoto Protocol, and every year of delay sees dozens more coal plants brought online.

Carbon capture is also untested on a commercial scale. To have confidence in the commercial viability of CCS, we'd need to build at least 20 commercial plants over the next 10 years,[6] in different countries. We need to test varying geologies for storage, along with different legal structures. The only commercial project on the books, the American FutureGen plant, was cancelled by the Bush administration in 2008, though a renewed commitment from the Obama administration seems likely.

Finally, CCS takes up space, and not all coal plants can be easily expanded. A coal plant might need to double in size.

There are novel approaches that try to *use* the carbon instead of burying it. US-based Calera, for example, is attempting to make building materials such as cement. Turning the CO_2 into a valued industrial commodity might get around the problem of added cost. But these technologies, like carbon capture itself, are still unproven.

The biggest problem for CCS is cost. Every coal plant must be retrofitted with equipment to capture the carbon, and burn one third more coal to power that equipment. We'll need an absolutely massive network of pipelines to carry the carbon to a place it can be buried. That is far more expensive, in my view, than replacing those coal plants with deep geothermal.

No doubt CCS will play a role in energy production, and some plants will eventually run carbon-free. There's too much big money behind coal to think otherwise. But it can't change the face of the entire coal industry. It's one small piece of a big puzzle. Worse, it can distract us from clean technologies that don't produce carbon in the first place.

But if we're going to stay hooked on some fossil fuels, CCS is the only way to do it. As Sir Nicholas Stern, the UK's expert on the economics of climate change, puts it: "In the medium term, this is the only real option for maintaining demand for hydrocarbon energy sources."[7] In places like India and China, CCS could provide some relief.

CCS is like a painkiller: It may appear to take the pain out of our fossil fuel addiction, but it comes with one nasty side effect: We run the risk of not feeling the need to quit at all.

Carbon Sequestration

Burn It and Bury It

Imagine if we could burn coal or natural gas without emitting any carbon, capturing it before it went out the stack and burying it deep underground. Would we still need to kick the fossil fuel habit? Probably not, at least not for a while. Carbon sequestration—also known as carbon capture and storage (CCS)—is the concept behind what's optimistically called "clean coal." The rough idea: Burn it and bury it.

Can CCS solve our energy dilemma? It's controversial. Fans of carbon capture see it as a magic bullet: Coal remains the backbone of our energy industry, and the problems of climate change disappear, along with all that smoke. To its critics, CCS is just an excuse for business as usual—a never-ending research project delivering nothing but misplaced optimism and reasons for inaction. Who's right?

Carbon capture is expensive. You need to burn a lot more coal to produce the same amount of electricity.

The truth lies somewhere in the middle. We can't afford to ignore any technology that lowers carbon emissions, and CCS holds particular promise for China and India, which are building coal plants at a furious pace. But the critics have a point. CCS is unproven on a commercial scale, and it's decades away from widespread adoption. For it to work, we need to build expensive infrastructure, yet there's no economic incentive to do so. Worst-case scenario: We pin our hopes (and resources) on CCS, and find it can't deliver.

Carbon capture can't be an excuse *not* to kick the fossil fuel habit, no matter how promising.

How does it work? Remove the carbon dioxide before it goes up the stack, before[1] or after[2] combustion. Compress it, and force it deep underground into a suitable storage spot.

Where do we store it? Old oil and gas fields, saline aquifers (underground saltwater deposits) and the deep ocean can all hold carbon dioxide. At the high pressures found deeper than half a mile (800 metres) down, carbon dioxide goes "supercritical," acting more like a liquid than a gas. Natural gas deposits were stable for millions of years, so supercritical carbon dioxide buried in old fields will theoretically stay put. But deep-ocean storage is dangerous. If the buried carbon were ever to dissolve,[3] the resulting acidification of the water would be devastating.

CCS is happening in a few places already. Since 2000, the American-based Dakota Gasification Co. has been sending carbon dioxide through a pipeline almost 200 miles (322 kilometres) across the Canadian border, to Weyburn, Saskatchewan, where it's pumped into an old oil field. Some of the CO_2 dissolves in the oil, making it less viscous (and easier to pump), and the rest builds pressure to squeeze out more oil. Norway's Statoil has been burying carbon dioxide for years, in a saline aquifer under the North Sea seabed.

Sounds great. What's the problem? First off, carbon capture is expensive. You need to burn a lot more coal to produce the same amount of electricity.[4] Plus, there's the cost of transporting the carbon from potentially far-flung coal plants to a storage facility and pumping it deep underground.

Potential and Pitfalls

Transportation is a hard nut to crack. Biofuels won't do it. And while electricity could replace liquid fuels, we'd still need to produce huge amounts of clean electrons: Replacing gasoline engines alone (no diesel) with electric motors in the US would mean roughly doubling[15] electrical production. It's difficult enough to replace existing production.

The potential of cycling is clear—it's carbon-neutral. But before bikes can go mainstream, many cities are going to need to spend big on cycling infrastructure: bike lanes, cargo space on trains and buses, plenty of parking, and showers to greet riders at work. We also need to persuade existing cycling cultures, like India and China, not to abandon their bikes for cars—increasingly difficult as the middle class in both countries continues to grow.

High-speed trains can replace some short-haul air travel and a whole lot of car trips. But building all those tracks takes time, money and political will (no high-speed train has ever been built without public support and

Copenhagen was the Union Cycliste Internationale's first official Bike City. Over 36% of its citizens commute by bike. Many of the paths are separated from traffic and have their own signal system. A new 62-mile (100-kilometre) citywide "greenways" network is currently being developed.

Smart urban design is the bedrock of clean transportation.

money). The maglev train works like a charm, but it's prohibitively expensive. Regular high-speed trains along the lines of the TGV are the way to go.

As for cars, electric ones are clearly better than gas-powered, since we have the option of powering them with clean energy. But they're no cure-all—we still have to produce all that electricity in the first place, and that could be tricky. An added benefit to electric cars is the role they'll play in building the Energy Internet (see Chapter 10). So if we *must* drive, let's drive electric cars. But it's

still better to leave them at home.

The real key here is the need for smart cities—the way they're designed is the starting point for clean transportation. A smart city grows upward, not outward. It charges cars to drive downtown. It builds transit that people *want* to ride and makes room for bicycles. High-speed trains connect one city center to another. Smart cities make it easy to get around—making life richer and more dynamic in the process.

So, smart urban design is the bedrock of clean transportation. Yet, so many cities and suburbs are badly designed—and we don't get another chance. We're stuck with what we've got.

The Trillion-Dollar Question:

So, what do you get for $1 trillion?
Say we split the cash in half—$500 billion to bikes and transit in the 50 biggest cities, and $500 billion to high-speed trains linking them. Allotting $1 billion in each city for cycling infrastructure and programs could put 85 million[16] people into the saddle. And spending $9 billion in each city for transit could result in 7.5 billion[17] fewer car trips each year. The other $500 billion would build about 20,000[18] miles (32,000 kilometres) of high-speed track—more than enough to build a serious American network.

The Taiwan High Speed Rail network opened in 2007 and spans the west coast of the island from Taipei to Kaohsiung. An express train now covers the 208-mile (335-kilometre) journey in 90 minutes, compared to the four and a half hours it took before.

Airships

Here's something far out—or rather, high up. Imagine crossing the ocean or touring Africa from the air, floating along in the lap of luxury as you watch the ground pass by. An airship is a giant structure held aloft by a gas lighter than air—like helium or hydrogen—with a range of up to 6,000 miles (10,000 kilometres). Even using a traditional engine for power, airships cut the energy needed to travel by air by up to 90%.[14]

It's still hypothetical. Although airships have been in use for almost a century, for everything from military surveillance to sky-high advertising during sporting events, no one's offering commercial, long-distance tours—yet. There's no reason to think we won't soon be taking trips above the treetops.

The downside is that airship passengers have to be patient. Current speeds are about 80 miles an hour (130 kilometres per hour), which means Paris to Toronto in a couple of days. But really, is that so bad? Why are we always in such a hurry? Traveling by airship, we'd arrive home from our overseas vacations relaxed—and ready to hop on a bike.

> Why are we always in such a hurry? Traveling by airship, we'd arrive home relaxed— and ready to hop on a bike.

Millennium Air Ship is developing the Skyfreighter, a maneuverable, lighter-than-air "heavy-lift" vehicle that can deliver massive cargo loads worldwide. Vertical takeoff and landing will allow it to serve remote areas that have no airport facilities—and it's even amphibious.

Smart Cities

Smart cities build density, not sprawl. They're designed so that residents don't have to get in the car to buy a carton of milk, and they include public transit that people actually want to ride. Good transit is not demeaning and slow, and only on offer for people who can't afford cars; it's faster and cheaper than driving. Decent transit is the only way to slow the flow of cars in our cities.

But as long as drivers don't have to pay for road access, our cities will continue to choke on cars. Electric cars alone aren't the answer—they still bring most transit to a crawl, and they won't stop traffic jams.

The most basic rule of the free market says: If something is scarce—like space on downtown roads—make people pay for it. When London's mayor, Ken Livingstone, installed cameras

> Skymeter can make our roads just like any other commodity—subject to market forces.

around the city to identify cars and charge them a fee for entering downtown, there were howls of protest. But it worked. Cars and buses moved faster, emissions[13] went down, and London's air cleared up. The same goes for similar programs in Singapore and Milan.

Canada's Skymeter has a solution that makes London's system look archaic. The company makes smart meters for cars—a GPS system that can track any car, anywhere. Governments could charge different amounts depending on the street and time of day. Cities can use the technology to change traffic flow, and insurance companies can use to charge by the mile. It can even charge for parking. What Skymeter can do is make our roads just like any other commodity—subject to market forces.

Singapore, the second most densely populated city-state in the world, is perfect for public transit. Its Mass Rapid Transit system opened in 1987 and now spans the entire island, with 70 stations and 1.5 million riders daily. It's the smart way to get around.

Slowing the Flow

People and goods[12] will always flow—traveling and trading with our economic partners is part of what makes us human. But it can be absurd. People in downtown Manhattan sip bottled water from Fiji. In my hometown, near Niagara Falls, Canada, they ship peaches to California, even as California ships peaches right back to us. We travel thousands of miles just to make a sales call, and commute vast distances every year, by ourselves, in vehicles that weigh several tons.

Thinking about *why* we travel or ship goods is just as important as *how* we do it. Whatever else we do, one thing is for sure: We need to slow the flow—of the stuff we buy, the incessant overnight business trips and the cars that clog our streets. Less is more.

The Virtual Trip

The business trip is standard fare for us suit-wearing folk. Cab to the airport. Fly across the country. Check into a crappy hotel. Wake up. Shake someone's hand, chat for an hour, then fly home. For a bit of "face time," we put up with a lot. And we use a lot of energy.

With Cisco's TelePresence, you can avoid the whole miserable experience. TelePresence is to video-conferencing what Mark Phelps is to swimming—so life-like that people on the other side of the planet look like they're sitting right in front of you. Life-sized high-definition video and three-dimensional sound bring them to life, but little details bring them even closer. The desks in one TelePresence room seem to be an extension of the desks in the other, and the rooms have identical décor. It's so real that when I tried out the technology at Cisco's headquarters in Silicon Valley, I couldn't help but turn around to look when someone entered the *other* room.

Thinking about *why* we travel or ship goods is just as important as *how* we do it.

If that's not enough, just wait for the holographic version of TelePresence. It'll allow you to replicate all the elements of face time—body language, a handshake—that make developing rapport so much easier. Why fly when you can send your holographic twin?

Cisco's TelePresence creates a live, face-to-face communication experience. Now firms can nurture interpersonal relationships without the need for travel—and their people spend less time away from home and family.

Conservation

NURTURING THE NEGAWATT

In 2000, when California faced rolling brownouts, the US government declared the need to build a coal-fired power plant every week to keep up with demand. Instead, Californians lowered their energy use by the equivalent of 10 power plants—in under a year. They produced "negawatts" faster than new plants could put out megawatts.

Efficiency and Conservation

An Introduction

"Turn out the lights!" That was a constant refrain in my childhood home, heard whenever I wandered from one room to another. My mother, who grew up in the UK during the Second World War, saw conservation of any kind as a virtue: turning down the thermostat in winter, carpooling and, yes, flicking out the lights when you leave the room. Conservation means going without or changing your behavior to make do with less. So far, though, the world has shown that it's unwilling to give up anything in order to kick our fossil fuel habit.

If conservation means doing without, efficiency means doing something smarter, with the same result. A house is more efficient when it's insulated, because it holds in heat. A diesel engine is more efficient than gasoline, because it wastes less energy on heat and light. Efficiency is like an athlete— think of Olympic runner Usain Bolt, whose easy stride avoids unnecessary and ungainly movements. That's efficiency: energy used gracefully, focused on a single purpose.

If conservation means doing without, efficiency means doing something smarter, with the same result.

And it works. You've heard of the megawatt, but have you heard of the *negawatt*? That's the term coined by energy expert Amory Lovins to describe the power of my mother's flipped switch or the grace of an efficient process. Not using a watt of energy is the same as producing one, but cheaper and easier. They may not be as sexy as a shiny new power plant, but negawatts have nevertheless been the single largest[1] contributor to the US energy sector since 1975—bigger than nuclear, coal or oil. Persian Gulf oil has contributed less than 10% the energy delivered by negawatts since the OPEC crisis.

Still have your doubts about the power of the negawatt? Harken back to the year 2000, when California faced rolling brownouts. The state was in a panic, and then-Vice-President (and fan of coal) Dick Cheney declared the need to build a power plant every week to deal with the problem.[2] The White House announced that more than 1,000 new power plants were required nationwide. "Pump up the supply!" was the cry.

Quietly and quickly, however, Californians lowered their energy use rather than face more brownouts. One-third of them cut usage by 20%. Within the first six months of 2001, Californians had lowered their consumption by the equivalent of 10 power plants. They produced negawatts faster than new plants could put out megawatts—and developers put their plans for new plants back on the shelves.

Energy expert Amory Lovins, who coined the term "negawatt," is cofounder of the Rocky Mountain Institute. His 4,000-square-foot home features thick stone walls, a greenhouse garden and passive solar heating— racking up a monthly electricity bill of just five bucks.

Many of the graceful ways to save energy have other benefits, too. For example, planting shade trees not only reduces cooling costs, but it can also enhance the value of the property and contributes to the overall improvement of air quality.

When Jimmy Carter reacted to the OPEC crisis of 1979 by initiating new rules[3] for automotive fuel efficiency, Americans churned out negawatts so fast, they changed the face of global oil production. In less than a decade, the oil market shrank by 10%.

Negawatts require conservation and efficiency. Together, they are the cheapest,[4] fastest and biggest new source of energy available.

If conservation means changing our behavior, we'll need a strong price signal to make it happen (see "A New Economics"). Until we pay more for power, we'll continue to cool our movie theaters so much that half the crowd wears sweaters, and our office buildings so

> Negawatts require conservation and efficiency. Together, they are the cheapest, fastest and biggest new source of energy available.

much that people put electric heaters under their desks. My mother is not typical—most of us will not turn out the lights until we have to.

This book celebrates technology, and that's what drives efficiency—new, more graceful ways of using energy, performing tasks without waste, and reducing energy without sacrifice. We've already seen some examples: geo-exchange heating and cooling, mass transit, smart buildings. Here are a couple more: planting shade trees that can reduce indoor cooling requirements by almost 50%, and painting flat roofs white to reflect heat. There are thousands of others.

What follows is just a taste.

American Superconductor's high-efficiency cable system in Long Island, New York, can carry 10 times more power than a conventional underground system. Installed in 2008, it delivers enough electricity for nearly 300,000 homes—under a single city sidewalk.

183

HVDC Transmission

In the late 1800s, two great energy pioneers fought a battle over how to move electricity. On one side was Nicola Tesla, champion of alternating current (AC), where power swings constantly from positive to negative voltage. On the other side, Thomas Edison was fighting for a constant, direct current (DC). Tesla won the day, and for good reason. Over short distances, AC is more efficient. But more than 100 years later, Edison may finally have his way, at least for cross-country transmission.

Sending power over long distances—especially using AC—means losing some of that power to resistance. Transmission losses total about 7%, but that's mainly over short distances—from power plants to the cities and homes they feed. If we're trying to send power farther, like solar from the American southwest to New York, those losses get much higher.

For the thousands of kilometres required for cross-country transmission, DC wins hands down.

That's where high voltage[5] direct current (HVDC) comes in. Sending power over DC lines results in less loss due to resistance than using AC, and there's a critical distance[7] at which DC beats AC—for anything over a few hundred miles, DC wins. For the thousands of miles required for cross-country transmission, it wins hands down. You can also send more power over a single, thinner[8] cable with HVDC, reducing the amount of money required to install it in the first place.

International powerhouse ABB is emerging as the leader in HVDC technology. The Swiss company is currently building the longest and biggest HVDC transmission line ever, in China. It will carry 6,400 megawatts of power over more than 1,240 miles (2,000 kilometres). ABB has also built the longest underwater HVDC cable, a 360-mile (580-kilometre) connection between Norway and the Netherlands.

The Swiss company ABB is emerging as a leader in HVDC technology. Its latest transmission system greatly increases the reliability of power grids and offers numerous environmental benefits. This is a shot of an HVDC light phase reactor.

The Bosphorus Bridge in Istanbul, Turkey, has the longest span of any suspension bridge outside the US. A fully computerized LED lighting system installed in 2007 illuminates the bridge with a panorama of changing colors and patterns.

LED Lighting

We took a look at my own project, the Planet Traveler Hotel, in Chapter 3. Since our goal is to build North America's lowest-carbon hotel, you'd think the last thing we'd do is light the whole place up at night. But we're using LED lighting, the most efficient lighting around. Using one-tenth the energy of an incandescent bulb to produce the same amount of light, LEDs can last more than 50 times longer. The technology is so efficient, we can light up the entire hotel, inside and out, for the same amount of energy as it takes to run a two-slice toaster.

Using a regular incandescent or halogen bulb is akin to building a campfire for light—the light is just a by-product of heating up

> Using a regular incandescent or halogen bulb is akin to building a campfire for light.

the filament until it's white-hot. LEDs (and their close competitor, the compact florescent bulb) are just the opposite: The energy they use goes directly to making light.

How do they work? LEDs are like computer chips: A semiconductor is injected with impurities, or "holes," which are atoms missing an electron. When a passing electron falls into a hole, it releases a photon, or light. Almost all the energy used to move the electrons gets emitted as light, not heat.

The pitfall is that LED lighting is expensive. Our lights will eventually pay for themselves, but not for many years. It's also a new and growing industry, so the leaders haven't emerged just yet.

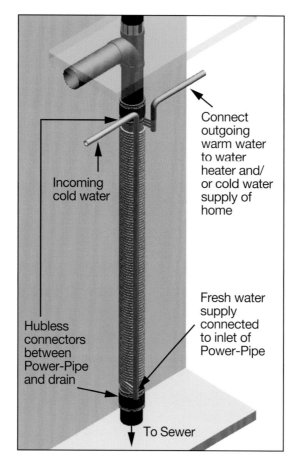

Connect outgoing warm water to water heater and/ or cold water supply of home

Incoming cold water

Fresh water supply connected to inlet of Power-Pipe

Hubless connectors between Power-Pipe and drain

To Sewer

The copper-wrapped Power-Pipe can capture as much as two-thirds of the heat that would normally go down the drain. It offers huge potential savings for industrial processes that require lots of heat, like food preparation, pulp and paper, and brewing.

The Power-Pipe

As someone who loves a long, steamy shower, I've watched a lot of hot water go down the drain. I can use some solar thermal to fill the hot water tank, but I'm still heating up the sewer as much as my shower. A small company based in Waterloo, Canada, has a simple solution: Replace your drain with a Power-Pipe and send all that heat right back to your hot water tank.

How does it work? The Power-Pipe is a long, copper drainpipe wrapped in copper tubing. As gravity-driven water swirls down the drain, it clings to the sides of the pipe (the same principle as the swirling water in a flushing toilet). Meanwhile, water heading for the hot water tank—to replace what the

Power-Pipes can grab nearly two-thirds of the heat going down the drain.

shower is using—is running through the copper tubing. Copper transfers heat, so that incoming water is preheated by the stuff going down the drain. It's called "drain water heat recapture," and it couldn't be simpler.

Home showers are just the start. The real potential is in industrial processes that require lots of heat, like food preparation, pulp and paper, and brewing. Power-Pipes can grab nearly two-thirds of the heat going down the drain. There *is* a pitfall: The drainpipes in existing buildings are typically hidden behind walls or under floors. The added hassle and cost of renovations makes the technology a harder sell.

Cogeneration

Most of the energy in a power plant gets spewed out the chimney as waste heat, just like the exhaust of your car. It's a by-product, thrown out like trash. We're making electricity and heating the sky. We can do better than that, by using that waste heat to power buildings or to make more electricity. Cogeneration—also known as combined heat and power (CHP)—can raise the efficiency of a power plant from one-third to nearly 90%.

The easiest way is called "district heating"—pouring all that waste heat into nearby buildings. In New York City, more than 100,000 buildings are heated with steam from seven local cogeneration plants. Cogeneration plants exist all over Europe, with Denmark leading the way. The nation gets more than half of its energy from waste heat. It's not just hot air, either. During the summer months, heat can be fed into "absorption chillers"— big refrigerators that run on heat to cool buildings. A *tri*-cycle plant adds an extra step: The exhaust heat is first used to create steam and generate more electricity, while the final exhaust goes to district heating and cooling. Double-dipping on waste heat.

It sounds easy, and it is. There's a problem, though: The power plants need to be close to the buildings they heat, but most of our

Most of the energy in a power plant gets spewed out the chimney as waste heat. It's a by-product, thrown out like trash.

electrical production takes place far from urban centers. That's why most cogeneration plants are small and scaled to power office buildings, a condo tower or one local neighborhood. Then there's the WhipserGen, a Stirling[9] engine that runs quietly in your basement, providing heat and power for a single home. It's a furnace, boiler and electrical utility all in one.

The potential? In Germany, half[10] of all electrical production could come from cogeneration, and there's no reason to think other countries couldn't do the same. British writer George Monbiot points out that the amount of heat wasted by UK power plants is roughly equal to the energy that's used for household heating.[11]

The Ribatejo combined-cycle power plant, located 18 miles (29 kilometres) northeast of Lisbon, Portugal, has three gas-fired combined-cycle units, each rated at 390 megawatts. It was completed in 2006, after Portugal opened its electricity sector to competition in 2003.

Toronto's Deep Lake Water Cooling

Toronto sits on the shore of one of the world's largest and deepest lakes. Having swum in Lake Ontario many times, I can attest that even the surface is cold—even at the height of summer! Water at the bottom of the lake remains a constant 39 F (4 C) year-round. Meanwhile, as the sun shines on the glass-walled office towers that dominate Toronto's downtown skyline, huge air conditioners roar to life, working to keep them cool. Hmm…loud, energy-sucking air-conditioners running alongside a huge body of cold water that stretches as far as the eye can see. There must be a better way.

> The idea is simple: Use the cold water of Lake Ontario to replace the air-conditioning needs of the downtown core.

There is. In 2004, Toronto's Enwave Energy turned on the Deep Lake Water Cooling system. The idea is simple: Use the cold water of Lake Ontario to replace the air-conditioning needs of the downtown core. It's like the district heating and cooling systems we've just seen, but using lake water as a source of cool air.

How does it work? Remember geo-exchange from Chapter 3? It's much the same. Enwave pumps 4 C water from 280 feet (85 metres) deep and three miles (five kilometres) out, passing it through heat-exchangers before sending it to Toronto's water system. That cools a chilled-water closed loop, which runs through the downtown core. Buildings reject heat into that loop using their own heat-exchangers.

It works beautifully, saving an estimated 60 megawatts on a hot summer's day. That's enough to power 60,000 homes. Some critics worry that Enwave is injecting the lake with unnaturally warm water, but the company takes in only enough to fill Toronto's water needs, so it's not having a major impact on the lake.

In 2004, Enwave Energy sank intake pipes 280 feet (85 metres) deep into Lake Ontario to provide cooling for Toronto's downtown office towers. The water, which remains 39 F (4 C) year-round, passes through heat-exchangers before entering the city's water system.

The Internal Combustion Engine

President Carter's Corporate Average Fuel Efficiency standards may have increased the overall fuel efficiency of America's fleet by 20%, but we lost those gains with loopholes big enough to drive an SUV through. By 2003, the efficiency of the Ford fleet was no better than it was during the time

Double the mileage for the same amount of gas. That's like comparing Usain Bolt to George Costanza on the 100-metre dash.

of the Model T, and the SUV was America's champion. Not the wisest move. Inefficiency was part of what brought the once-great American car companies to their knees in 2009.

How efficient could we make cars? In Europe, even the troubled US automakers are way ahead. DaimlerChrysler and General Motors each produce family sedans that get close to 80 miles per gallon (three litres per 100 kilometres). Volkswagen sells a four-seater that gets about the same, and it has

By 2003, the efficiency of the Ford fleet was no better than it was during the time of the Model T, and the SUV was America's champion.

also premiered an ultralight diesel that gets almost 300 miles per gallon (less than one litre per 100 kilometres). In comparison, a Hummer gets 10 miles per gallon, and the US average is around 20. Disgraceful.

Volkswagen's BlueMotion technology reduces fuel consumption and emissions with longer gear ratios, aerodynamic fine-tuning and engine modifications. The Polo BlueMotion is the most fuel-efficient five-seater in Europe, at 3.8 litres of diesel per 100 kilometres (62 miles per gallon).

President Obama has seen the light. His new fuel-efficiency standards will drop American oil consumption by 1.8 billion barrels annually. That's more than US imports from Saudi Arabia, Libya and Venezuela combined. The bottom line? The American Academy of Sciences stated in 2001 that cost-effective efficiency gains could double the average efficiency of US vehicles, without sacrificing performance or safety.

Double the mileage for the same amount of gas. That's like comparing Usain Bolt to George Costanza on the 100-metre dash. Who would you rather watch?

Potential and Pitfalls

Negawatts are not just for the virtuous. Underrated and overlooked by an energy industry obsessed with production, they're the largest source of energy—and the cheapest, too. According to energy experts Amory and Hunter Lovins, it's possible to reduce energy used by developed countries by at least half, for two cents per saved kilowatt hour. Negawatts will *really* take off when the Energy Internet lets utilities participate (see Chapter 10). Total potential? Half our energy use worldwide.

But here's the irony: Negawatts are so effective, they can be their own worst enemy. Efficiency and conservation often reduce energy demand so quickly and steeply that the price of power comes crashing down. And when that happens, people stop making

Negawatts are overlooked by an energy industry obsessed with production, but they're the largest source of energy—and the cheapest, too.

negawatts. We've seen it happen four times since the 1973 OPEC crisis. Negawatts need to be integrated into a larger strategy.

When Californians ended their energy crisis in 2000 by cutting their power consumption, they didn't do it out of the goodness of their hearts. They did it because they faced brownouts and spiking energy costs. Conservation may be adopted by some—like my mother—as a virtue in its own right, but for global uptake, we're going need an ongoing, constant price signal. Efficiencies are driven by the same pricing signal.

There's some truth to what Dick Cheney said in 2001: "Conservation may be a sign of personal virtue, but it is not a sufficient basis for a sound, comprehensive energy policy." Cheney's response was to pump up coal production and other fossil fuels—not exactly the basis of a sound, comprehensive energy policy.[12] But a culture of conservation and efficiency does require a price signal to ensure that our self-interest, as well as our virtue, drives us to make negawatts.

The Energy Internet will automate negawatt production, making sure that customers and

Total potential of conservation? Half our energy use worldwide.

utilities are paid to produce them. That refrain from my childhood—"Turn out the lights!"—will come as an electronic signal straight from the utility. Contrary to what Cheney has said, conservation *will* become the basis of a sound, comprehensive energy strategy.

Overhead power lines are generally underutilized because loads are restricted to accommodate climatic extremes. Real-time monitoring by companies like the Valley Group allows transmission capacity to be raised by 15% to 30%, alleviating network congestion.

The Trillion-Dollar Question:

So, what do you get for $1 trillion?
More than half of the energy used by the developed world can be eliminated at an average cost of two cents per kilowatt hour. For $1 trillion, we could buy a reduction equal to the entire energy use of the G7 nations. Realistically, though, we can only eliminate half of that energy use. That means that G7 consumption could be cut by 50% for $500 billion a year. Negawatts are the single best weapon in the fight against carbon.

Negawatts accrue when people get turned on to energy efficiency and conservation—like at the biannual Solar Pentathlon in Washington, DC, where 20 teams of university students compete to design and build the most energy-efficient solar-powered house.

191

The End of Easy Oil

Saving for the Future

Imagine that all the oil in the ground is sitting in a giant bathtub. Over millions of years, the tub filled up—drip by drip—as organic material dropped to the bottom of the oceans, sank underground and was pressure-cooked into oil (or natural gas, if it sank deep enough). Today, we're clearly draining the tub faster than it's being filled. There was about two trillion barrels of oil in there before we started dipping into it. There's about a trillion[1] left.

So, when should we start worrying about the end of oil? When there's a million barrels left in the tub? A billion? Perhaps when there's 10 years' worth left, or 20. Seeing as we're draining the tub at a rate of about 35 billion barrels a year, that means we have more than 30 years[2] of oil left. Why worry now?

> We need the oil that's left to help support our petrochemical industries. The last thing we should do is burn it.

It turns out that the time to start worrying is when the tub is half full—right about now. Why? That's when the rate at which we produce oil starts to decline, while demand continues to rise. This causes a large—and permanent—spike in the price of oil. If supply drops by 2% or 3% a year, and demand rises at the same rate, that's a 5% shortfall. We'd need to replace half the oil supply in a decade, while dealing with a severe economic shock. A price shock can happen quickly, but replacing infrastructure takes decades. We're simply not prepared for this.

Back in the 1950s, geophysicist Marion King Hubbert predicted that oil production in the lower 48 states would peak around 1970, then go into permanent decline, precisely at the point when half the known reserves had been used up. He was derided at the time, but Hubbert was dead right. He used three arguments to make his prediction, and they apply equally well to world production today.

Hubbert's first argument links the rate of oil discovery to a prediction of total reserves. Picture a rising curve showing how fast oil is being discovered. One year, you find a billion barrels, the next, 10 billion. At some point, that number starts to decrease. Hubbert figured out how, given that point, you could predict when discovery of new reserves would stop altogether—no more new oil. All you do is make some reasonable assumptions about the shape of the curve. The rate of discovery of oil predicts the size of the bathtub. Turns out it's about two trillion barrels.

Next, Hubbert assumed that over the long term, the rate at which oil is pumped from the ground would follow a bell-shaped curve. It starts off slowly, increasing over time to a peak, at which point the pumping starts to slow down. That was the case for the lower 48, and it looks to be true for many of the world's large oil fields, like those in the North Sea and Mexico. Without any fancy math, you can predict when the peak will occur, as long as you know the rate at which oil has been produced and how much is in the tub.

Put those two arguments together, and they point to one thing: We'll hit peak oil sometime this decade.[3] From there, supply tightens permanently.

There's a third argument that leads to the same result. Hubbert noticed that the rate of oil discovery predicted the rate of consumption a few decades later. In other words, when the rate of discovery starts to slow, consumption will follow suit roughly 30 years later. We're set to hit the slowdown right about now.

All this points to trouble, and soon.

What about a big oil discovery—wouldn't that change things? Not by much. Say we *did* find a big one—something like the Ghawar field in Saudi Arabia, the biggest find ever, at just under 90 billion barrels. That would move the peak back by just a year[4] or so.

Major oil companies worldwide have spent billions of dollars looking for just such a field. But the odds of finding one get smaller every year. In 2006, when Chevron discovered the Jack field in the Gulf of Mexico, the media got pretty excited. Yet, even the most optimistic estimates put the field's reserves at just 15 billion barrels[5]— enough oil to push peak production out by less than *three months*.

We'll hit peak oil sometime this decade. From there, supply tightens permanently.

Unconventional oil, like the tar sands of Alberta, could also put off the crash, but not by much. Aside from the environmental concerns, it would take decades to develop them enough to really put a dent in world supply. We don't have that long.

The OPEC-induced oil shock of 1973 led to panicked lineups at gas stations. This time, it won't be temporary, and it won't be artificially induced. The high oil prices of 2007 are just a hint of what's to come. The crazy thing is, we need the oil that's left to help support our petrochemical industries. Plastics, pharmaceuticals, fertilizers— almost all of the organic chemicals we use come from oil. The last thing we should be doing with the oil that's left is burning it.

TEN

The Ener

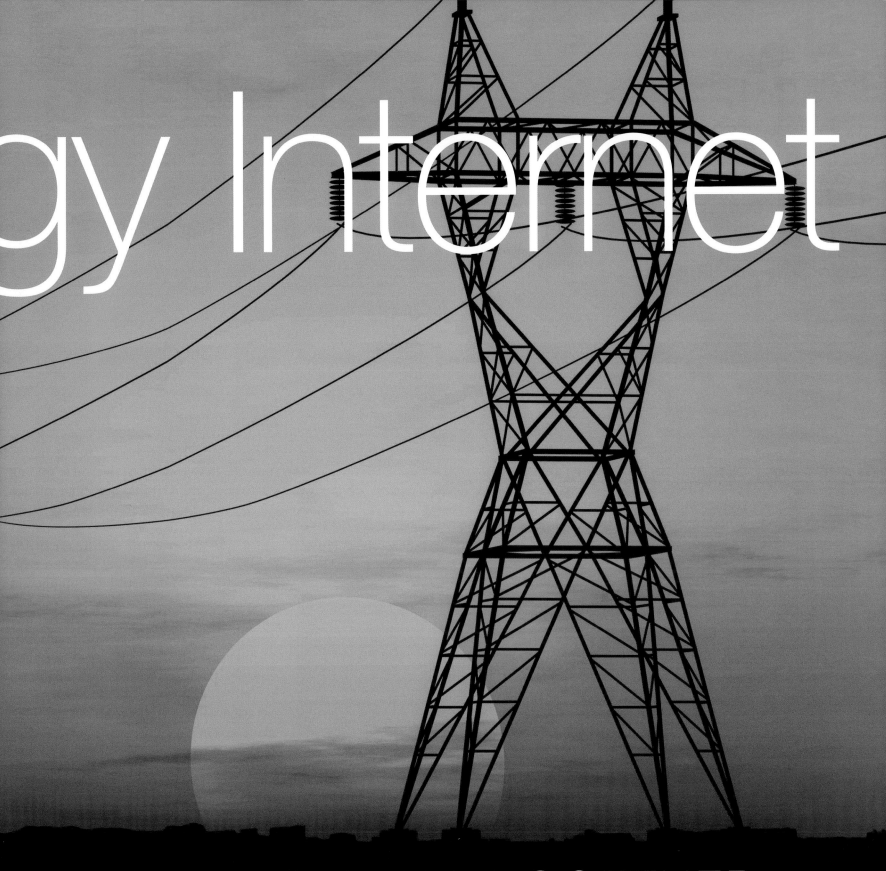

gy Internet

PUTTING IT ALL TOGETHER

The Energy Internet

An Introduction

In the 1950s, families gathered around television sets as big as lounge chairs, their rabbit-ear aerials capturing signals broadcast by the big networks. TVs haven't really progressed much since then—they're still "dumb." That is, they're nothing more than passive receivers at the end of a one-way street. Sure, you can change the channel or turn down the volume, but compared to your computer, a TV has no real smarts. Our electrical system is just as old—and just as dumb.

The power plants and cables that make up the electrical grids of the industrialized world are arguably the largest machines ever built. Constructed around the time TV and radio were still considered high-tech, they were designed in much the same way: Houses and factories passively receive energy sent over the grid by big, centralized power plants. You can turn off a light bulb or turn down the thermostat, but there's no *communication* and no *storage*. It's a one-way street.

Just as the Internet forever changed the way information is made, shared and stored, so the Energy Internet—sometimes called the smart grid—will change the way we produce, distribute and store energy. Bringing together computers and communications, clean power and energy efficiency, the Energy Internet is an Internet of *things,* an interconnected web of smart homes, appliances, cars and power plants.

When your home joins the Energy Internet, it taps into a huge network of energy exchanges happening in real time all across the country. Your dishwasher, for instance, will negotiate with the utility for the best rates, and switch on when power is clean and cheap. The utility will talk to your thermostat and hot water heater, and you'll scarcely notice as it temporarily turns one down when the grid gets overloaded.

On a grander scale, utilities will bring up tidal power on the west coast when the wind

> ## Just as email needs the Internet, renewable power will only work with an Energy Internet.

dies down in the east, or turn off biogas plants in New York when the sun is shining brightly in Nevada. Efficient high-voltage DC lines (HVDC) will distribute that power across continents. Rooftop solar panels and windmills, even the electric car sitting in your driveway, will form part of a new, countrywide grid of distributed production and storage.

Sounds cool, but the lights go on now. Can't the old grid do the job? The simple answer is no. Just like email needs the Internet, large-scale renewable power will only work in conjunction with an Energy Internet. We can't kick the fossil fuel habit without it. Let's find out why, and take a look at what the world might look like with a smart grid.

But first, let's take a look at how our grid got stuck in the Television Age.

Families in the 1950s gathered around television sets as big as lounge chairs. TVs have progressed a lot since then, but our electrical system hasn't. It still just cranks out megawatts, with no communication or storage. It's a passive, one-way street.

London's coal-fired Battersea A Power Station was built in the 1930s. Its identical second half, Battersea B, was completed in the 1950s. Although unused since 1983, it remains one of London's best known landmarks, thanks in part to the exposure it got from the Beatles and Pink Floyd.

Your local grid is designed like a giant wheel, taking power from a central plant and spreading it outward. It's not easy to plug in renewables out on the spokes of the wheel.

The Way It Is

Stuck in the Television Age

Our utilities[1] are a legacy from another era, a time when energy was cheap, carbon dioxide wasn't a problem, and computers were the size of warehouses. They are dumb, closed and disorganized, and run by brute force.[2] It's difficult for renewables to muscle their way onto this scene.

Since utilities are paid[3] to make power, not conserve it, they meet increased demand with more supply. After all, what company wants to sell less[4] of its product? Utilities add power plant after power plant—many of which spend most of their time sitting idle. That's because the utilities build enough plants to meet *peak* demand, which we may only hit for a few hours each year.

When Germany beat England in penalty kicks in the World Cup in 1990, English fans drowned their sorrows in a cup of tea. Plugging in all those kettles at the same time demanded enough energy to power a city of a million people. That can bring a grid to its knees. How to respond? "Most of the flexibility is provided by fossil fuel power stations,"

Our utilities are from another era, when energy was cheap, carbon dioxide wasn't a problem, and computers were the size of warehouses.

says Stewart Larque, spokesman for the UK National Grid. Imagine a massive Christmas-decoration factory that sits idle all year, then churns out enough decorations for every house the day before Christmas. That's how our grid meets demand for electricity.

The utilities couldn't reduce demand by much even if they wanted to. They can't change the price from moment to moment—or communicate that price to the customer. Nor can they turn off unnecessary equipment, or force those kettles to feed into the grid more slowly. That requires two-way communication.[5] Dumb grids mean more brute force.

Dumb grids are closed grids—they can't connect to a bunch of small and medium-sized renewable projects spread out over hundreds of miles. Your local grid is designed like a giant wheel, taking power from a central plant and spreading it outward. It's not easy to plug in renewables out on the spokes of the wheel.

On a national scale, grids are like a hodge-podge of tangled wires that can't effectively distribute power over long distances. The US grid is one of the worst offenders, with more than 3,000 local utilities tangled up into three large, regional grids. As *New York Times* columnist Thomas Friedman puts it, sending power from the east coast to the west coast is like "trying to drive across America, from New York to Los Angeles, without our interstate highway system—taking just state and local highways—and using only county maps to figure out where you were going."[6] We need to move renewable energy from where it's made—places like the sunny Mojave Desert and the windy Great Plains—to the cities that need it.

Utilities add power plant after power plant—many of which spend most of their time sitting idle. That's because the utilities build enough plants to meet peak demand, which we may only hit a few hours each year.

199

The Energy Internet, like the World Wide Web, will be a maze of interlinked computers spanning the globe. Their scale will vary from massive banks of equipment, like this power plant control panel, to tiny microcomputers regulating energy flow in your kitchen.

The Way We're Going

The Energy Internet

The Energy Internet is an Internet of *things*—cars, appliances, power plants—woven together into a choreographed dance of energy by a humming buzz of power lines and wireless communication.

Think of the Energy Internet as a mix of three scales of grid: national, regional and local.

Renewable-energy power plants, transmission lines, electrical meters, appliances, and even the solar panels on rooftops and electric cars in driveways will be able to talk to each other in real time, while sharing power. Their conversation will be about electrical loads, wind speeds and energy prices. Companies like General Electric, IBM and Cisco are already developing the language the Energy Internet will speak.

Power plants may play a starring role, but this dance gives equal time to transmission, storage and consumption. From the dishwasher in your kitchen, all the way up to giant offshore wind farms, no part of the Energy Internet acts in isolation, but rather, as part of a coordinated whole. Demand for energy will change based on the power that's available. The power that's available will depend not just on the wind, sun and tides, but also on demand itself and how much energy has been stored.

Think of the Energy Internet as a mix of three scales of grid: national, regional and local. The national scale lets large renewable

No part of the Energy Internet acts in isolation, but rather, as part of a coordinated whole.

plants compete with coal and nuclear, by allowing them to act in concert and back each other up. The regional scale makes it easy for lots of smaller, local renewables to plug in. And the local scale completely changes how we demand energy and lets every customer play in the power game.

The Energy Internet will manage the transmission of massive volumes of power between countries and continents. This will require a new generation of systems and equipment, like this 550-kilovolt circuit breaker being tested by Siemens in Berlin.

In September 2008, Siemens completed testing of the world's first 800-kilovolt HVDC converter transformer. It was built for the Yunnan-Guangdong high-voltage DC transmission system in China, one of two with the highest rated capacity in the world.

The Supergrid

Making the Intermittent Regular

Highly efficient HVDC transmission lines will link renewable energy plants spread across continents—not just to the cities that need it, but also to each other. It's called "grid balancing," and it makes renewable energy production more predictable and reliable. When one energy source diminishes, another comes online. As wind in one region dies down, for example, it may pick up thousands of miles away. When the tides turn on the west coast, hydro or solar power in the east comes online. Grid balancing also includes storage, often in the form of pumped hydro,[7] which can act as a backup to the whole system.

> Renewables have always been criticized for just not being reliable enough. The Supergrid puts that issue to rest.

That's still a ways off. But there are exciting projects happening right now. Europe's Airtricity is planning a network of underwater HVDC cables—called the Supergrid—to tie together offshore wind farms all around Europe, from the Atlantic to the Mediterranean. Covering an area large enough to contain different weather patterns,[8] the Supergrid is expected to increase the capacity factor of offshore wind farms from 40% to 70%,[9] as well as to provide a single, continent-wide electricity market. The first phase of the project, covering the UK, Germany and Holland, is expected to provide enough electricity for eight million homes, and the grid portion will cost more than $2 billion. There are already HVDC lines across the English Channel and in the US.

The high-powered DESERTEC Foundation, based in Berlin, envisions much more than just wind farms (see Chapter 1). Add large-scale solar throughout North Africa, biomass in France and geothermal from Iceland. Then add storage, so that when the wind howls over the Atlantic, water flows uphill in Norway's pumped hydro storage reservoirs. Each of these power sources knows just what the others are up to and coordinates the power loads across many different sources. This is the backbone of the Energy Internet.

European leaders are already committed to the idea, particularly those in the UK and France. And US President Barack Obama and Jon Wellinghof, head of the Federal Energy Regulatory Commission, have both caught the Supergrid bug, which means HVDC lines may soon crisscross America. "There's 500 to 700 gigawatts of developable wind throughout the Midwest," says Wellinghof, and "enough solar in the southwest, as we all know, to power the entire country. It's a matter of being able to move it to loads."[10]

Supergrids like these require vision, capital and big engineering resources. But this is just the sort of large-scale, multisourced grid we need to catapult renewable energy production from a niche industry into something that can compete head-to-head with nuclear and coal. Renewables have always been criticized for just not being reliable enough. The Supergrid puts that issue to rest.

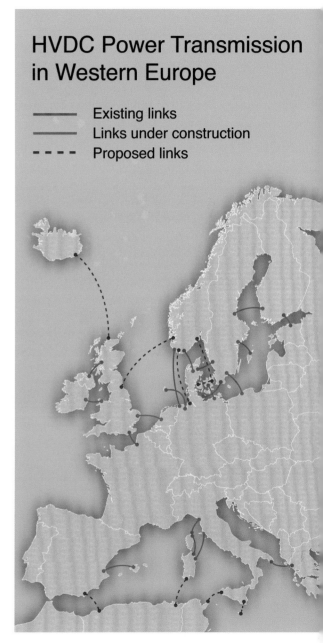

HVDC Power Transmission in Western Europe

——— Existing links
——— Links under construction
- - - - Proposed links

Undersea HVDC transmission cables will be the vital link between countries in Western Europe's proposed Supergrid. It is expected to increase the capacity factor of offshore wind farms from 40% to 70% and eventually lead to a single, continent-wide electricity market.

The Regional Grid

Building a Two-Way Street

In the existing grid, power from central plants flows one-way though a tangle of ever-smaller wires. Those wires weren't designed to *take in* power; they were designed to *deliver* it. But renewable energy will be composed of lots[11] of smaller plants scattered

Smart power electronics will help create a two-way street for electricity. When power is available, energy flows one way. When power is needed, it flows another.

across the grid—tidal turbines, community-owned wind farms, solar panels. Called "distributed production," it requires two-way wires. The Energy Internet, like the Internet itself, is about *access.*

Distributed production will include releasing power that was previously stored. Thousands of fuel cells and hydrogen tanks that have replaced the backup diesel generators in buildings across the country will do double-duty—storing power for backup, but releasing some into the grid at peak demand. Fuel cells[12] produce electricity from hydrogen, but can also run in reverse, producing hydrogen when fed electricity. They're like powerful batteries, with storage capacity limited only by the size of the hydrogen storage tank. Fuel cells clearly need a two-way street.

Smart power electronics will help create a two-way street for electricity. When power is available, energy flows one way. When power is needed, it flows another. Renewable energy production becomes "plug and play,"

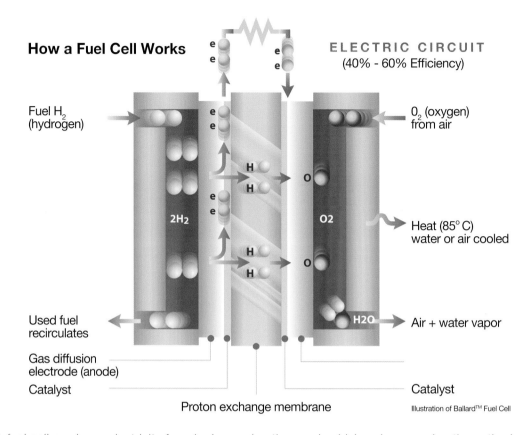

How a Fuel Cell Works

ELECTRIC CIRCUIT (40% - 60% Efficiency)

Fuel H_2 (hydrogen)

O_2 (oxygen) from air

2H2

O2

Heat (85° C) water or air cooled

Used fuel recirculates

H2O — Air + water vapor

Gas diffusion electrode (anode)

Catalyst

Catalyst

Proton exchange membrane

Illustration of Ballard™ Fuel Cell

A fuel cell produces electricity from hydrogen (on the anode side) and oxygen (on the cathode side), which react in the presence of a catalyst (electrolyte). When hydrogen reaches the catalyst, it separates into protons (hydrogen ions) and electrons. The free electrons, produced at the anode, are conducted in the form of a usable electric current.

anywhere and anytime. Creating regional two-way grids for energy is a big job. If

Thousands of fuel cells across the country will do double-duty—storing power for backup, but releasing some into the grid at peak demand.

building a national grid is like building a new house, updating the regional grid is like a

long, complicated renovation.

Everything that's connected to the Energy Internet, from power electronics to wind farms to fuel cells, will be embedded with sensors and constantly monitored. Power flowing at every point will be measured. That's a lot of real-time information to manage, and California-based Silver Spring Networks is getting ready to do just that. Partnering with electronics and communications companies like GE, ABB and Cisco, it's building the software a utility will need to manage this new "Internet of things."

ABB has a system called "HVDC Light" that transmits power underground, underwater, and over long distances. The environmental benefits include invisible power lines, neutral electromagnetic fields, oil-free cables and compact converter stations.

Millions of tiny computers will control the Energy Internet—each component will have a chip inside that talks to the grid. All that intelligence will enable utilities to adjust demand, just like they adjust supply. The best part is, you'll hardly notice.

The Local Grid

Matching Demand to Supply

Imagine if your air conditioner, refrigerator and washing machine were smart enough to bid for energy, turning on only when it's cheapest. You'd barely even notice—your fridge, for instance, might power down for a few minutes, but the light would still flick on when you opened the door. Your air conditioner might turn off, but the fans would still circulate air. Your coffeemaker's element might turn off for seconds at a time, but the pot would stay hot.

Now picture your electric car as a smart, miniature power plant that charges up in your driveway at night when energy is cheap, and sells power back to the grid while you're at work. It's smart enough to hold on to enough power to get you home. And if you plug it into your friend's outlet, the utility knows whom to bill for the power. Same goes for the solar panels on your roof—they'll sell power to the grid during the day, when you're not using the energy they produce.

The local grid is where the Energy Internet really shows its smarts. It doesn't take much—each component has a chip inside that talks to the grid. But all that intelligence adds up, letting utilities adjust demand just like they adjust supply. The best part is, you'll hardly notice. We saw in the last chapter that negawatts, reducing energy demand, is the single most effective energy source available. The Energy Internet is what really ramps up the negawatts.

It's called "demand response," and doing it in real time is just as important to renewable energy as production. Demand decreases during peak load, eliminating the need for all that standby power. When wind farms pick up at night, demand increases to make

Major appliance manufacturers are rushing to develop IP-enabled devices to work with the Energy Internet. Whirlpool says some of its products will be smart-grid capable as early as 2010.

sure every bit of that clean power is used. If there aren't enough dishwashers waiting for cheap, clean energy, then millions of cars across the country store it, releasing it back when demand rises again. (By the way, those smart dishwashers aren't far off—appliance-maker Whirlpool has announced that all of its appliances will be compatible with the Energy Internet by 2015.)

How important is demand response? In California today, the last 10% of power production is used less than 1% of the time. That means that if the state could adjust demand for only 57 hours a year, one-tenth of its power plants could be mothballed. That's just the start. Some studies show that new American generation capacity required by 2030 can be cut roughly in half[13] with aggressive demand management.

The Energy Internet turns customers into mini-utilities. And just like mobile phone companies, utilities will start to offer all sorts of different deals. "Clean and Green" might emphasize nighttime consumption. "Mini Utility" might put your car and solar panel at the center of your own grid, and "Keep It Simple" might ignore all demand response—but cost a lot more.

Potential and Pitfalls

The Energy Internet is not optional. If renewables are going to hit the big leagues, it's absolutely crucial. All three scales of grid—national, regional and local—add a piece of the puzzle. The vagaries of the wind and sun are washed away in a continent-wide, balanced grid. Cities become utilities, because the big buildings are all equipped with fuel cells. Coal plants no longer sit idle, waiting for all of England to plug in their kettles at halftime. And consumers rule—their coordinated demand response is equivalent to the biggest power plant on the planet.

The best thing about the Energy Internet is that it doesn't require a lot of new inventions, but simply the application of existing technologies. One pitfall, however, is the sheer scale required—the Energy Internet is going to cost a lot. Each mile of HVDC transmission costs about $1 million (and that doesn't include the connecting equipment). Connecting wind and solar plants across continents requires thousands of miles of HVDC transmission. Upgrading all the power electronics of the regional grids is also expensive—some estimates are as high as $500 billion for the US alone.

Another pitfall is that there's not a lot of experience in real-time operation of continent-wide, distributed power production systems. There are bound to be a few complications along the way.[14] The Energy Internet is a huge

> The best thing about the Energy Internet is that it doesn't require a lot of new inventions, but simply the application of existing technologies.

interplay of software, wireless devices, homes, factories, power plants, transmission lines and customer responses. Even if each were well understood on its own, it shouldn't surprise us if unforeseen behavior emerges as all these components are brought together. A new systems engineering theory will probably result.

But the potential is enormous. Without the Energy Internet, we'll be stuck in the Television Age. With it, our energy infrastructure will finally enter the 21st century: smart, connected, versatile—and clean.

The Trillion-Dollar Question:

So, what do you get for $1 trillion?
Roughly, a smart grid that covers America or Europe.[15] That means renewable energy could be created almost anywhere and be distributed right across the country or continent. Utilities could talk to customers in real time, reducing demand by as much as 50%.

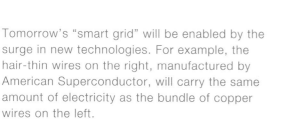

Tomorrow's "smart grid" will be enabled by the surge in new technologies. For example, the hair-thin wires on the right, manufactured by American Superconductor, will carry the same amount of electricity as the bundle of copper wires on the left.

Imagine a possible world in 2050: smart, connected, versatile—and clean. The Energy Internet now efficiently manages the interplay between wireless devices, homes, factories, power plants, transmission lines and customers. At last, we've managed to kick the fossil fuel habit.

209

Postscript: The World in 2050

What would a future free of fossil fuels look like? How might we get there? Here's a fanciful flight, fueled by optimism...

As the sun rises over northern Africa, hundreds of giant solar fields come to life, each one big enough to replace an old-fashioned coal plant. Some begin to work when the sun is low on the horizon; others use stored heat to pump power 24 hours a day. Much of it goes to Europe—the first jurisdiction to rely entirely on clean energy—via a network of cables that crisscross the continent. Though these solar fields cover just a tiny fraction of the Sahara, they supply almost half of Europe's energy needs.

Our cities are far smarter—cars no longer dominate urban centers.

Europe's cable network also connects with other types of renewables, like wind power generated by the jumbo-jet-sized blades on massive turbines, both on land and in the sea. During the night, those turbines charge millions of electric cars, thousands of giant sodium sulfur batteries, and fill the tanks of countless fuel cell generators with hydrogen. Utilities also capture power from the clock-like regularity of the tides and even from waves. The vagaries of weather are buffered by storage, and distribution over space and type of energy source.

It took North America a decade to catch up to Europe, but soon the American southwest provided solar power to the entire continent, and the windswept Great Plains hosted thousands of massive turbines. Both coasts contribute tidal power, and hydro pulls a big load. Once Canada figured out that clean energy was cheaper than melting tar (as long as you put up the same amount of capital), it soon emerged as a renewable-energy superpower. All of North America is bound up in a single, massive Energy Internet.

Back in 2009, most experts expected the growth in carbon emissions to come from what was then known as the developing world (they're called "newly developed nations" now). But innovative financing from developed nations, mostly the US and Europe, unleashed a flood of clean technology. Once we'd committed both capital and technology, the newly developed nations finally capitulated to demands that they keep their carbon emissions in check.

In those countries—especially China and India—deep geothermal is now the dominant source of energy. The technology first went big in China when it became clear how hard it would be to replace thousands of coal plants with something that would pump out the same amount of power with the same reliability. Nuclear cost too much. Large-scale wind and solar were reliant on the Energy Internet, and since there wasn't enough capital to replace their coal plants *and* the distribution system, that had to wait. Carbon capture and storage wasn't a good fit, either, because China's coal plants were so far apart.

Negawatts continue to be the best new power source.

So, retrofitting with deep geo was the only option. Besides, a global team of researchers had perfected deep geo long before carbon capture, once the US got serious about funding it. Led by the champions of deep geo—namely, the engineering department at MIT—huge numbers of coal furnaces were replaced by a couple of deep holes and a heat-exchanger.

As for the predicted increase in energy use—from new devices and more people—it was offset with reduced demand. We don't build new supply for peak power anymore, since the Energy Internet smoothes out the spikes. Negawatts continue to be the best new power source. That means only power production that existed in 2010 had to be replaced. Without negawatts, we never would have gotten here.

Huge numbers of coal furnaces have been replaced by deep geothermal holes and heat-exchangers.

Biomass is no longer used to produce electricity. What little we have is used exclusively for liquid fuel production. Even our best efforts couldn't stop *all* warming, so the global food supply is constrained. We didn't manage to irrigate the entire Sahara, but large parts of coastal Mexico and Africa are now used for halophyte production—plants that love saltwater. We rotate winter crops on traditional farms, and once unproductive land now grows fuel crops. Algae exploded when Exxon got into the game, after its successful 2009 experiment, and algae farms dot the landscape. We don't produce biofuel anywhere near the scale we once pumped conventional oil, but it's enough to keep us in liquid fuel—mostly for boats and planes.

While we couldn't fix suburb-dominated urban planning overnight, our cities are far smarter than they were in 2009. Cars no longer dominate urban centers. Even US cities—like New York and Los Angeles—started using GPS to track and charge drivers, since electric vehicles did away with gas taxes. The rate you pay depends on the type of car you drive—the bigger it is, the steeper the levy. Tax breaks for cyclists got lots of people into the saddle, and in Toronto, there are even covered bike lanes for winter riding. These days, it's considered sophisticated to ride a bike.

Thanks to tough new building codes across North America and Europe, no building constructed after 2020 used anything other than geo-exchange for heating and cooling—if it required such a system at all. Likewise, a massive retrofit program introduced around the same time reduced energy use in buildings by 75%. And any buildings erected after 2030 are net-zero, sucking no energy from the grid.

How did all this happen? In short, it cost us many trillions of dollars, along with a huge overhaul of our industrial sector and massive political will at every level of government, worldwide.

So, what finally turned the tide? Most people point to COP15, the climate negotiations held in Copenhagen in 2009, where world leaders tried to come up with the first global treaty to replace the original Kyoto Protocol. That's when the United States, under then-President Barack Obama, finally took the lead on climate change, and we began to do more than talk about kicking

All of North America is bound up in a single, massive Energy Internet.

the fossil fuel habit. Though arguably the spike in oil prices of 2011—when the cost of a barrel shot up to $200—had something to do with it, along with better education on climate change.

continued…

Postscript: The World in 2050

Before COP15, leaders in China wouldn't even *talk* about limits on carbon emissions. The argument was that they needed to continue feeding their growing industrial machine, and the government feared that it would fall too far behind the West if it were constrained. But threats of sanctions on carbon-heavy industries, and promises of clean technology transfer, finally got them on board. India joined in when President Obama acknowledged the country's moral argument: that each person had the same right to emit carbon, regardless of when and where they were born.

At COP15, countries across the globe began the long political process that would reduce carbon emissions by 80% by 2050. The great drought of 2020 increased the target to 100% by 2050.

COP15 may have brought the world together on carbon reduction, but it was money that got the job done. The economic recovery that followed the Great Recession of 2009-'10—and in particular, the sustained spike in oil prices that came with it—finally got Big Business on side, and the real work began.

The economy boomed, and the growth in clean infrastructure kept employment high for decades.

A new, clean energy infrastructure needed lots of patient capital, and that came from two places. Governments around the world began issuing bonds—green bonds, climate bonds, energy bonds—that all amounted to the same thing: Savings were redirected to clean energy. But the *really* big money came from the world's largest pension funds, which collectively managed assets of more than $100 trillion. Starting around 2020, they realized that their long-term ability to pay members was directly linked to the health of the climate, and they started moving assets to clean energy. Pension funds were the slow-moving giants that saved the game.

Oil is no longer the cause of wars, and pumping it no longer requires massive military support. The Middle East is no longer an area of strategic military importance, since most countries are now entirely energy-self-sufficient. The economy boomed starting in 2020, and the sustained growth in clean infrastructure kept employment high for decades.

The 10 clean technologies in this book are a roadmap of where to go. Getting there is up to all of us.

This scenario is imaginary. But it could happen. The first thing we need to do is realize that a world free of fossil fuels is both possible and necessary. Then, we need to commit the necessary resources and get to work. Because this is not the only possible world in 2050—and the alternative is not pretty.

We can do it. Humankind can now bring to bear unprecedented levels of engineering and scientific talent, industrial might, political arm-twisting, international diplomacy and financial clout. It will be painful at times; all transformations are. And it will be frightening, as the true scope of the problem becomes clear. *But we can kick the habit.* The 10 clean technologies in this book are a sort of roadmap of where to go. Getting there is up to all of us.

Please be part of the solution. Your kids and grandkids will want to know where you stood on the issue, because it will dominate their personal and professional lives. Understand why we need to kick the fossil fuel habit. See that there *are* solutions, but know that they're difficult to achieve and require effort.

Talk to your friends, neighbors and coworkers. Because we're not going to solve this problem if we don't all believe it's necessary—and possible.

—Tom Rand, December 2009

Endnotes

The Endnotes have been carefully prepared to provide supporting evidence for the many facts quoted and claims made in this book. We hope they will enhance your understanding of the subject and enjoyment of the book

Preface

1 Margaret Thatcher, Nov. 8, 1989, speech to United Nations General Assembly (Global Environment). See www.margaretthatcher.org/speeches for a full transcript.

2 How fast must we do it? By 2030, we need to bring our carbon emissions down to near zero if we are to avoid some pretty scary positive feedback effects, like the melting of the permafrost and the release of the massive amounts of greenhouse gases it contains.

3 As quoted in G. Dyer, *Climate Wars*, pg. 157

4 See "Cheap Money – Enter the Green Bond" for just one idea on how to accelerate the movement of cheap capital.

One: Solar

1 One end of this range comes from the US Energy Information Agency (US EIA) (http://www.eia.doe.gov/oiaf/aeo/assumption/pdf/electricity.pdf#page=3). Its estimates are tempered by analysis of current, real, commercial-scale projects.

2 Includes cost of fuel only. Operating costs for coal and large solar plants are assumed to be similar, with the major difference being the cost of fuel.

3 Lower end: US EIA. Upper end of this range: Alliant Energy Corp. announced that a small, 300-megawatt coal plant to be built in Wisconsin will cost an estimated $1.2 billion. Duke Energy revised construction costs for a single 800-megawatt coal plant in North Carolina to $1.8 billion. These costs include no carbon sequestration.

4 According to the US EIA, total coal used in the US for electrical generation was around one billion tons. Total electricity generated was two billion megawatt hours. Cost of coal in 2008 was $35 per ton. So, the cost of the coal input is $0.0175 per kilowatt hour.

5 The lower end is large, commercial PV systems (in line with US EIA), and the upper end corresponds to single-home installations. This accounts for none of the significant cost reductions expected over the next several years. By 2012, these costs should be half what they are now.

6 Based on the Toronto installation example, capital cost per kilowatt (thermal) is just over $1, or $134,000 for 120 kilowatts-thermal (source: Manufacturer Enerworks rate each panel at two kilowatts-thermal). Smaller installations will be more expensive due to installation costs, so the estimate on capital costs is between $1 and $3 per watt-thermal of capacity.

7 Lower end: The Nevada One project, rated at 64 megawatts, cost $260 million (just over $4 per watt). The proposed 553-megawatt Mojave Solar Park is estimated to cost $2 billion (just under $4 per watt). The US EIA also agrees with this number ($3.7 per watt).

8 OPEC Production is 30 million barrels a day, or 11 billion barrels per year. 11,000 square kilometres required = 4,230 square miles. Connecticut is 4,845 square miles, land only, or 5,543 square miles, including water.

9 11 and 20 megawatts respectively

10 New solar PV cells have the new record, at just over 40%.

11 Rated at 10 to 25 kilowatts

12 500 megawatts to start, scaling up to 850 megawatts

13 According to Stirling: eight per acre

14 Even in northern latitudes, like Toronto, Canada, a 178-square-metre installation produces 134,000 kilowatt hours per year (hence it's a conservative estimate—southern latitudes would produce more energy per square metre). That comes out to 45 billion kilowatt hours per year, or the energy equivalent of more than 28 million barrels of oil.

15 Compare to 20% to 40% for solar PV and over 30% for concentrated solar. A more fair comparison, however, might be to crops for biofuels, which convert much less than 1% of the sun's energy to a useful form.

16 That means if it's rated at 200 megawatts, it would produce, on average, between 80 and 100 megawatts every hour of every day, year-round.

17 100 gigawatts (source: http://www.guardian.co.uk/environment/2008/jul/22/solarpower.windpower?gusrc=rss&feed=environment). Note: It appears that initial plans for the grid come in around $80 billion, and the solar farms the rest.

18 The Fort Hills project, a tar sands development run by Petro-Canada, has estimated capital costs of $130,000 per barrel per day of capacity (source: http://www.moneyweek.com/investments/commodities/are-canadian-tar-sands-the-answer-to-our-oil-needs.aspx). This is equivalent to three billion barrels of oil per $1 trillion of capital expenditure. Looks comparable—even favorable—to the low end of solar. But that's *only the capital cost for the infrastructure.* You then have to pay for all the energy to melt the tar, upgrade it, refine it, etc., which amounts to over $25 a barrel. So the three billion barrels will have an additional annual cost of $75 billion. For the accountants in the room: The present value of that annual cost, over just 20 years and at 5%, is another $1 trillion. So, the effective rate of oil production is only 1.5 billion barrels a year for that $1 trillion. Concentrated solar could deliver around 1,000 billion kilowatt hours per year on a $1-trillion investment (see "Concentrated Solar"). This is equivalent to 600 million barrels of oil—but this energy is already in a useful form. The oil from the tar sands needs to be burned in an engine or turbine, and we'll only get one-third of it out as useful work. So the two come out about the same.

19 They're not quite the same—solar thermal for hot water wins at 1,000 billion kilowatt hours. Concentrated solar is second, right on the 1,000 billion kilowatt hours mark, and solar PV is third, at around 600 to 1,000 billion kilowatt hours. But they're pretty close—why? Seems odd, given they're very different technologies. Concentrated solar is currently more cost-effective than solar PV and will probably retain a slight lead, but solar PV is coming down in price fast. Solar thermal is the simplest—it requires no

continued...

Solar is already fast becoming cost-competitive with coal-based production. With economies of scale, lower capital costs and a price attached to emitting carbon, solar is clearly positioned to compete with our dirtiest source of electricity.

Endnotes

One: Solar ...continued

intervening turbine, for example—but that simplicity seems to be offset by the fact that installations are smaller and therefore have more economic overhead. The necessity of a turbine for large-scale concentrated solar electrical production, which would only operate at about 30% to 40% efficiency, is overcome by the scale of installation.

[20] **Concentrated solar energy output:** Let's look at three projects: an existing project, and two planned projects.

1) The Nevada One project, rated at 64 megawatts, produces an estimated 134 M kilowatt hours annually (source: http://www.nevadasolarone.net/press-releases/ACCIONA-Connects-to-the-Nevada-Grid) and cost $260 million. A trillion dollars would translate to 515 billion kilowatt hours annually.

2) The proposed 553-megawatt Mojave Solar Park is estimated to cost $2 billion. At a 25% capacity factor, this translates to 605 billion kilowatt hours for $1 trillion.

3) The European Solar Project: If the 200 gigawatts (100 gigawatts for $500 billion, so 200 gigawatts for $1 trillion) produced in the European "supergrid" plan above had a 25% capacity factor, you would get 438 billion kilowatt hours annually.

So each way of looking at it comes up with somewhere between 400 and 600 billion kilowatt hours every year, for the lifetime of the plants. If we assume that mass production of materials, advances in surface materials and lower-cost debt capital (as the perceived risk associated with this technology comes down, or with government risk-rates in play) can cut the costs by half, we get somewhere between 800 and 1,200 billion kilowatt hours annually.

Solar PV energy output: On small installs, the solar cells themselves cost around $4,000 per kilowatt of capacity, but that's not installed. Each installed kilowatt of capacity costs $8,000 to $12,000 and generates 800 to 2,000 kilowatt hours per year, depending on whether they're installed in cloudy England or sunny Australia. Take the average of these numbers, crank the calculator, and it comes out around 150 billion kilowatt hours annually for $1 trillion. (Calculation: $1 trillion ÷ $12,000 = 83,333,333 > 800 kWh = 66.7 billion kWh annually [low end] and $1 trillion ÷ $8,000 = 125,000,000 > 2000 kWh = 250 billion kWh annually [high end]). Large, utility-sized installations are more efficient. The installation at Nellis Air Force Base cost $100 million to build, is rated at 14 megawatts and generates over 25 million kilowatt hours per year. That's 250 billion kilowatt hours annually for $1 trillion. (Calculation: $1 trillion ÷ $100,000,000 = 10,000 > 25 million kWh = 250 billion kwh).

We can assume costs will come down sharply, and efficiencies will go up with economies of scale and newer technology. The president of Sharp Corp. expects those costs to come down by half in the next few years alone (source: http://www.cleanbreak.ca/2006/08/31/solar-pv-prices-halved-by-2010-sharp/), and one company, Arise Technologies in Germany, is already shipping solar chips at $2.50 per watt (source: http://research.dundeesecurities.com/Research/APV120408.pdf). The concentrated solar PV systems are also significantly cheaper to build, since mirrors are cheaper than chips. It's not unreasonable to assume costs will come down fourfold,

so let's quadruple those numbers to get between 600 and 1,000 billion kilowatt hours annually.

Solar thermal for hot water: A large-scale project in Toronto, Canada, that cost $134,000 is a 60-plate installation covering 178 square metres. These panels generate 134,000 kilowatt hours per year. This translates to the equivalent of 1,000 billion kilowatt hours a year for a $1-trillion investment (source: private correspondence on actual solar thermal installation). With some economies of scale, and assuming slightly warmer climates, this would easily double.

[21] The United States currently gets half of its electrical production from coal, and that amounts to 2,000 billion kilowatt hours (source: http://www.eia.doe.gov/cneaf/electricity/epa/figes1.html). Electrical production from $1 trillion worth of solar would amount to somewhere between 600 and 1,200 billion kilowatt hours annually, depending on whether it were concentrated solar (high end) or solar PV (low end).

Two: Wind

[1] As quoted in G. Dyer, *Climate Wars*, pg. 43

[2] Light from the sun is like a rainbow, but all mixed together to make white. As the light passes through the atmosphere, air molecules scatter primarily the blue part of that rainbow, in all directions. Those scattered blue bits hit our eyes and give the sky its wonderful shimmering blue color. It's the missing blue parts make the sun appear yellow, since yellow is what a rainbow looks like if you take the blue away.

[3] See "Solar"

[4] See "Solar"

[5] See "Solar"

[6] See "Solar"

[7] Micro-Wind: source, Helix Wind. This includes grid connection.

[8] Onshore wind: Capital costs vary depending on the size of the wind farm. US EIA estimates capital costs of $1,340 per kilowatt installed. Canada's Department of Natural Resources estimates that equipment comprises 76% of a wind farm's capital costs—the raw cost of a large turbine is around $1,000 per kilowatt, so that would agree with the US EIA estimate. Lower range is $1,300 per installed kilowatt. Note that this is the cost of *rated* output: Wind farms generally operate at only around one-third capacity—that is, they produce, on average, about one-third of their rated output, year-round. Let's acknowledge that with an upper range of $4,000.

[9] Offshore wind: US EIA estimates capital costs of $2,547 per kilowatt. Capacity factor in deep-sea will be higher—say, 50%—so an upper range of $5,000 per kilowatt.

[10] *New Scientist*, Oct. 11-18, 2008, pg. 34, corroborated by http://www.ocean.udel.edu/windpower/ResourceMap/index-world.html. Note: This

continued...

Endnotes

Two: Wind ...*continued*

is calculated as the amount of wind energy converted to electrical power that can be captured by wind turbines placed in areas where it's practical to capture the wind. For example, only areas on the continental shelves are considered potential development sites, not the open ocean. The point is that this is a realistic engineering analysis, not a theoretical pie-in-the-sky analysis.

[11] Source: Canadian Wind Energy Association, corroborated by UN estimates of 14 gigajoules (approximately 4,000 kilowatt hours) per North American household of electricity requirement. Assuming a capacity factor of 30%, the Clipper would generate 10 megawatts 365 days a year, 24 hours a day, times 30%. That equals 26 million kilowatt hours, or 6,500 homes (see http://www.bwea.com/pdf/ref_three.pdf for estimates of realistic capacity factors ranging from 20% to 40%).

[12] Source: *Renewable Energy*, G. Boyle, pg. 276, and US National Wind Coordinating Committee, 1999

[13] Installed capacity of 3,000 megawatts

[14] Source: "American Wind Energy Association Report," World Changing, pg. 175

[15] See the Pickens Plan at http://www.pickensplan.com/theplan/

[16] Source: British Wind Energy Association, *UK Offshore Wind, Moving Up a Gear*, pg. 5

[17] Source: Associated Press, Dec 9, 2008

[18] The air passing over the wing splits into two streams, one over the wing and one under. The curve on the top of the wing forces the air passing over it to travel just that bit further than the air passing under it, which can go in a straight line. That means the air molecules are spread just a bit further apart during their travel over that wing, and that creates lower pressure. That lower pressure creates a vacuum (suction) and pulls the wing upward, creating lift.

[19] http://www.skysails.info/index.php?id=472&L=2

[20] Source: http://www.risoe.dk/rispubl/reports/ris-r-1608_186-195.pdf

[21] Total electrical energy use worldwide is 18,000 billion kilowatt hours per year (source: US EIA, http://www.eia.doe.gov/iea/elec.html). Forty percent is 7,200 billion kilowatt hours. At a 25% capacity factor, total install capacity needs to be 7,200 billion kilowatt hours ÷ 365 days ÷ 24 hours x 4 = 3.3 billion kilowatts of installed capacity, or around 1.6 million two-megawatt turbines.

[22] As quoted in G. Dyer, *Climate Wars*, pg. 132

Climate Science I – The Basics

[1] There are other greenhouse gases—methane, nitrous oxide and water vapor, among others—but for simplicity I'll stick to carbon dioxide, as it contributes more than 60% of the greenhouse effect.

[2] For a historical account of this discovery, see http://www.aip.org/history/climate/co2.htm

[3] See Siegenthaler et al., "Stable Carbon Cycle—Climate Relationship During the Late Pleistocene," in *Science*, Vol. 310, Nov. 25, 2005. Also: http://cdiac.ornl.gov/trends/temp/vostok/jouz_tem.htm

[4] Sometimes the temperature goes up first, before the carbon rises, which caused some people to doubt the link. What this shows, though, is the existence of "feedback mechanisms," where an increase in temperature causes something to happen (like the melting of permafrost that holds stored carbon) that releases more carbon. See "Climate Science III – The Complex Stuff" for details on feedback.

[5] By oceans, forests, etc.

[6] World Meteorological Organization, "Extreme Weather Events Might Increase," press release, July 2, 2003. See also http://www.greenfacts.org/studies/climate_change/l_3/climate_change_2.htm#3

[7] For a full account of what might happen in the climate, see *Heat* by G. Monbiot, and for the geopolitical sphere, see *Climate Wars* by G. Dyer.

[8] The IPCC was saddled at the outset by a need to generate an unusually high degree of consensus—near unanimity—before it publishes any results. It takes time to build that consensus, and the outcome is rendered very conservative. It also takes a great deal of time to go through the rigorous peer-review process. The end result is they use data that is, literally, years out of date. For the 2007 report, field data from the turn of the century was used.

Three: Geothermal

[1] Tidal power is the other exception.

[2] The deepest exploratory holes dug in the Earth's surface are only about 7.5 miles (12 kilometres) deep.

[3] Heat and temperature are two different, but related, things. Temperature is *not* energy, but is a measure of the *intensity* of the energy. Heat is energy—a measure of the total kinetic energy of the molecules of a substance. Generally speaking, the higher the temperature, the higher the heat content. But here's an important difference: A lot of something at a low temperature can contain as much heat as a little bit of something at a high temperature. So heat can be "high-quality" (or high-temperature), and it can be "low-quality" (or low-temperature). Just because something has a low temperature doesn't mean it doesn't contain heat.

[4] *The Future of Geothermal Energy; Impact of Enhanced Geothermal Systems (EGS) on the United States in the 21st Century*, © 2006, Massachusetts Institute of Technology, MIT-led interdisciplinary panel, J.W. Tester (chair).

[5] Strictly speaking, there's an equilibrium of sorts near the surface (less than 60 feet, or 20 metres or so), in which a small degree of solar energy is present as well. Beneath that point, however, almost all the heat comes from that inner nuclear battery.

[6] How long depends on two factors. The first is how much heating or cooling that's needed—the load, type and size of building, insulation, where it's located, etc. The second is what's called the "thermal conductivity" of the ground; that is, how fast heat is transferred to and

continued...

There's enough harvestable wind out there to provide five times the world's electrical consumption. But sometimes the wind doesn't blow, so large-scale grid balancing will be needed to increase the percentage of wind's contribution.

The real promise of geothermal is EGS (enhanced geothermal systems). Conservative estimates of the accessible geothermal energy in the US: 3,000 to 30,000 tImes the country's total energy needs. Similar abundance exists everywhere in the world.

Endnotes

Three: Geothermal *...continued*

from the pipe. If the pipes hit an underground aquifer, for example, much less pipe is needed, since water has a very high thermal conductivity. A typical 3,000-square-foot (278-square-metre) home might need 1,200 to 1,400 feet (365 to 425 metres) of buried pipe.

[7] The loop can be horizontal, laid along a trench, or it can be installed in vertically drilled holes. Horizontal loops are cheaper, but need more area and must be at least 10 feet (three metres) below ground. Vertical loops are normally installed to save space in dense areas.

[8] The heat pump uses compressors, just like a refrigerator, to remove heat from the glycol solution through a heat-exchanger. A refrigerator moves heat from the inside of the fridge to the room; the heat pump moves heat from the glycol solution to the building.

[9] Since all of the energy the building uses is now electricity, if the grid is supplying renewable, zero-carbon electrons, the building has essentially eliminated any carbon footprint. While this may be unlikely for existing grids, it *is* possible—that's the point I'm trying to make in this book!

[10] Two to five years for a commercial installation, a few more for a house.

[11] By "greenest," we mean something specific: an 80% reduction in carbon emissions from business as usual. Without geo-exchange, there was absolutely no possibility of reaching that target, since it was—by far—the lion's share of the carbon-reduction target.

[13] About 10% of carbon dioxide, and less than 1% of others (source: Boyle, pg. 375).

[14] Average US household electrical use is around 11,000 kilowatt hours per year (source: http://www.eia.doe.gov/emeu/recs/recs2001/enduse2001 / enduse2001.html). One metric ton of coal can provide approximately 2,200 kilowatt hours (source: US EIA; approximately two billion megawatt hours were produced from 1 billion US short tons of coal in 2007. That's 2,200 kilowatt hours per metric ton). Therefore, 70,000 metric tons generates 154 million kilowatt hours, or 14,000 household years of electrical power.

[15] For a full, technical update on the Soultz project status at time of writing, see: http://pangea.stanford.edu/ERE/pdf/IGAstandard/SGW/ 2009/genter.pdf

[16] Assuming an average cost of $12,000 per household, spread across condos and homes, 83.3 million households get installed. There are approximately 105 million households in the US (source: US Census Bureau).

[17] Approximately 70% of energy use is for heating/cooling (space and water). Geo-exchange lowers heating/cooling energy use by 75% (actual amount varies according to electrical source and original heating source). Total energy reduction would be 80% (portion of population) multiplied by 70% (heating/cooling portion), multiplied by 75% (energy savings), or 42% of total residential energy use.

[18] Total US household energy use is 22,000 trillion BTUs (source: US EIA, http://www.eia.doe.gov/emeu/states/sep_sum/html/pdf/sum_use_all. pdf). Annual savings would be 9,240 trillion BTUs, or the equivalent of 1.6 billion barrels of oil a year (one barrel of oil equals 5.8 million BTUs. Source: US EIA).

[19] Costs of EGS are divided between exploration and drilling, construction of power plant and present value of future re-drilling. There are two ways of generating an estimate: First, assume the cost of large-scale EGS to be similar to existing geothermal—the holes may be deeper, but EGS benefits from economies of scale, ease of site location, proximity to transmission and ongoing improvements in drilling technology. Estimate: $1,057 (lowest cost according to the US EIA), $1,150 to $3,000 (Renewable Energy Policy Project), $1,663 (MIT) per kilowatt of capacity. Average equals $1,600 per kilowatt of capacity. Second, MIT estimates that 65% of the final cost of EGS electricity per kilowatt hour is due to carrying costs of initial capital investment ("MIT Report," pg. 9-9), available at long-term average of around 8% ("MIT Report," pg. 9-37). The break-even price for EGS is around six cents per kilowatt hour, if deployed on a large scale ("MIT Report," pg. 9-38). So, capital carrying costs are 65 percent multiplied by six cents, or 3.9 cents per kilowatt hour. Assuming a 90% capacity factor, one kilowatt of capacity generates 7,884 kilowatt hours per year. Capital carrying costs are 7,884 kilowatt hours multiplied by 3.9 cents, which equals $307 per kilowatt hour, per year. Amortize this payment over 30 years and the up-front capital is $3,491 per kilowatt. Take the average of the two methods, and you get approximately $2,500 per kilowatt. So, $1 trillion gets you 400 gigawatts of capacity.

[20] The US uses around four million gigawatt hours a year (US EIA)—400 gigawatts at 90% capacity can produce more than three million gigawatt hours a year.

Climate Science II – The Complex Stuff

[1] Pat H. Bellamy, et al, "Carbon Losses from All Soils Across England and Wales 1978-2003," in *Nature*, Vol. 437, Sept 8, 2005

[2] Chris D. Jones, et al, "Strong Carbon Cycle Feedbacks in a Climate Model with Interactive CO2 and Sulphate Aerosols," in *Geophysical Research Letters*, Vol. 30, May 2003

[3] Methane is about 20 times as effective as carbon dioxide at trapping the sun's heat. When I say it will effectively triple the amount of carbon, I mean that the amount of methane released will have the same heating effect itself as twice the current levels of carbon dioxide.

Four: Biofuels

[1] See "Climate Science I" for an account of the role carbon dioxide plays in global warming.

[2] Phelps consumes up to 12,000 calories while training, compared to the average 2,500.

[3] Plants grab less than 1% of the solar energy reaching their fields, and that *continued...*

Endnotes

Four: Biofuels ...continued

energy must then be converted to a useful form. Compared with solar thermal or photovoltaic, plants are quite inefficient. They also require water, labor and often fertilizer. Their advantage is price. Plants are cheap solar collectors.

4 It is, strictly speaking, much more complicated than this statement implies. There are an enormous number of intermediate steps and complicated cellular mechanisms involved in the digesting and metabolizing of our food, and the food we eat clearly consists of much more than mere sugars. However, it is not unreasonable to characterize our very complicated set of metabolic pathways in this way: We oxidize chemical energy that originally derives from the sun.

5 Source: G. Boyle, *Renewable Energy: Power for a Sustainable Future*, pg. 109

6 See "Climate Science I"

7 http://www.theglobeandmail.com/servlet/story/RTGAM.20080721.wfarms21/BNStory/ National/

8 UK capacity is approximately 70 gigawatts.

9 An alcohol is like a hydrocarbon, but with a bit of oxygen thrown in.

10 Source: G. Boyle, *Renewable Energy: Power for a Sustainable Future* pg. 140. Also, here is a heavyweight paper that started the firestorm of controversy over ethanol: http://petroleum.berkeley.edu/papers/patzek/CRPS416-Patzek-Web.pdf

11 According to the US EIA, "competing uses would limit biodiesel production from yellow grease to 100 million gallons per year (6,523 barrels per day)." Competing uses are things like animal feedstock. Even without competition, the total potential production is well under 25,000 barrels per day. The US consumes over three million barrels of diesel per day (source: US EIA). So waste oils can meet less than 1% of total supply.

12 Soy produces about 0.4 metric tons of oil per hectare. There are 30.5 million hectares of land dedicated to soy production in the US (source: http://www.greenergy.com/perspectives/Soy.pdf). Therefore, the total *potential* production of soy-based oil under current land-use patterns is 12.2 million metric tons. The US consumes 3.21 million barrels of diesel fuel per day, or 1.171 billion barrels per year. A barrel of fuel = 0.13637 metric tons (source: http://www.eia.doe.gov/kids/energyfacts/science/energy_calculator.html). Therefore, around 160 million metric tons of diesel are required, and total conversion of the soy oil would replace about 7.6% of US diesel demand. This figure includes *none* of the diesel requirements to produce, process and transport the soy, or any of the fossil fuels required for fertilizer. Given that the CO_2 emissions savings from biodiesel versus diesel is 62% (source: http://www.greenergy.com/perspectives/Soy.pdf), we can assume that it takes one barrel of fossil fuel to produce three barrels of biodiesel. This drops the replacement percentage to only 4.7%. If

we then consider that the energy content of biodiesel is less than that of diesel, the figure drops further.

13 *Industrial mustard crops for biodiesel and biopesticides*, by K.S. Tyson, J. Brown and M. Moorab, National Renewable Energy Laboratory

14 G. Dyer, *Climate Wars*, pg. 107

15 See "Third-Generation Fuels" for details

16 Source: *New Scientist* magazine, April 8, 2008

17 Genetic engineering is a complicated topic outside the scope of this book. Briefly, however, what one might do is take a gene (a single, functionally defined piece of the genome, or DNA) from the DNA of one organism—say, a cow—that appears to perform a specific task or express a particular *phenotype*. A phenotype might be blue eyes or webbed feet. Whether or not single genes match up to single phenotypes is not straightforward; this is a caricature. Splice that gene into the genetic structure of another organism (say, a bacteria or a type of corn). The hope is that the new organism would then inherit some of the "donor" organism's features. Spider genes have been spliced into goats, for example, to produce milk that contains the high-strength fibre of a spider web. Individual genes are often associated with single enzymes or protein production. Thus, splicing in a particular gene might result in cells producing a desired enzyme. Genetic engineering is fascinating and complex—but *highly controversial*. I am not going to enter that debate here, other than to note the following: Introducing novel genetic changes into an organism without taking into account the knock-on effects of that gene or organism's potential entry into the ecosystem at large is irresponsible and perhaps quite dangerous. This is particularly the case with very small life-forms such as bacteria.

18 For those who love the fancy stuff, *Clostridium phytofermentans*

19 Source: *New Scientist*, "Fungal diesel could revolutionize fuel production," November 2008

20 The first, from microbes found in hot springs, breaks the cellulose down into little bits. Next, a gene from a fungus breaks those bits into pairs of sugar molecules. Finally, a gene from microbes in cow stomachs separates those pairs into simple sugars.

21 Source: *New Scientist*, "Biofuel Corn Makes Cow Bug Enzyme to Digest Itself," April 8, 2008

22 As quoted in G. Dyer, *Climate Wars*, pg. 126

23 Take soy production of 0.4 metric tons, or 125 gallons, per hectare. The entire US landmass is 930 million hectares, giving a theoretical maximum of 119 billion gallons of biofuel. It would take 140.8 billion gallons of biofuel to replace US petroleum. That's more than the US land mass. Palm oil production, which generates 20 times the amount of biofuel per hectare, would require about 7% of the landmass. Since only 19% of the landmass is arable, that's more than one-third of the arable land mass.

continued...

Biofuel is no magic bullet. Biofuels will only change the game if we spend as much money building vast fields of bioreactors and irrigating deserts with saltwater as we do finding and defending our sources of oil.

Hydro is a present-day, viable and large-scale renewable alternative to coal. Given what's at stake if carbon levels get too high, and all else being equal, large-scale hydro should proceed as fast as we can put up the dams.

Endnotes

Four: Biofuels ...*continued*

[24] Source: "Pond-Powered Biofuels: Turning Algae into America's New Energy," *Popular Mechanics*, March 29, 2007. The National Renewable Energy Laboratory had a program looking into algae for energy, until the Bush administration shut it down.

[25] Algae contains 30% to 60% oil, compared with 20% for soy (source: http://www.thefreelibrary.com/ Seashore+mallow+seen+as+biodiesel+source-a01610723024).

[26] From the conclusion of the paper "Halophytes Energy Feedstocks: Back to Our Roots," by R.C. Hendricks and D.M. Bushnell: "As an example, if the Sahara Desert (8.6 × 108 ha) were made capable to support halophyte agriculture...and if production were increased to 100 bbl/ha-yr of bio-oil, it alone would supply 421.4 Q, or 94% of the 2004 world energy consumption."

[27] Irrigating the Desert: According to Wynne Thorne, "Agricultural Production in Irrigated Areas" in *Arid Lands in Transition*, Harold E. Dregne, editor, AAAS (1970) pp. 31-56: The weighted average for medium to large irrigation projects is around $98,000 per square kilometres. This ranges between $56,000 to $177,000 per square kilometre. These are 1970 prices, so let's triple the median to around $300,000. This is for land that doesn't need clearing, but it's also for land to which you need to supply fresh, not salt, water. So $1 trillion might convert more than three million square kilometres to irrigated land. Since the Sahara is about nine million square kilometres, and that could provide almost all our energy needs, the three million figure corresponds to one-third of our energy needs. But oil is only one-third of that, so it could replace roughly all of our oil consumption.

Converting the Fuel: According to the US EIA (http://www.eia.doe.gov/oiaf/analysispaper/biodiesel/), "A new biodiesel plant is estimated to cost $1.04 per annual gallon of capacity." So, the same $1 trillion could build factories that could produce 23 billion barrels of bio-oil a year. That's pretty close to what we use now.

Putting it Together: So to irrigate the land and to process the oil, it would take $2 trillion to replace all our oil. So $1 trillion would replace half.

Five: Hydropower

[1] While other options are slowly coming online, for example big flywheels and massive sodium-sulfur batteries (see Chapter 10), these are not yet changing the game at the level of utility-scale electrical production.

[2] Turbines vary in size from around one to 20 feet in diameter, and there are any number of shapes. By far the most common is called a Francis turbine, invented by American James Francis back in the mid-1800s. Unlike the water wheels of old, the Francis turbine is completely underwater, and is shaped so that water is guided around an inner wheel shaped like a snail's shell, hitting the turbine blades at a steep angle, then flowing along the blades and out an inner channel. The turbine is designed to spin so that the speed of the blade is just less than the speed of the incoming water. Two other designs are worth mentioning. If the water flow is slow but large (a large river and small dam, for example), then a turbine blade shaped like a traditional propeller is used. For very high-pressure turbines, like those of the Hoover Dam, "impulse" turbines are used, where the high-pressure water is sprayed in a jet onto spoon-shaped cups that ring the turbine. Impulse turbines are not submerged, but are strangely reminiscent of those water wheels of old!

[3] Turbines have a number of "poles," or sets of magnets and coils, that are activated on rotation. A magnet passing through a coil generates moving electrons. The spinning of the turbine is set such that a set of poles is activated each time the alternating current changes direction. If the grid cycle is 60 Hz, and there is only one set of poles, then the turbine will spin at 60 cycles a second. That's unusually fast for a submerged turbine, so they generally have many more poles. If a turbine had 20 sets of poles, it would have to spin at only 360 rpm.

[4] See Note 1 above

[5] It's a loose definition, since small reservoirs and dams are sometimes used. Although the definition could include a project like Niagara Falls, that's not really in the right spirit!

[6] See Note 1 above

[7] One kilowatt hour of coal-based electrical production in China takes 0.366 kilograms of coal (source: National Development and Reform Commission of China). Three Gorges produced around 81 terawatt hours in 2008, so 30 million metric tons of coal were avoided. Since coal produces three times its weight in CO_2, then 90 million metric tons of carbon dioxide were avoided.

[8] Canadians use a total of around 24 billion litres of gasoline a year (source: Environment Canada: http://www.ec.gc.ca/soer-ree/English/Indicators/Issues/Transpo/Tech_Sup/ptsup4_e.cfm). Gasoline emits 2.4 kilograms of CO_2 per litre. That's 55 billion kilograms of CO_2, or 55 million tons.

[9] Estimates: Three Gorges Dam was estimated to cost about $40 billion, at 22,500 megawatt capacity ($1777 per kilowatt). The US EIA. estimates the cheapest hydro resources in the US could be developed for about $2,000 per kilowatt of capacity (http://www.eia.doe.gov/oiaf/aeo/assumption/pdf/electricity.pdf#page=3). The proposed Lower Churchill Falls project in Newfoundland, Canada, is estimated to cost about $8 billion, building capacity of 3,000 megawatts (so $2,667 per kilowatt of capacity). The average of these figures is around $2,150 per kilowatt. Run-of-river is more expensive, since the projects generally have smaller economies of scale and a higher proportion of costs associated with transmission. Let's say run-of-river is three times as expensive, at around $6,000 per kilowatt of capacity. If the $1 trillion is split between large-scale and run-of-river, we get about 250 gigawatts of capacity.

continued...

Endnotes

Cheap Money – Enter the Green Bond

1 Not *all* the cost, of course; there are operating costs. Some renewables, like biofuels, also require the cost of the input material. But by and large, the cost of credit is the single greatest factor in pricing renewable energy.

2 According to a national poll commissioned by myself and some colleagues on the Action Canada Green Bonds Policy team, 81% of Canadians support the idea of a Green Bond, and 62% say they would buy them. I'm sure other countries' citizens feel the same way!

Six: The Ocean

1 There's a bit of a cheat going on here. The water that comes out of the Spout is not ocean water, but freshwater originating from a small trickle that enters the hole. Nevertheless, it is the *force* of the air shooting that water up and out of the Spout that is so impressive and is of interest here.

2 The explorer Steve Fossett had planned to reach the depths of the Marianas Trench in a ship called the Deep Flight Challenger. Unfortunately, his plane crashed in the Sierra Mountains just weeks before the ship was to be tested.

3 Also called the Global Ocean Conveyor (which sometimes refers to the Gulf Stream itself), it is technically known as an example of "thermohaline circulation" ("thermo" referring to heat, and "haline" to salt). This very large-scale movement of water is the result of a complex set of circumstances. Roughly speaking, warm waters of the tropics move along the surface of the ocean due to wind and ocean currents. When that water hits northern climes, it becomes denser as water evaporates and the temperature drops. Eventually, it plunges to the bottom, forcing a conveyor-like motion, slowly returning south along the bottom. This global movement of water brings warmth from the southern oceans to places like northern Europe, which would be much colder without the added heat.

4 It is feared that the Great Ocean Conveyor might one day cease to function, as melting ice adds freshwater to the northern oceans, making the surface water less dense and eliminating the "plunging down" action that is the basis of the conveyor-like motion.

5 There are actually a number of separate sets of circular motion beneath the traveling wave that get smaller with depth.

6 Often what's called a "Wells Turbine," which spins in either direction, so it doesn't matter if the air is blowing in or out.

7 This is an example of conservation of energy. A wave's energy remains the same, until it is dissipated as noise or heat when it breaks, or as it gets larger with more wind energy. That means it has the same amount of potential energy (the amount of water above a flat sea level) as it's forced up the narrow channel. The result is that the wave height increases as its width decreases.

8 Roughly speaking, the Gaia hypothesis is the idea that the Earth and its many systems—atmospheric, geological, ecological, etc.—form a single, self-regulating system. It is grounded in rigorous scientific analysis, rather than the sort of hand-waving often associated with it in popular culture. The atmosphere, for example, was conditioned over millions of years by life that came before us, revealing a deep inter penetration between the atmosphere that life finds itself within, and life itself. Gaia theory is, at bottom, a repudiation of the idea that the Earth can be viewed from a purely reductionist perspective—that is, the whole really is more than the sum of its parts. See James Lovelock's writings for a fascinating account of the real thing.

9 And, to a lesser extent, the sun's gravitational pull.

10 A differential equation is one that describes how something changes over time. Laplace's equations shows that, given a sheet of water of a certain thickness and some other physical constants (like "g"—the force of gravity at the earth's surface), the surface of that sheet of water will change its morphology (or shape), resulting in horizontal flows away from a peak. Those horizontal flows are tidal currents.

11 Kinetic energy is proportional to the square of the velocity times the mass. If water is 800 times as dense, its kinetic energy at a given speed is 28.24 times as much. Therefore, to get an equivalent kinetic energy of water flowing at 15 kilometres per hour, you need air flowing 28.24 times as fast, so 424 kilometres per hour.

12 See G. Boyle, pg. 310-311

Seven: Smart Buildings

1 Some Passivehauses do have small, supplementary heating systems, typically in the heat-exchanger. That said, the top-up heating is minimal and must meet the Passivhaus standard of a maximum of 15 kilowatt hours per square metre, per year.

2 The 12-story Washington re-skinning project cost $60 million. That's $5 million per story. The entire building is 565,000 square feet (52,000 square metres), so each story is 47,000 square feet. That means re-skinning it cost about $100 per square foot. But that's a one-off, and a new idea. Let's assume that, once mass production gets involved, and the process and materials are streamlined, the cost comes down by three-quarters, to $25 a square foot. So, the $1 trillion could re-skin 40 billion square feet. Let's assume that each person requires 500 square feet of living space and 250 square feet of working space. Total population whose living and working space can be re-skinned is 40 billion divided by 750, or more than 50 million people.

We could easily cut our buildings' energy use in half. Since buildings consume around 40% of our power, that means smart buildings could lower our total energy use by one-fifth.

High-speed trains are serious competitors to short-haul flights and make driving seem primitive. A network of high-speed trains linking North American cities would be expensive, but it would do wonders.

Endnotes

Nuclear – Fission and Fussion

1 Including decommissioning and construction of the plant, carbon emissions can be as high as one-third of fossil-based plants. However, any plant—including renewables—requires construction, and that's not an entirely fair comparison. The processing of the fuel does require energy, but it can come from nuclear or renewables, so it doesn't add to the carbon total.

2 The used reactor vessel does become contaminated with radioactivity, but this a tiny and incidental by-product.

3 Another common, naturally occurring radioactive element. The ability to use thorium more than doubles the amount of available fuel.

4 The world produces between 7,000 and 11,000 metric tons of waste a year. Yucca mountain is designed to hold 70,000 metric tons.

5 If nuclear is to play a significant role in weaning us off of fossil fuels, that's the sort of increase we'd need to see. Right now, nukes produce about 6% of the world's electricity (source: International Energy Agency). If world electrical production rises by 50% by 2030 (source: US Energy Information Administration), and nuclear's share rises to one-third, say, then total nuclear production needs to increase eight-fold.

6 Source: *U.S. May Never Need More Nuclear, Coal Plants, FERC Head Says*, report by T. Seeley, Bloomberg News, April 22, 2009.

Eight: Transportation

1 Not without a bold plan: Like irrigating the Sahara desert for saltwater plant production (see Chapter Four). There's not enough arable land for both food and fuel.

2 While there are theoretical options for planes (hydrogen, perhaps) and boats (massive fuel-cells) these are not practical. I'll assume these will be the last mode of transport to leave the liquid fuel behind.

3 There are currently almost 10 million cars in China. At the same level of per-capita car ownership as the US, that number climbs to almost a billion. If those cars burn fossil fuels, it's really bad news. If they go electric, it's still a problem. Cleaning up China's electrical grid, replacing coal plants with clean energy sources, is already difficult. If we add the energy needed to charge up all those cars, the job becomes gargantuan.

4 In the US, the average length of commute is over 10 miles (16 kilometres); in Canada, it's much less—only 4.7 miles (7.6 kilometres). Source: http://www.industrializedcyclist.com/nhts.pdf and http://www.cbc.ca/consumer/story/2008/04/02/commute-statscan.html

5 Although the election of a new mayor, Boris Johnson, may put that spending in doubt.

6 As quoted in the *New York Times*, July 28, 2009.

7 Source: R. Kemp, *Transport Energy Consumption*, Lancaster University, 2004.

8 Ibid

9 Source: American Automobile Association

10 An electric car can be powered by batteries or by a hydrogen fuel-cell. Batteries will win—see "Hydrogen – An Energy Vector".

11 The power plant, like almost all power plants, will run at around one-third efficiency. That means you need to burn the equivalent of three kilowatt hours of coal to get one kilowatt hour of electricity. Then you have to charge and discharge the battery, which means further losses. Let's say you need four times the thermal energy from coal to run that electric car. Regular combustion engines are around one-third efficient. Therefore, you'd emit more carbon by burning coal to charge the battery than you would using a regular engine.

12 For better or worse. The benefits and drawbacks of global trade are hotly contested, and this is not the place to settle that debate. But it's clear that global trade is neither entirely good, nor entirely bad. The way we set up global commerce defines much of our effort to alleviate both poverty and environmental degradation. The idea that totally unrestricted trade is a complete answer to either issue is finally going out of fashion. In terms of climate change, the increase in global shipping directly increases carbon emissions. But unrestricted global trade can also cause "carbon leakage." If one country imposes restrictions on carbon emissions, their industry might move to a country with fewer restrictions. This is one of the reasons countries like the US are so unwilling to unilaterally fight climate change.

13 In all three cities, there was an immediate drop in carbon emissions of over 10%.

14 Source: A. Bows, K. Anderson, P. Upham, *Contraction and Convergence: UK Carbon Emissions and the Implications for UK Air Traffic*, Tyndall Centre Technical Report Number 40, 200, pg. 23, as discussed by G. Monbiot, 2006, pg. 185-86

15 The US uses 390 million gallons of gasoline for motors daily (source: US Energy Information Agency). That is equivalent in thermal energy to 14 billion kilowatt hours per day, or 5,110 billion kilowatt hours annually. Total US electrical production is 4200 billion kilowatt hours annually (source: US EIA). So, slightly more electrical energy is needed than is contained in all of the gasoline. But gasoline motors are only one-third efficient, while the electrical motor is much higher (around 90%). That reduces the amount of electrical energy we need by about two-thirds. That's offset by the inefficiency of charging a car's battery (say, 50%, dependent on battery type). So the two figures are, in the end, roughly equivalent.

16 London's plan calls for $1 billion over 10 years to go toward a full-scale facelift of the city to make it more bike friendly. Initiative include a rental bike scheme, bike parking in underground stations, as well as the transformation of the city to include bike lanes and areas that are cycle-only zones. For that $1 billion, they expect to get 1.7 million daily trips by bike. Since London is so far behind on cycling, it's safe to assume their goals can be matched by 49 other large cities.

17 Obviously, this figure will vary wildly from city to city, and depending on whether it's spent on buses, rail or streetcars. Let's take an area with mixed-use transit for an averaging effect. British Columbia has a budget of approximately $12 billion for a massive expansion of its public transit, including both rapid transit rail lines and buses. The goal of the plan is to increase ridership by 200 million trips annually. So, let's say our $9 billion per city has the same pro-rata effect, increasing ridership by 150 million trips annually, per city. So 7.5 billion car rides go away.

continued...

Endnotes

Eight: Transportation ...*continued*

[18] Rates for building track in the US varies from $22 million to $132 million per mile, a lot of the variance coming from the cost of obtaining the necessary real estate (source: The US Government Accountability Office). Let's take a rate near the low end, since a project of this size would be covering spans of the US well outside the more expensive corridors and would bring significant economies of scale: say, $25 million a mile.

Carbon Sequestration – Burn it or Bury it

[1] Modern coal plants use "gasification," which means the coal is first subject to very high temperatures, which splits it into carbon monoxide (CO) and hydrogen (H_2). The CO reacts with water to form carbon dioxide and more hydrogen. The carbon dioxide can be separated and captured before burning the hydrogen.

[2] The most common method is to bubble the exhaust gases through chemicals called ethanolamines, which absorb almost all the carbon dioxide. Heating the mixture releases the absorbed carbon dioxide, effectively removing and capturing it.

[3] Since the carbon needs to be stored essentially forever, while it sits in the ocean it will always remain a threat to ocean life. That's a hefty risk to take.

[4] According to the IPCC, between 10% and 40% more coal needs to be burned to get the same power output under CCS. This is because of the extra energy involved in capturing and compressing the carbon dioxide. See G. Monbiot, 2006, pg. 86.

[5] New plants are near the lower range, and retrofits near the upper. Source: McKinsey report as referenced in N. Stern, *The Global Deal: Climate Change and the Creation of a New Era of Progress and Prosperity*, 2009, Perseus Books Group, pg. 106. Other estimates include the US IEA at $35 to $60 by 2030.

[6] Source: International Energy Agency, as referenced in N. Stern, 2009, pg. 171

[7] N. Stern, 2009, pg. 36

Nine: Efficiency and Conservation

[1] One way of measuring energy efficiency is to measure the amount of energy used to produce a dollar of GDP—called "energy intensity." Between 1975 and 2000, energy intensity in the US dropped 40%, and since 1996 has been the fastest-growing energy source. See A. Lovins & H. Lovins, "Mobilizing Energy Solutions."

[2] See *New York Times*, May 6, 2001

[3] The CAFE (Corporate Average Fuel Efficiency) rules dictated mandatory fuel efficiency averages for a car-makers' fleet of vehicles.

[4] It's estimated that the cost of reducing energy use in the developed world can be achieved at two cents per kilowatt hour, for up to half of all energy use. Source: A. Lovins, *Negawatts, 12 Transitions, Eight Improvements and One Distraction in Energy Policy 24, no. 4*, pg. 331-343.

[5] There's a reason electricity—whether it's AC or DC—is sent at high voltage. Power losses are proportional to current squared. So if you can reduce the current, keeping the power the same, you can reduce the loss. Since power equals voltage times current, you can increase the voltage, decrease the current, and keep power constant.

[6] HVDC loses about a constant 3% per 600 miles (1,000 kilometres).

[7] The exact distance will depend on a number of factors: cable type, voltage levels, and type of equipment used to convert to DC and back again.

[8] One reason the cable can be thinner is due to the "skin effect." With AC, the current tends to cluster around the outside shell of the cable, and the middle part is wasted. This does not happen with DC, and the entire cable is used to pass current.

[9] See Chapter One. A Stirling engine is an external combustion engine requiring heat to be present on the outside of the cylinders.

[10] See http://www.gtai.com/homepage/industries/energy-efficiency-sector/chp-industry/

[11] See G. Monbiot, *Heat: How to Stop the Planet From Burning*, pg. 135

[12] See *New York Times*, May 6, 2001

[13] Negawatts at two cents per kilowatt hour are available in the developed world up to a half of total energy use (source: see H. Lovins above). So, $1 trillion buys 50 trillion kilowatt hours. Total energy consumption of all kinds of the G7 is about 180 quadrillion BTUs, or 180 times 1015 BTUs. One BTU equals 0.293 watt hours. So total G7 energy consumption of all kinds is 54 times 1015 watt hours, or 54 trillion kilowatt hours. The US is responsible for 100 quadrillion BTUs, or 29 trillion kilowatt hours. Only half of that energy can be turned into negawatts. In other words, we couldn't possibly spend that $1 trillion in a year.

The End of Easy Oil – Saving for the Future

[1] The amount of oil in the ground is a controversial measurement by any standard. Also called "known reserves," much of the oil that is thought to exist is based on numbers reported by countries who have every reason to inflate them. They're hard to confirm. In the 1980s, the OPEC countries suddenly increased their known reserves (without reporting any significant discoveries!) when their quota was linked to reported reserves. What they actually have in the ground may not be as much as they say. The former head of exploration and production at giant Saudi Aramco, Sadad al-Huseini, has publicly stated that known worldwide reserves may
continued...

Most of the energy in a power plant gets spewed out the chimney as waste heat, just like the exhaust of your car. Cogeneration—also known as combined heat and power (CHP)—can raise the efficiency of a power plant from one-third to nearly 90%.

229

Highly efficient HVDC transmission lines will link renewable energy plants spread across continents. It's called "grid balancing," and it makes renewable energy production more predictable and reliable. When one energy source diminishes, another comes online.

Endnotes

be overstated by as much as one-quarter. Also, what sort of oil is to be included is not always clear. Heavy oil, the tar sands and what's known a "shale oil" are supposed to be in addition to the trillion-barrel figure.

2 BP reports the R/P ratio—the ratio of reserves to production—as being 40 years. That's a pretty standard figure.

3 Even if the time of the peak is off by a few years, the basic lesson remains: There will be a time, sometime soon, when oil production will begin to drop off. If demand continues to rise, we have a big problem.

4 World oil consumption is around 35 billion barrels a year. So, adding 90 billion barrels to the mix gets us 45 billion pre-peak barrels, or just over a year of consumption.

Ten: The Energy Internet

1 I'll use the US as an example, but the process throughout the industrialized world is quite similar—particularly in Canada and Europe.

2 Not to denigrate utilities *tout court*! Cheap, reliable and continuous power is the lifeblood of our economy, and that is what the utility model has managed to deliver. The problem is that we're entering a new era of carbon constraint, and the utility model we have will no longer suffice.

3 A utility normally sells power at a price set by a local rate board. The rate is set so that it pays back the utility for the investments it has made to meet expected demand, plus a reasonable profit. That means the utility is motivated to spend money on more power plants. It's not only more fun to run a bigger company, but they're guaranteed to generate a profit based on the size of those investments. The more power plants they build the more profit they make.

4 Now that grids occasionally get overloaded, there are some programs designed to reduce peak load—called *demand reduction*—but these efforts are weak at best. Until the utility is directly motivated to reduce demand, building another power plant will always be their first choice.

5 The few "smart meters" around today barely scratch the surface, and are used mainly for remote meter-reading and time-of-day charging. The communication that's required starts with smart meters, but it needs to get past the meter and into the home. This is known as "behind the meter."

6 T., Friedman, *Hot Flat and Crowded: Why we Need a Green Revolution— and how it can Renew America*, 2008

7 See Chapter 5. Pumped-storage means using excess electrical production to pump water uphill to storage reservoirs. Later, that water is used for conventional hydropower.

8 The idea is that the wind farms take advantage of Europe's natural geography, over which areas of high pressure are normally separated from areas of low pressure by several hundred kilometres. From a slightly more technical perspective, the locations of the wind forma are negatively correlated with respect to wind availability. That means that when wind is not blowing in one place, it will be blowing somewhere else.

9 The capacity factor for a wind farm—a measure of how much energy it produces as a portion of how much it *could* produce—is affected by two variables. How much and how hard the wind blows is the factor that first comes to mind. It's also affected by how much energy can be used when the wind is blowing. If the wind howls all night long, but there is no demand for the energy, that brings the capacity factor down. The Supergrid is meant to ensure that when the wind blows, it can be used somewhere.

10 See *U.S. May Never Need More Nuclear, Coal Plants, FERC Head Says*, Bloomberg News, April 22, 2009

11 According to the National Energy Technology Laboratory in the US, more than 120,000 of these distributed generating plants (each supplying less than 50,000 homes' worth of power) can be expected to be connected in the US alone over the next couple of decades. So we'd better figure out a way to get them connected.

12 See "Hydrogen" for details about fuels cells and hydrogen storage.

13 "Energy efficiency programs on the grid can reduce generation capacity from 214 GW to 111 GW by 2030," Dundee report.

14 I hardly see this as a problem; this is exactly the sort of engineering problem we humans excel at.

15 According to the Dundee report, it will take about $300 billion to upgrade transmission in the US and $500 billion for distribution (national and regional grids). Add a couple hundred billion for the local grid. In Europe, the initial lines for the DESERTEC proposal come in at around $60 billion. One can assume that's just the start, so let's call it $300 billion, like the US—the area of Europe is smaller, but those lines will have to cross water more often. Assume the rest of the infrastructure is roughly proportional to population, and it comes out near the US figure of $1 trillion.

Acknowledgements

There are a number of people I'd like to thank for their help in making this book a reality: Dave Clark was a tireless Creative Director who brought the words to life on the page, and sourced the amazing photographs. Chris Smith, for checking all my words to ensure I told no untruths. Dawn Calleja, for rendering continuous improvements to the prose. MaRS Discovery District for supporting the project, and giving me the time and space required to finish.

To all the scientists and engineers, upon whose work this topic rests.

Finally, to all those who work to make this world a better place, and believe that—somehow, still—truth and ingenuity might yet save our backsides.

Photo Credits

We are very grateful to the forward-thinking organizations and talented individuals whose creative efforts have made an enormous contribution to this book. We acknowledge and thank you for doing your part to help make the book meaningful, colorful and engaging.

Cover: Jun Li, Shutterstock
Pg 2/3: Jon Gibbs

One: Solar

Pg 10/11: xJJx, Shutterstock
Pg 12: (top) Elpis Ioannidis, Shutterstock, (bottom) Paul Paladin, Shutterstock
Pg 13: Jarno Gonzalez Zarraonandia, Shutterstock
Pg 14: Otmar Smit, Shutterstock
Pg 15: DOE/NREL – Bill Timmerman
Pg 16: DLR/Markus Steur
Pg 17: (top) Falk Kienas, Shutterstock, (bottom) DOE/NREL – Sandia National Laboratories
Pg 18: (top) DOE/NREL – Pat Corkery, (bottom) DOE/NREL – Warren Gretz
Pg 19: ACS-Cobra Group
Pg 20: Abengoa Solar
Pg 21: PSA – CIEMAT
Pg 22: Stirling Energy Systems
Pg 23: (top) Infinia Solar Systems, (bottom) Stirling Energy Systems
Pg 24: (top) GreenVolts, Inc., (bottom) DOE/NREL – Warren Gretz,
Pg 25: DOE/NREL – Tom Stoffel
Pg 26: DOE/NREL – Dave Parsons
Pg 27: (top) Mondial Energy Inc., (bottom) DOE/NREL – Jean Ku

Pg 28: Schlaich Bergermann Solar
Pg 29: DLR/Steur
Pg 30: (both) DESERTEC, Trans-Mediterranean Renewable Energy Cooperation
Pg 31: DOE/NREL – Robert McConnell

Two: Wind

Pg 34/35: Kriss Russell, iStockphoto
Pg 36: Andrey Prokhorov, iStockphoto
Pg 37: James Steidl, Shutterstock
Pg 38: Kavram, Shutterstock/Peter Zaharov, Shutterstock
Pg 39: Mike Carter
Pg 40: Anyka, Shutterstock
Pg 41: (top) Jason Cheever, Shutterstock, (bottom) Stephen Strathdee, Shutterstock
Pg 42 & 43: Clipper Windpower
Pg 44 (top) Bret Atkins, Shutterstock, (bottom) WhalePower
Pg 45: Nextera Energy
Pg 46: Siemens Energy
Pg 47: DOE/NREL
Pg 48: Brian A. Jackson, Shutterstock
Pg 49: (top) Mike Carter, (bottom) SkySails
Pg 50: Helix Wind
Pg 51: Southwest Windpower
Pg 52: Magenn

Pg 53: Sky WindPower
Pg 54: DOE/NREL
Pg 55: Vestas Wind Systems

Three: Geothermal

Pg 58/59: John R. NcNair, Shutterstock
Pg 60: Chad Bontrager, Shutterstock
Pg 61: Videowokart, Shutterstock
Pg 62: Valery Shanin, Shutterstock
Pg 63: Brewster Well Drilling
Pg 64: Wyggeston and Queen Elizabeth I College
Pg 65: Tomasz Borowicz
Pg 66: (both) Jo-Anne McArthur
Pg 67: Rob Broek, iStockphoto
Pg 68: Eli and Ric, iStockphoto
Pg 69: Graham Prentice, Shutterstock
Pg 70: DOE/NREL – Warren Gretz
Pg 71: Tomasz Borowicz
Pg 72: Geodynamics Limited
Pg 73: Geopower Basel AG
Pg 74: (top) Alexander Laws, iStockphoto, (bottom) Grétar Ívarsson
Pg 75: Conor Quinlan, iStockphoto
Pg 76: Giovanni Consani. iStockphoto
Pg 77: Geodynamics Limited

Photo Credits ...*continued*

Four: Biofuels

Pg 80/81: K. West, Shutterstock
Pg 82: Tomasz Borowicz
Pg 83: Copestello, Shutterstock
Pg 84: DOE/NREL – Gerry Harrow
Pg 85: DOE/NREL – Warren Gretz
Pg 86: Jim Parkin, Shutterstock
Pg 87: CropEnergies AG
Pg 88: Karl Naundorf, Shutterstock
Pg 89: Max Blain, iStockphoto
Pg 90: Qteros
Pg 91: (top) Mascoma, (bottom) Eduardo Rivero, Shutterstock
Pg 92: Michigan State University
Pg 93: (both) Range Fuels
Pg 94: Szefei, Shutterstock
Pg 95: Alexander Gitlits, Shutterstock
Pg 96: Georg Hanf, iStockphoto
Pg 97: Harry Huang, Shutterstock
Pg 98 (top) Elena Gueno, iStockphoto, (bottom) Kevin M. Kerfoot, Shutterstock
Pg 99: CropEnergies AG

Five: Hydropower

Pg 102/103: Commit, Shutterstock
Pg 104: Cathy Steen, iStockphoto
Pg 105: Dpaint, Shutterstock
Pg 106: Elora Mill Inn
Pg 107: Joanna Pecha, iStockphoto
Pg 108: L. Freytag, iStockphoto
Pg 109: Nalcor Energy
Pg 110: Ontario Power Generation Inc.
Pg 111: Elena Elisseeva, Shutterstock
Pg 112: Thomas Barrat, Shutterstock
Pg 113: Artefficient, Shutterstock
Pg 114: Tomasz Borowicz
Pg 115: Martin Maun, Shutterstock
Pg 116 & 117: Statkraft
Pg 118: Wetsus
Pg 119: Peter Frank, iStockphoto
Pg 120: Tony Tremblay, iStockphoto
Pg 121: Pichugin Dmitry, Shutterstock

Six: Ocean

Pg 124/125: Dropu, Shutterstock
Pg 126: Voith Hydro Wavegen Limited
Pg 127: Eric Bartlett

Six: Ocean ...*continued*

Pg 128: Tomasz Borowicz
Pg 129: Armin Rose, Shutterstock
Pg 130: Eric Gevaert, Shutterstock
Pg 131: Voith Hydro Wavegen Limited
Pg 132: Checkmate Seaenergy Limited
Pg 133: Pelamis Wave Power Limited
Pg 134: Robert Rushton, iStockphoto
Pg 135: Linn Barringer
Pg 136 & 137: Marine Current Turbines Limited
Pg 138: Kris Unger/Verdant Power Inc.
Pg 139: OpenHydro Tidal Technology
Pg 140: DOE/NREL
Pg 141: (both) Lockheed Martin
Pg 142: Pelamis Wave Power Limited
Pg 143: Lunar Energy Ltd.

Seven: Smart Buildings

Pg 146/147: Alexandre Zveiger, Shutterstock
Pg 148: Craig Cozart, iStockphoto
Pg 149: David H. Seymour, Shutterstock
Pg 150: Architekt Martin Wamsler
Pg 151: Kirsten Jacobsen, Earthship Biotecture
Pg 152: Solares Design Build Inc.
Pg 153: Hufton & Crow, Sheppard Robson
Pg 154: Co-operative Financial Services
Pg 155: Somerset Partners
Pg 156: Kirsten Jacobsen, Earthship Biotecture
Pg 157: ArchMan, Shutterstock

Eight: Transportation

Pg 160/161: Tito Wong, Shutterstock
Pg 162: Manfred Steinback, Shutterstock
Pg 163: Saponjic, Shutterstock
Pg 164: Alan Tobey, iStockphoto
Pg 165: Peter D., Shutterstock
Pg 166: Mura, iStockphoto
Pg 167: Andre Klaassen, Shutterstock
Pg 168: Tesla Motors
Pg 169: ZENN Motor Company
Pg 170: Don Victorio, Shutterstock
Pg 171: Cisco Systems, Inc.
Pg 172: Ken Toh, Shutterstock
Pg 173: Millennium Air Ship, Inc.
Pg 174: Shi Yali, Shutterstock
Pg 175: Grant Dougall, iStockphoto

Nine : Efficiency and Conservation

Pg 178/179: Travelife, iStockphoto
Pg 180: Byron W. Moore, Shutterstock
Pg 181: Rocky Mountain Institute
Pg 182: Jorge Salcedo, Shutterstock
Pg 183: American Superconductor
Pg 184: ABB Inc.
Pg 185: Senai Aksoy, Shutterstock
Pg 186: (both) RenewABILITY Energy Inc.
Pg 187: Siemens Energy
Pg 188: Enwave Energy
Pg 189: Volkswagen AG
Pg 190: Nexans – The Valley Group
Pg 191: DOE/NREL, Warren Gretz

Ten: The Energy Internet

Pg 196/197: Svetlana Tebenkova, iStockphoto
Pg 198: Rene Mansi, iStockphoto
Pg 199: Simon Whitehead, iStockphoto
Pg 200: Svetlana Tebenkova, iStockphoto
Pg 201: Idee One, iStockphoto
Pg 202: Alexander Gatsenko, iStockphoto
Pg 203: Siemens Energy
Pg 204: Siemens Energy
Pg 205: Tomasz Borowicz
Pg 206: Ballard Power Systems Inc.
Pg 207: ABB Inc.
Pg 208: Vasil Vasilev, Shutterstock
Pg 209: Whirlpool Corporation
Pg 210: American Superconductor
Pg 211: Nikada, iStockphoto

Endsnotes

Pg 214: Solel Solar
Pg 217: Siemens Energy
Pg 218: Eli and Ric, iStockphoto
Pg 221: Terrance Emerson, Shutterstock
Pg 222: Bill Lawson, Shutterstock
Pg 225: Keith Wheatley, Shutterstock
Pg 226: Christian Lagereek, iStockphoto
Pg 229: Siemens Energy
Pg 230: Siemens Energy
Pg 234: Tatiana Grozetskaya, Shutterstock
Pg 238/239: Lars Lentz, iStockphoto
Back Cover: René Mansi, iStockphoto

Geothermal is one of our most abundant sources of clean energy. This hot river, in the Valley of Geysers, on Russia's Kamchatka Peninsula, winds through the second largest concentration of geysers in the world. The remote valley, now a World Heritage Site, is best reached by helicopter.

Index

*Note: Page numbers in **bold** indicate pictures or diagrams.*

continued...

Index ...*continued*

*Note: Page numbers in **bold** indicate pictures or diagrams.*

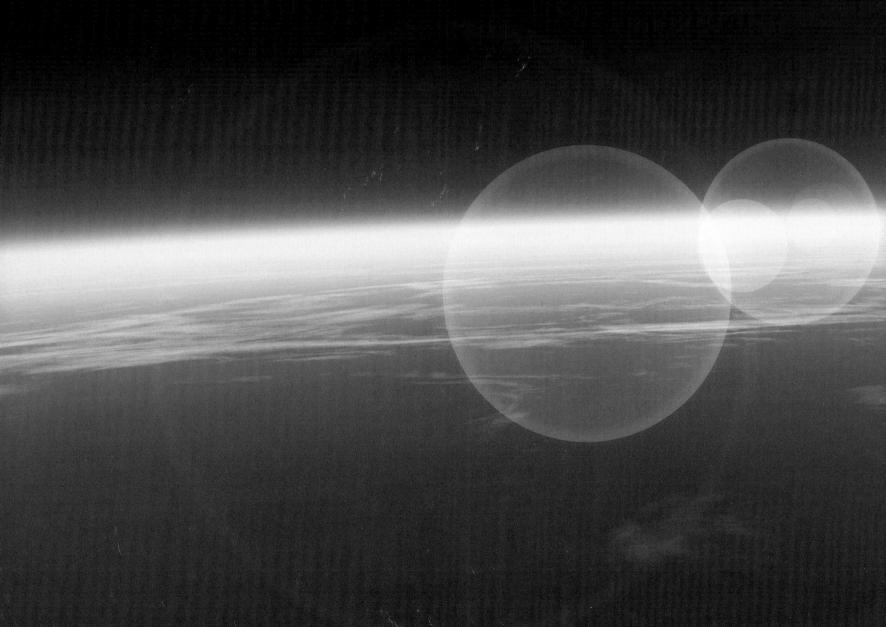

When it comes to the future, there are three kinds of people:
those who let it happen, those who make it happen, and those
who wonder what happened."

—*John M. Richardson, Jr.*

239